D0068339

GUACONOMICS

Dipping a Chip into America's
Besieged Party Bowl

Guaconomics: Dipping a Chip into America's Besieged Party Bowl

By Jeremy Bagott

First Edition

Band of Investment Publishing Co.
Ventura, California

ISBN-13: 978-0-9997107-2-2 (paperback)
ISBN-13: 978-0-9997107-3-9 (Kindle)

10 9 8 7 6 5 4 3 2 1

BAND OF INVESTMENT PUBLISHING CO.
2674 East Main Street, Suite E-504
Ventura, California, 93003

Email inquiries or comments to:
BOIPublishingCo@gmail.com

Disclaimer: This publication is meant to provide accurate, authoritative information regarding the subject matter covered. It is sold with the understanding that neither the publisher nor the author is engaged in rendering legal, accounting or investment counseling or any other type of professional service. If expert assistance is required, the services of a competent professional should be sought.

ACKNOWLEDGMENTS

For their kindness and treasured friendship, the author embraces Dave and Julianne Smith. He is a man of arts and letters, and she, a woman of arts and letters. The author genuflects to Frank Matcha, a linguist and raconteur with whom the author has collaborated on many rogue endeavors.

This book would not have been possible without the keen insights, boundless energy and frequent rescue provided by Cassandra, Rob, Hannah and Rick.

For running his periodic columns over the past few years, the author is deeply grateful to editors Mike Dunbar, Kevin Modesti, John Martin, Nels Jensen, Kyle Peterson, Jim Braun, Blanca Gonzalez, Bill McEwen, Donald Luzzatto, Ken Maryanski, Adam Steinhauer, Charles Crumpley, Mark Wright, Dan Hatfield, Carol Trice, Jay Schneider and Joel Fox.

The author dedicates this book to Irene and to the lingering spirit of Hunter S. Thompson, Tom Wolfe, William Jennings Bryan and Norman Borlaug.

"His specialty was alfalfa, and he made a good thing out of not growing any. The government paid him well for every bushel of alfalfa he did not grow. The more alfalfa he did not grow, the more money the government gave him..."

— Joseph Heller, *Catch-22*

"Before we go back to organic agriculture, somebody is going to have to decide what 50 million people we are going to let starve."

— Earl Butz
Secretary of Agriculture
Nixon and Ford administrations

"Nuts!"

— Gen. Anthony McAuliffe, U.S. Army
(reply to a German surrender demand
during the Battle of the Bulge
in World War II)

United States of Agriculture

Corn and Soybeans under Spacious Skies

As a trade war intensifies, the Corn Belt, built for the global economy and subsidized by the taxpayer, spans much of western Indiana, Illinois, Iowa, Missouri, eastern Nebraska and eastern Kansas.

'Udderly' Squeezed

Awash in a global dairy glut, farmers in top dairy states California, Wisconsin, Idaho, New York and Pennsylvania thin their herds and work off-farm jobs. Meanwhile, California and New York enact laws that lead to more dairy failures.

Northwest Beatdown

Battling Mother Nature, farmers in fertile regions of the Northwest are under attack by state governments that impose increasing layers of regulation and taxes on them. Meanwhile, globalization leaves them exposed.

Peanut Gallery

Favored by farm bills past and present, growers in the six major states of the Peanut Belt produce nearly all of the U.S. peanut crop. The states are Georgia, Florida, Alabama, Texas, South Carolina and North Carolina.

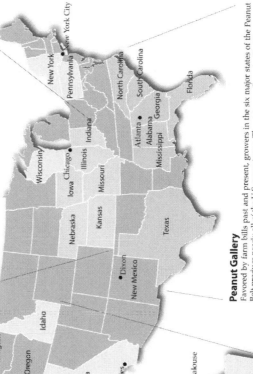

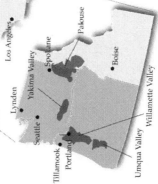

California Even Nuttier

San Joaquin Valley

The unintended consequences of globalization and California's regulatory state have led to more than a million acres of tree nuts in the San Joaquin Valley, part of the state's vast Central Valley. The San Joaquin includes all or part of seven southern counties: Kern, Kings, Fresno, Madera, Merced, Stanislaus and Tulare counties.

Central Valley

The Central Valley, which includes the San Joaquin Valley, constitutes 17% of the nation's irrigated land. It includes all or part of 19 counties: Butte, Colusa, Glenn, El Dorado, Fresno, Kern, Kings, Madera, Merced, Placer, San Joaquin, Sacramento, Shasta, Stanislaus, Sutter, Tehama, Tulare, Yuba and Yolo.

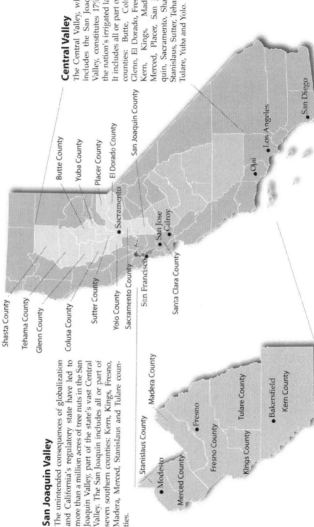

Shasta County
Tehama County
Glenn County
Colusa County
Sutter County
Yolo County
Sacramento County
San Francisco
Santa Clara County
San Jose
Gilroy
Sacramento
El Dorado County
Placer County
Yuba County
Butte County
San Joaquin County
Los Angeles
Ojai
San Diego

Stanislaus County
Madera County
Modesto
Merced County
Fresno
Fresno County
Kings County
Tulare County
Bakersfield
Kern County

Mexico: Agave, Limes and 'Green Gold'

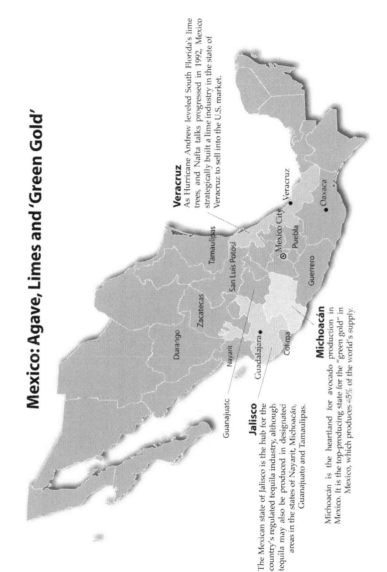

Veracruz

As Hurricane Andrew leveled South Florida's lime trees, and Nafta talks progressed in 1992, Mexico strategically built a lime industry in the state of Veracruz to sell into the U.S. market.

Jalisco

The Mexican state of Jalisco is the hub for the country's regulated tequila industry, although tequila may also be produced in designated areas in the states of Nayarit, Michoacán, Guanajuato and Tamaulipas.

Michoacán

Michoacán is the heartland for avocado production in Mexico. It is the top-producing state for the "green gold" in Mexico, which produces ≈5% of the world's supply.

Contents

Prologue   i

Chapter I
Forty Acres and a Harvesting Drone   1

Chapter II
Deconstructing the 'Sunion'   25

Chapter III
You Are Now Entering Santa Clara County   42

Chapter IV
Mandarins in the Garden of Good and Evil   58

Chapter V
The World's Nuthouse   94

Chapter VI
The Guac Is My Copilot   115

Chapter VII
Wings over America   129

Chapter VIII
Doritos Throwdown   139

Chapter IX
Cork-ucopia   155

Chapter X
Agave Blues   162

Chapter XI
Hoppy Welfare Queen   176

Chapter XII
Wheys and Means   192

Chapter XIII
Fifty Shades of Nuts   **215**

Chapter XIV
One World under Hummus   **224**

Chapter XV
An Inconvenient Fruit   **232**

Chapter XVI
Peanut Republic   **245**

Chapter XVII
Jacked Crustaceans   **258**

Epilogue   **271**

Index   **292**

Prologue

These are surreal times. Most people today have no connection to where their food comes from. This would have been unimaginable in America four or five generations ago. Farmers constituted half the country's labor force in 1880. As recently as 1950, a full 12 percent of workers called themselves farmers. Today, it has just slipped below one percent. Never in human history has so much food been produced for so many by so few.

I didn't set out to write the magnum opus on guacamole, tortilla chips, suds, salty nuts, cheese, hummus and buffalo wings during the late-Obama and early Trumpian era (well, actually, I did, but then thought better of it as the data mounted). The food and drink I touch on in this book are those that people have lavished on me in orgiastic quantities at get-togethers for March Madness, Fourth of July, Super Bowl, Cinco de Mayo and assorted other pretexts for merriment. These are the same things I'm compelled to serve my guests in return. In writing this book, I come to the realization that food production in America is at the brink of an Elon Musk-style – nay, a Lindsay Lohan-style – meltdown. As I write this in 2018, salvos have been exchanged in a trade war with China; Washington has levied tariffs on $250 billion worth of Chinese goods. Beijing has retaliated against U.S. agriculture. Farmers gird their loins. The federal government, brandishing the only instrument it knows, shovels piles of taxpayer money at ag in an attempt to remedy a problem it largely created by subsidizing big-ticket monocrops in the first place.

As the trade war with China heats up, the Irony Genie has escaped the bottle. The world's biggest pork producer, the Chinese conglomerate WH Group, is now eligible to offload a potential geyser of bacon, franks, short ribs and pork butts into the gaping maw of the U.S. federal nutrition assistance and child nutrition programs, which may soon be backstopping the Virginia-based-but-China-owned Smithfield Foods. (WH Group bought Smithfield in 2013.) Small American hog farmers are up in arms over the prospect, while food banks are reported to be overflowing even now.

But a few words on what this book isn't:

The book isn't meant to yuck your yum. It's not the "Silent Spring" for the condo-commando intent merely on firing up the barbie and having a good time. I aim to sow no bumper crop of alarm. I don't want you silencing your next viewing party with the contents of this book or acting sanctimonious. You're above that kind of showmanship. Also, I didn't set out to be the den mother of a death cult or to inspire the next Armageddon-themed Norwegian black metal anthem.

The book isn't a poison-pen letter, either; I didn't set out to plunge a pitchfork into anyone or anything. There are no truly odious characters in it. Most are just people going about their daily business, though sometimes in extreme ignorance, sometimes unwilling to see the big picture. Of course, the book might hector the fawning politician, cloying crony or acquisitive fraudster – people hurting food production and knowing it. But that's the exception, not the rule. Whether you've stopped to ponder it or not, there are enormous contradictions in what kinds of food and drink we humans need for nourishment and how government uses its powers to subsidize the things we probably shouldn't be consuming so much of. But all in all, there are more saints than sinners in the world of food production.

After leaving journalism in the late 1990s, I began appraising real estate, much of it in California's agricultural San Joaquin Valley and along the state's fertile coastal plain. I've interviewed hundreds of farmers, land brokers and ag consultants connected to the nation's besieged farmscape. In valuing ag land for more than a few unpopular public projects, I learned that farmers don't shrink from telling you what's on their mind. You can count on it. Their unvarnished comments can make for bleak reading.

The good news? The American party platter is still alive and well. For now, you should dip chip or hoist hefeweizen boldly. In fact, the cautionary tone of this book, juxtaposed with the current abundance, may seem like someone painting a mustache on the Mona Lisa. Just know that the many tentacles of corporate welfare, the regulatory state, vertical monopoly formation and the blind zeal of globalization are sharing the guac bowl alongside you (sometimes double- and triple-dipping).

This book is about the forces of distortion and disruption buffeting many foods and slowly limiting their availability. Hidden risks are being nurtured. Food production has become more perilous, and we are sleepwalking into trouble on several fronts. Stables need to be mucked out. Even science has been as much a bane as a blessing to ag of late. We've learned that globalization is more than buying the world a Coke.

Amid it all, there are success stories, and this book is as much a celebration of those as a jeremiad for the foods becoming less accessible, more expensive and less able to be produced in America.

This book is a roundup of the people and places directly involved in bringing a handful of shared-consumption foods to a party platter near you. I want food production in America to be diversified, healthy and booming. I never want you to dip a chip and come up dry. If that happens someday, you should know the forces that led to it.

So, I give you the Baedeker to the state of nuts, avocados, limes, wings, corn chips, tequila, beer, wine, cheese, hummus and shrimp. I threw in garlic and onions because they're everywhere in shared foods. A final item is the mandarin orange. I realize it may be too healthy to make its way into many party spreads, but its rise is a spectacular one, so indulge me on that.

Chapter One

Forty Acres and a Harvesting Drone

IN 2013, FIAT CHRYSLER stirred emotions mightily when it resurrected a snippet from the late broadcaster Paul Harvey's "So God Made a Farmer" speech and set it to a two-minute ad for Ram Trucks.

Extolling the grit of the American farmer, the spot aired during the fourth quarter of Super Bowl XLVII. It featured stills of farm life set to the conservative commentator's smoky, salt-cured baritone. Sure, the ad may have also featured a few images of Ram trucks proving their mettle down on the farm patch, but the messaging didn't eclipse the message. It was a paean to the agrarian spirit, rural values and the farm work ethic.

Polling showed that many viewers found it to be the best Super Bowl ad that year. Reports surfaced of aging farmers with parched skin and calloused hands — some fourth- and fifth-generation farmers — being moved to tears by the commercial. It was a testament to the power of words and pictures. It laid out the story arc of their lives and awakened something deep and essential in our collective breasts. Not since the populist spirit whipped up by Willie Nelson, Bob Dylan, John Mellencamp and the Nitty Gritty Dirt Band in the first Farm Aid concerts in the 1980s, or the oratory of William Jennings Bryan a hundred years earlier, had the average American couch potato been reminded that a whole world might exist outside his 9-to-5 routine in the city. In a case of life imitating art, farm-state Senator Charles Grassley of Iowa was quick to make political hay of the publicity created by the ad. He told reporters he hoped the people of America would finally wake up and appreciate the nation's family farmers. It was tough not to be swept up by it.

As if on cue, the killjoys on the Washington Post's editorial board threw cold water on the whole thing. Days after the Super Bowl, they pronounced modern farmers wealthy, addicted to government handouts and undeserving of tribute. "Actually, farming no longer resembles the hardscrabble family enterprise of so much mawkish marketing," claimed the Post's editors. "Much of it is dominated by large operators supplying not only the U.S. dinner table but also far-flung export markets." Of the Post's subscribers in the Farm Belt, it's unlikely many called that day to extend their subscriptions.

But both the Norman Rockwell view of the American farmer, summed up in Harvey's words, and the Post's cynical view of the American farmer as a welfare slouch bore elements of the truth.

Such is the confused organism agriculture has become, in no small part thanks to government meddling. Surviving as a small farmer in the United States is now like trying to master the fictional Kobayashi Maru test (warning: "Star Trek" reference), that no-win training scenario at the Starfleet Academy. Suffice it to say, the confusion has been building since the U.S. government saw the need to protect farmers from the banks and railroads in the 1890s. Meanwhile, the Trumpian trade war with China, Mexico, Canada and the European Union has meant America's big-ticket monocrops are becoming less sellable in the very countries they've been set up to service. With the nation running big budget deficits, the federal government will be less inclined to throw growers a lifeline and will have to engage more than it already does in picking winners and losers in the farmyard. Add to this a shambolic feast of regulations and taxes that key U.S. ag states are now inflicting on their farmers. The incessant tinkering with market mechanisms and its unintended consequences put many corners of the nation's food supply at risk.

But America's agrarians – caught between the Scylla and Charybdis of cut-throat globalization and the ever-expanding regulatory state – *are* tough as nails and have remained tough in the face of these forces. But as tough as they are, it hasn't stopped a die-off of small farms. From 2007 to 2012, the nation lost 55 a day. Almost 100,000 farms disappeared from the American landscape during that time, according to the U.S. Census of Agriculture. Soon, there will be fewer than two million farms in America. Small farmers are being plowed under.

In lockstep with the trend, the concentration of cropland ownership has snowballed over the past 30 years. The median farm size — the size that marks the middle of the distribution for cropland — was 589 acres in 1982. But by 2012, it had reached 1,234 acres. This consolidation has not only been massive and continual but has occurred in almost all states and for all crops.

Farmers don't seem to have the numbers or the spare time any more for even the gesture politics of the past, like driving their tractors to the state capital to clog traffic for a day (punctuated by the burning of a few tractor tires outside the statehouse for added drama). Seed, fertilizer and equipment costs are at all-time highs, and a grain and dairy glut now swamps the market, causing many to operate in the red as I write this in 2018. It has led U.S. agrarians to sow the fewest acres of winter wheat in more than a century, reported the Wall Street Journal.

"No one just grain-farms anymore," Deb Stout told the Journal's Jesse Newman and Patrick McGroarty in 2017. Stout's sons, Mason and Spencer, farm the family's 2,000 acres in Sterling, Kansas. Spencer also works as a mechanic, and Mason as a substitute mail carrier. "Having a side job seems like the only way to make it work," she said.

Some farmers can't make existence itself work. The Centers for Disease Control and Prevention found in a 2012 study that farmers had the highest suicide rate of any profession it tracked, with about 85 suicides per 100,000 people. The category also includes ranchers, fishermen and lumberjacks. The suicide rate for agricultural workers was nearly five times higher than that of the general population. American farmers commit suicide at twice the rate of veterans (who kill themselves at an already elevated 35.3 suicides per 100,000 people) or of police, firefighters and corrections workers (at 31 per 100,000). The study speculated isolation, stress, work-home imbalance, lower income, lower education levels and lack of access to health services as causes. Many farmers are hanging on by their fingernails. The reality is that food production is becoming an activity that is done in isolated places by a dwindling number of people, many of them multigenerational, some failing, some troubled enough to end it all.

The premise of that accretion of benefits that has come to be called the "farm bill," renewed twice a decade, is that farmers and ranchers are exposed to unique risks and play a unique role in feeding the nation. But elected officials inject sops and special-interest patronage into the bills, stand idly by as seed and chemical companies merge and dominate markets, allow U.S. farmers to be undercut by cheap foreign produce with no possibility of competing on price, and allow integrated global behemoths to suffocate our system of free enterprise. The farm bill was conceived during the Great Depression and is today dedicated to the proposition that some farmers are more equal than others.

Adding to the misery, progressive state governments in farm states like New York, California, Oregon and Washington enact taxes, fees and regulations that make everything more expensive for ag, often without studying the effects these burdens have on national food production or farmers' livelihoods. State officeholders representing urbanized districts – many of them yoked to identity politics or assorted *au courant* rights movements – increasingly lack basic economic literacy. Their ignorance about commodities and where food comes from seems only surpassed by that of their constituents. Many of the latter are urbanites with limited attention spans who, on social media, will level maudlin accusations about America descending into totalitarianism, then, a few hours later, will post selfies from a Florence and the Machine concert.

Meanwhile, dubious policies that ignore supply and demand – those focused on solving urban ills and climate change through government edict – are causing big trouble for agriculture. (On the latter note, agriculture, which requires predictable growing conditions, is a net *victim* of climate change, not a net perpetrator.)

Politicians have begun vilifying agriculture only because it plays well to their urbanized constituents. Ag makes a great *bête noire*. After all, this mysterious world, filled with its clutter, its foul smells and its strangely wheeled contraptions, is alien to most voters these days; it could also harbor – heaven help us – factory farms. (In reality, all farms, big or small, dense or sprawling, organic or non-organic, are factories – food factories. The thought that some farms aren't is only a comforting mythology. The only exception might be the vanity vineyards and gentlemen cattle ranches owned by retired CEOs and celebrities.)

Globalization and the ever-increasing burden of taxation and regulation on ag, especially at the state level, have forced small farmers to sell out to ever-larger ag concerns – bank foreclosures speed the process – and then the selfsame lawmakers responsible for the policies that led to this scaling up of farms go on to decry agriculture for having grown too big. They then enact further legislation, inadvertently causing yet more consolidation. In the Empire State, well-heeled constituents in the Cash Belt along the Hudson River have prodded state lawmakers to enact one-size-fits-all legislation that is helping to decimate New York State's dairy farmers in far-flung places like Cayuga, Genesee and St. Lawrence counties. In 2006, the state had 6,000 dairy farmers. By 2016, the number of dairy farmers had fallen by nearly a quarter to 4,600.

In Olympia, Washington, lawmakers recently debated Senate Bill 6529. The bill, innocent of any basis in plant pathology or entomology, would have forced farmers in the Evergreen State to give the state government one week's notice before spraying their fields. The problem, berry farmer Rob Dhaliwal told the Capital Press, is that mummy berry, botrytis fruit rot, powdery mildew, aphids, mites, spotted-wing drosophila and other diseases and pests can get out of hand in much less time than a week.

The bio of the bill's sponsor, state Senator Rebecca

Saldaña, touts her background, promoting a menu of *de rigueur* themes and touchpoints – "worker and immigrant advocacy, transit equity, women's rights, social and racial justice [and] environmental justice." She has climbed the greased rope of Democratic politics in the Evergreen State, beginning as a union organizer. No one is doubting her dedication to Washington State's downtrodden, but one might be forgiven for questioning her familiarity with brutes like the spotted-wing drosophila, an insidious creature that infests many fruit crops in North America and Europe just when fruit starts to ripen. Her bill requires a one-week waiting period from the time a farmer discovers a pest, canker, blight or wilt and when the farmer can treat for it (after filing the correct paperwork, of course). The notion that agricultural pests or pathologies can always wait a week before treatment is preposterous.

Could Saldaña's passion be redirected from ag to, say, job training and public safety for her 37th District? For places like the downwardly mobile Bryn Mawr-Skyway, which the site roadsnacks.net named one of the "10 Most Ghetto Cities in Washington for 2018"? Folks in Skyway currently ride out the crime waves and pray for annexation by Seattle. Nearby Renton has also become a problem child in her district. The city earned a rating of 3 in a recent crime index in which a score of 100 is considered safest. In Renton, even her constituents of the four-legged variety are winding up on crime-victim lists. As I write this, locals were following the story of Rex, a dog who was shot three times during a home invasion. (In case you're wondering, Rex underwent surgery and "came through well," said the vet. So, there's that.)

Having built a meteoric political career as a voice for the disenfranchised, Saldaña – who became the majority whip during the writing of this book – is now disenfranchising those in the state who farm soft summer fruit like cherries, blueberries, blackberries, raspberries, peaches, nectarines and grapes. Asked by a lawmaker to rate the threat of her bill to agriculture on a scale from one to 10, Eastern Washington wheat farmer Nicole Berg answered "10." Farmers generally have an aversion to hyperbole. When a farmer tells you a problem will be a "10," you listen. Another farmer suggested Olympia's ideology-infested statehouse might stand a good pelting with pupae-infested Bing cherries. To many farmers, Saldaña's bill, with its awful presumption, seemed to know no bounds. Wafting up from it was the unmistakable stench of, well, mischief. If he could reason, Rex, the canine crime-victim, would puzzle over Saldaña's foray into ag, he would.

The big and obvious reality in Washington State is that even rollicking frontmen in Soundgarden tribute bands; mewling identitarians; kale-smoothie-drinking Prius drivers; aging nü-metal aficionados; private-equity virtuosos, their Gulfstream G550s hangered at Paine Field south of Everett; and tatted neo-Trotskyites must all consume a certain number of calories from nourishing food on a daily basis. Another obvious reality: Agriculture isn't a competitor with tech, aerospace and other industries in the Evergreen State – it's a precondition for those industries to thrive since aeronautical engineers, corporate procurement managers and aircraft skin polishers, like everyone else, must consume nourishing food. If these workers can barely afford housing in the Seattle area – which is the case for a growing number – spikes in food prices could send them into RV living (see the chapter "You Are Now Entering Santa Clara County").

"The state of Washington is run by three counties," said Rick Gastelum, business manager at the Washington Farm Bureau, "Snohomish, King and Pierce." As the saying goes among the state's world-weary farmers: To win a statewide election, all the votes you'll ever need can be seen from the top of the Space Needle. Swaddled in natural fibers and perched in Belgian gastropubs, vinyl-record stores, tattoo parlors, hookah dens and single-location coffee shops, Seattle's hipsters; along with its aloof techies; Facebook-addicted civil servants; twentysomethings with beards not seen since the Rutherford B. Hayes administration; kundalini yoga instructors; rage-projecting grannies, their locks of frizzed gray hair splayed, *comme il faut*, across the shoulders of sequined "#Resist" T-shirts; and foppish postmoderns astral-projected from the Weimar Republic are unwittingly calling the shots on what crops can be grown in the Palouse or the Yakima Valley.

Occasionally, some Luddite from the state's agrarian hinterland will question the effects on farmers of new taxes aimed at getting people to carpool on Interstate 5 in Everett or providing family leave for teenagers working fast-food jobs in Kirkland. These dim bulbs are quickly dismissed as crackpots, for in the Evergreen State, voters are increasingly more concerned with nurturing their gut microbiomes than the macrobiomes in the state's fertile farm fields, which they take for granted.

One state to the south, growers on some of the richest onion soils in eastern Oregon report being forced across the border to Idaho to escape mandates uncritically embraced by that state's artisanal pickle-makers, deeply caring Pokémon GO enthusiasts, pop-veined social-science professors, "woke" ad agency interns and misery-loving boomers living in subsidized artist housing. A Portland Uber driver referred to one loitering pack of vaping top-knotted, man-bunned cosmopolites as "bro-hemians." In Salem, elected officials, policy analysts and ideological co-belligerents tut while deploying anti-capitalist jargon over soy lattes in Venmo-friendly coffee houses on streets with names like Liberty and

Commercial.

California, another breadbasket state, has effectively abolished the traditional "farm" and "nonfarm" payroll categories. Historians will look back and concur that the rot truly set in when the state enacted a high, one-size-fits-all minimum wage on the backs of its poorer, rural counties after little discussion with anyone, let alone the state's farmers. In those counties, this "minimum wage" is a mid-tier wage. It came alongside a new farm overtime law that did not take the harvest season's frenetic "make hay while the sun shines" possibilities into account. A Rubicon had been crossed, not simply with the $15 benchmark – that's just a number – but with the rubber-stamping, the hubris, the lack of circumspection, the belief in the gavel as a proxy for market functions. The governor wrapped farmworkers in a gentle statist caress but failed to point out to them that if their hands cannot fly nimbly enough through the citrus trees, asparagus stalks or garlic bulbs to warrant a value of at least $15 per hour, plus payroll taxes and benefits, these workers would have no ability to work, since farmers would simply re-crop to survive. The $15 benchmark is as much a productivity cut-off as a wage floor.

"This is Hugo Chavez, not Cesar Chavez," said an aging agrarian in a rich, spice-rubbed *basso profondo*. He said he rotates in and out of carrots and parsnips on cropland he leases near Bakersfield in Kern County. "These are people who get their history from Oliver Stone movies," he said of certain of the state's elected time-servers, dismissing them with a wave of an enormous leathery hand and a tauro-scatological utterance.

A 2016 University of California Extension study on the onion harvest put the true cost for non-machine field workers in the Golden State, including a payroll overhead of 40 percent, at $19.60 an hour. That hourly cost is slated to increase by 70 cents a year through 2022. The state's legislature rushed the $15 minimum-wage grenade through in less than a week before it was signed into law by the governor. But the $15 wage required of farmers in Modesto in the rural Central Valley is something entirely different from the same wage in the Silicon Valley. Agrarian California is a world apart from life in the state's affluent coastal counties. The state's experiment with big city public-union governance is having ill effects on ag and food security – for not just the state but the nation.

Instead of enriching pickers and ranch hands, California laws have nurtured hidden risk-taking as growers gradually move out of the hand-harvested field crops they can no longer grow profitably and into crops that can be mechanically harvested. As one row-crop farmer described the growing dystopia for California field-crop farmers and idled pickers in the wake of the $15 wage progression, "the juice is no longer worth the squeeze." The $15 minimum wage is a cost without benefit for ag.

The result of all this? Every four days in California, one square mile of bell peppers, squash, beets, carrots, parsnips, tomatoes, green onions, nectarines, cotton, alfalfa and grapes has been fed to the machine-harvested almond monocrop. There are now over a million acres bearing almonds in the Golden State with hundreds of thousands of acres more in the pipeline.

While the governments of Western ag states nibble at the golden goose's succulent white meat, farmers – unlike manufacturers – can't just pack up the soils their families have lovingly enriched over generations and move to nearby business-friendly states. In many cases, they're stuck and simply choose the course of least suffering. So, they plant almonds, and sometimes pistachios or walnuts, but mostly almonds. Some farmers sell their land to hedge funds, pension funds and endowments, who then develop it to almonds.

Ignorance of economics among California's officeholders is transcendent. Ignorance of government itself is pervasive. One aggrieved lawmaker in Sacramento recently demanded lobbyists provide her the race, gender and sexual orientation of everyone in their firms, accusing them of being blind to diversity. Her comments gave the impression she believed these firms might somehow be part of government and that officeholders were obliged to work with them and could audit them like a state agency. It was a wavelet of revelation.

Meanwhile, increasingly indignant workers in California's 150 professions that require licensing – from embalmers to appliance service contract sellers to landscape architects to auto mechanics – must demonstrate proficiency, pay a recurring fee and seek permission from time to time from entrenched boards, commissions, agencies and panels simply to earn a living. Contrast that with the state's elected officials, who need not demonstrate any particular mastery of government or economics. There is no required licensing, no continuing education standards, no standardized testing for them. And it shows.

This economic illiteracy made for a rich vein of irony in the Empire State. Gotham's era-defining "it" candidate for Congress took a break in 2018 from campaigning for a vast menu of cradle-to-grave "free" stuff with a ruinous $40 trillion price tag over ten years. The ineffable Alexandria Ocasio-Cortez, 28, wrote that she'd dropped by to say farewell to pink-slipped former co-workers at a restaurant where she had tended bar before running in the primary. Later, the eatery's co-owner, Charles Milite, told the New York Post he was shutting down due to New York's enormous hikes in the minimum wage — a big plank in Ocasio-Cortez's own platform. But unlike Milite's restaurant, most failing businesses, like most failing farms, disappear with no press coverage and in silence.

Officeholders tinker with market mechanisms in the ag world. In doing so, they create a food production hall of mirrors at the state level, on top of the distortions and perverse incentives created by federal farm bills – themselves worthy of a hundred years of screeds and scholarly discourses. The states don't recognize a corollary to their actions: When prices for a given crop don't support the pay and benefits they've capriciously awarded, these lawmakers engage in crop selection.

"We have two Californias," said former Bakersfield newspaper columnist Lois Henry. "One with all the political muscle that doesn't really understand what the other, with most of the resources, needs to continue operation."

When politicians require engineers to redesign toilets and washing machines or reformulate house paint, it results in toilets that must be flushed twice, washing machines that require the "heavy duty" cycle to clean ordinary clothes and house paint that must be reapplied every few years. In their most extreme form, hubris and autocratic decision-making can even kill; look no further than the largely self-inflicted Soviet grain famines of the 1930s. In their 2004 book "The Years of Hunger: Soviet Agriculture, 1931–33," writers R.W. Davies and S.G. Wheatcroft place the death toll at 5.5 million to 6.5 million.

Eclipsing even that episode of unfathomable human misery was the one that came thirty years later, in the wake of China's misnomered Great Leap Forward in the late 1950s and early 1960s. Scholars debate the number of deaths, but most agree on about 30 million. It was the deadliest famine in history. A prelude to the famine was something called the Patriotic Four Pests Health Campaign. For a son of a farmer, Mao Zedong cared little about the animal kingdom, let alone matters involving entomology and ornithology. Instead, he devoured books on the October Revolution in Russia and came under the influence of Karl Marx and the Communist Party of China. He knew everything about the power of simple messages and of peasant mobilization. He alone determined that if four pests — rats, flies, mosquitos and sparrows — could be eradicated, disease and hunger in China could be halted. He went as far as to call sparrows "tools of capitalism," since they picked away at the grain stores of the proletariat, each bird eating an estimated four pounds per year.

To that end, an enormous number of Chinese were mobilized to kill the Eurasian tree sparrow. Soldiers, students, civil servants and members of neighborhood committees — tens of millions of Chinese — set about hazing sparrows, destroying their nests and denying them roosts. Soon, whole flocks dropped from exhaustion in midair. The sparrow population in China plummeted and the species was driven to near extinction.

But one Chinese ornithologist raised questions about the wisdom of Mao's sparrow campaign early on, pointing out that sparrows ate insects that would be much more detrimental to rice yields than birds ever could be. Sparrows, as it turned out, were a vital cog in China's agricultural system, since they ate locusts, whose numbers subsequently exploded absent a primary natural predator. It was the locust outbreak that triggered the mass famine, which killed tens of millions of Chinese. It was made worse by other elements of the Great Leap Forward, such as deforestation and the overuse of pesticides.

The ornithologist who dared question the sparrow eradication and predicted the plague of locusts, Tso-Hsin Cheng, was declared a criminal, forced to wear a badge that identified him as a "reactionary." He spent a decade sweeping corridors and cleaning toilets. Later, he was kept in isolation in a cowshed, and all his belongings were seized, including his most prized possession, a typewriter.

What the Soviet and Chinese famines have in common is government coercion, destruction of entrepreneurial incentive, and widespread coverups and falsification of production data. No one is suggesting the United States is now at the brink of such misery, only that Americans have become increasingly ignorant of poor governance and the effects it is having on agriculture; it is all too often laced with arrogance and scapegoating.

* * *

Zephyrs and a cornflower blue sky at dawn portend a good growing day. The Rusty Wagon restaurant is a locally famous eatery on Hannegan Road in the middle of nowhere in Whatcom County, Washington. The diner is Texas-themed. Its walls and ceilings are leprous with Texas memorabilia and placards. It's a place where words come easily, the kind of place a politician running for office might wander into to press the flesh for the cameras with polite but skeptical constituents and then grab a plate of the eatery's substantial breakfast steak. Today it is serene. A handful of patrons populate the tables. Ambient luminescence, filtered through skylights, and conical glass pendants, bathe the place in a comforting morning glow. Two elderly men sit at a table near the wall. An elaborately carved cane belonging to one of the men leans against the rustic-style wainscoting. Tourists have not yet discovered the Rusty Wagon, at least not in the same way they huddle around restaurants off Guide Meridian Road and Grover Street in Lynden proper. Lynden, population 14,000, is the second-largest city in Whatcom County, the largest raspberry-producing county in Washington, which in turn is the largest raspberry-producing state in the nation. In an office along a tree-lined street of well-kept wood-framed clapboard houses, many with dormers and front-gabled roofs, can be found Henry Bierlink, executive director of the Washington Red Raspberry Commission.

"I don't sense urban lawmakers are hostile to agriculture, just very ignorant about it," said Bierlink.

When it comes to going head to head with certain of the state's elected officials, and the deputies and policy analysts who screen them, one suspects Bierlink lives by the advice of George Bernard Shaw to never wrestle a pig: "You get dirty, and besides, the pig likes it." He keeps his observations hedged with a slight kumbaya vibe.

"Washington, like other rapidly growing states, is characterized by stable rural communities [surrounded by] exploding urban populations where new economies are developing. This is a recipe for misunderstanding," he said.

"But the more we misunderstand each other the more we will be thinking we need to regulate behavior we don't understand. Farmers certainly feel misunderstood and overregulated," said Bierlink. His earnestness and regular-joe respectability come through, but so does his meaning.

"So, farmers are feeling marginalized, right?" I asked him. "Not sure if 'marginalized' is the right description, but sheer numbers make our job more challenging and require us to adopt new tactics – not exactly why most people went into farming." said Bierlink. There's enough portent in his words to warrant concern.

Wage and benefit *diktats* and layer upon layer of fuel and

fertilizer taxes, state income taxes, state corporation taxes, water-use restrictions, water fees and nuisance fees that affect operating costs are shrinking the diversity of America's crops and scaling up what's been called the "monoculture."

Besides treating farmers as a convenient target for regulation and taxation, officeholders – some merely reveling in the political game from deep in the weeds – are failing to ensure the free functioning of markets, a basic responsibility of government in a free society. It's the engine room of the whole thing. They're failing to protect the markets from the undue influence of trusts, syndicates and vertical monopolies that form in agriculture when government loses interest or gets bought off. Concentration of ownership gunks up free markets. Lawmakers refuse, or don't care enough, to keep them free and functioning. When growers, seed producers, consolidators, packing houses, distributors and cooperatives get too big, they can become mini-Standard Oils, cornering markets, fixing prices and brandishing their size to devour competitors and forcing problems upstream and downstream as they try to consolidate vertically and horizontally and shed risk. Nature rushes to fill a vacuum. How can politicians spot trust formation in agriculture if they remain ignorant of it or – as I suspect in some cases – ignorant of basic economics?

Dairy farmers are going out of business in Pennsylvania's top dairy county, Lancaster County, unable to meet expenses in the face of what they claim is empire-building by ever-larger milk cooperatives they say have assumed control of milk processing and have too much power. The Lebanon Daily News reported in 2018 that local agriculture leaders fear the next six months may bring an unprecedented sell-off of dairy herds in the county.

In Oregon, you don't just buy a dairy, a broker told me. You buy the *contract* the dairy has with a processor or co-op.

The dairy itself is a secondary consideration. An effect of state lawmakers taking ag for granted is they are no longer able or willing to identify trust formation within agriculture. (A clue to the current passion among officeholders and policy analysts in the Beaver State? Dominating the news at this writing, Oregon officials are agonizing over which species should prevail in the Columbia River as federally protected sea lions gorge themselves on federally protected salmon and steelhead.)

Like L.A. drivers scratching their heads at how the price of gas can go up while the price of crude goes down, dairymen – when they're not working their second or third off-farm job to make ends meet – sometimes try to understand the Byzantine formula processors use to set the price of milk. Most dairy farmers have no idea how buyers set their prices, so they shrug their shoulders and submit.

Simply because the climate and soil are ideal for certain crops in certain places, if lawmakers "gift" wages above what's feasible, farmers won't grow strawberries along California's fertile Central Coast. They won't grow Bing cherries in Washington's Yakima Valley or onions in eastern Oregon. Certainly, they won't grow these foods simply because we like – and need – to eat them as part of our human diet.

With labor-intensive crops like garlic and mushrooms, farmers won't grow these if the profit isn't commensurate with the risk – or if there is no chance for profit at all. It should be no surprise. U.S. farmers strain to compete with products from places like Mexico, Peru, Guatemala and China, where farmworkers make in a week what they make in the United States in a day.

But farmers are resilient. It's in their DNA. They will do as much of an end-run around high costs as they can as they focus on personal survival to the detriment of the whole. A classic "tragedy of the commons" is shaping up. Smaller farms – their owners no longer able to compete – are being assembled into larger ones; the new consolidated farms then grow a narrower variety of domestic crops, even if it threatens America's food independence and crop diversity. Farmers will also flock to crops for which they can receive federal price supports, now fashionably called "crop insurance."

All the while, demands on agriculture grow. By 2050, the global population will reach 10 billion people, requiring a 60 percent increase in worldwide agricultural productivity. The need for food security, the growing global population and shrinking natural resources – agriculture's big investment thesis – has become a cliché. It's been used as justification for all manner of actors to grow all manner of crops by all manner of methods – and sometimes receiving all manner of taxpayer money in the process. But make no mistake – cliché or not – the global population *is* growing, natural resources *are* shrinking, and countries *are* seeking to increase their own food security, and justifiably so. To survive, the small farmer needs to be an accountant, a healer, a scientist, a technologist and an accomplished professional gambler.

But what of the farm laborers?

Farm laborers, to the extent they're unskilled, have little chance of employment if their hands are idled by the rotors, claws and pincers of machines. Small farms are being bought up by larger ones, allowing greater economies of scale. Scaling up allows more mechanization, resulting in yet more idled pickers. It's been a vicious cycle. The small farmers at least have a better chance of hiring on with – or leasing their onetime land back from – whatever private equity fund, global ag concern or endowment happens to buy them out. Not so the farmworker. Maybe that was the idea all along.

Though the growing drumbeat of automation is a fact,

it's ironic that laws enacted glibly by urban lawmakers to help those at society's bottom rung are adding to their misery by eliminating work and limiting the availability of nutritious foods for those at the bottom rung, and everybody else.

It is the unwitting crop selection that is the far more dangerous unintended consequence. A wide breadth of domestic experience with diverse crops could disappear before our eyes as we accept the offshoring of a big chunk of our food supply. Diversity is otherwise preached as a great strength in every nook and cranny of American life. Scientists speak of the strengths of biodiversity. Yet the dangers of ignoring crop diversity aren't discussed. Our nation's food supply is much more vulnerable due to the vast monocrops that have developed in America's agricultural belts as globalization has become embedded in America's farm patch.

Farmers are at once being bludgeoned by climate politics and the *climate*. The cost to agriculture of ambitious climate programs at the state level means increases in the price of energy used in crop production – hikes in diesel fuel, gasoline, electricity and natural gas. The impact is the greatest where energy is needed for irrigation. In 2018, Washington looked like it would be the first state in the nation to tax carbon pollution. The bill lacked the one or two votes it needed to pass, according to the governor.

Such a tax would have increased off-farm transportation costs and penalized struggling farmers who drive long distances to their off-farm jobs. An energy tax would increase the cost of nitrogen fertilizer and other inputs and add to a list of ways Washington farmers are at a competitive disadvantage in the global marketplace. An extremely hot and dry summer in 2015 affected apples and cherries in the Evergreen State. The state's farmers got beaten up by Mother Nature. Then, for their troubles, they got beaten up by the state of

Washington, having to fight off the prospect of the carbon tax. Ironically, what kept the bill from passing was Washington's lawmakers' failure to agree on what to do with the revenue. Legislators in Hawaii, Maryland, Massachusetts, New Hampshire, New Mexico, New York, Oregon, Rhode Island and Vermont are examining similar bills. The indirect costs of government directives to combat climate change are predicted to eclipse direct costs and are estimated to account for about 70 percent of the total impact. Then there are the distortions in labor. Agriculture's current predicament is not all the fault of unappreciative urbanites and the politicians who represent them. It has long been an open secret in U.S. agriculture that about half of farm laborers are in the United States illegally. The Department of Labor, in its National Agricultural Workers Survey, puts it at 46 percent. Robert Guenther, senior vice president for public policy for the United Fresh Produce Association, a produce industry trade group, told the Washington Post in 2017 that he believes it's between 50 percent and 70 percent. This means what profitability has existed in some farm sectors has been based on a fiction. The labor, as a mobster might put it, "fell off the back of a truck." For eight years, the Obama administration prioritized border enforcement and stepped up deportations. Then the Trump administration came in and made this its calling card. The dependence on illegal labor is ag's own doing. Now the bill is coming due as the labor pool dwindles and reality sets in. A quick glance at the system that supplies largely illegal seasonal labor to farmers would be a made-to-order labor-racketeering case for any budding county D.A. or assistant U.S. attorney. Somehow, the practice came to be accepted.

Of the huddled masses who come to our shores legally thanks to Uncle Sam's largesse – over one million a year at last count – few agrarians seem to be among them. A sign of this: Despite heavy legal immigration into the United States over many decades, a graying trend among farmers has only accelerated, and America hasn't been able to replenish its dwindling farmer population. In 1982, the average age of the American farmer was 51 years old – already high. By 2012, the average farmer was older than 58, with over a quarter million U.S. farmers reporting in at 75 years old or older, according to the U.S. Census of Agriculture. In Oregon, farmers over the age of 70 made up the largest demographic, coming in at about 22 percent of all farmers in the Beaver State. We can't mint enough new farmers domestically, and we can't import our way out of the crisis through legal immigration.

It's no surprise that someone like Mary Kimball, executive director of the Center for Land-Based Learning, spends a lot of her time thinking about the problem. "It is what we talk about all the time," she told the Sacramento Business Journal in 2018. "It's a bad, bad, bad situation. There are a lot of people needed in the system." Farmers are aging out of the profession.

Farming in America doesn't necessarily require you to grow any crops either – or even to make fog on a mirror. According to the Government Accountability Office, between 2007 and 2011, Uncle Sam shelled out some $3 million in subsidies to 2,300 farms where no crop of any kind was grown. In a previous GAO report, more than 2,700 people whose gross income exceeded $2.5 million received more than $49 million in payments during a three-year period. Many should have been disqualified due to their high incomes.

The GAO also found the Agriculture Department had paid $1.1 billion between 1999 and 2005 to more than 170,000 people who were no longer alive. The report recommended the Agriculture Department work with the Internal Revenue

Service on a new verification system. That fix resulted in *just* $10.6 million being paid to farmers who had been dead for over a year between 2008 and 2012.

At this writing in 2018, the latest iteration of the farm bill is shaping up. The old bonds are being renewed among special-interest groups and political parties – conservative, liberal and all in between. Nothing unites Republican, Democrat and independent like a carve-up of ag welfare. Sketching out farm bills is a well-beloved parlor game.

Increasingly, farm households need to participate in the "gig economy." Median farm income earned by farm households is now less than zero. It was estimated to be negative $940 in 2016 and is forecast to decline further to $1,316 in the red in 2018, according to the Agriculture Department. In recent years, more than half of farm households have had negative farm income. The median off-farm income is forecast to increase 2.3 percent from $66,468 in 2016 to $68,011 in 2017, and another 2.8 percent in 2018 to $69,940. About 82 percent of U.S. farm household income, on average, is forecast to come from off-farm work, up from 53 percent in 1960, which must have seemed absurdly high even then. Brian Briggeman, an agricultural economist at Kansas State University, told the Wall Street Journal that most farmers couldn't repay the debts they incur to run their farms without an outside paycheck.

Farmers are grappling with the triple-whammy of globalization, changing weather patterns and enhanced government meddling. Food abundance, which Americans have taken for granted for decades, could end. Two of those forces are clearly the doing of man, not nature: Globalization, which pushes down prices on everything, and taxes and regulations, which push up operating costs on every aspect of bringing food to people.

Additional government meddling, in the form of sops to farmers, must then be brought to bear to rescue U.S. agriculture in the form of the farm bill. American agriculture has become a bus crash with the parts strewn across rural roads from Salinas to Cape Fear, visible to any acolyte wishing to take the time to see them.

If you doubt the role of globalization in all this, consider America's asparagus crop, which fell 61 percent between 2004 and 2014. Much of the decline is attributed to two trade agreements: The North American Free Trade Agreement and the Andean Trade Preference Act. These opened a floodgate of cheap, tariff-free asparagus from Latin America. Asparagus is uniquely dependent on human labor. According to the California Asparagus Commission, 75 percent of the production cost of asparagus is tied to human labor.

In the best of times, there are innumerable moving parts for any farmer, like rain, bank loans and crop prices. But these aren't the best of times. There are no winners when U.S. farming is driven offshore. While the consumer will benefit in the short term, it comes at a big increase in long-term risk to our food security. Meanwhile, the modern regulatory state brandishes only insouciance to the plight of the farmer, especially the small farmer. Ag needs to be respected and appreciated, not taken for granted or demonized. America's urban woes cannot be solved on the backs of food producers. If, for no other reason, because everybody needs to eat – even urbanites.

Many trends need to be reversed and many layers peeled back – which brings us to the "Sunion." Developed by Bayer Crop Science, it is a metaphor for all that is good and bad in modern-day agriculture. It is discussed in its tearless glory in the next chapter.

Chapter Two

Deconstructing the 'Sunion'

BROCCOLI IS MAN-MADE. You will never find broccoli growing in the wild. It was bred by Roman farmers beginning in the 6th century B.C. They bred it selectively from wild cabbage.

Like the Roman broccoli breeders, agronomists at Bayer Crop Science bred generation after generation of onion bulb over three decades, seeking out those that were least pungent using gas chromatography. They finally settled on a variety they now call the "Sunion" – touted as the first tearless onion.

"Onions that don't make you cry are finally here," blared a sophomorically exuberant food-section headline in the December 19, 2017, online edition of the Los Angeles Times. "There are few kitchen tasks more perilous than chopping with a sharp knife while blinded by onion tears," Times food writer Holly Van Hare effused. ABC's "Good Morning America," the Huffington Post and other media outlets issued over-the-top fluff pieces exalting the new onion variety.

The National Public Radio story got exceptionally fanciful, invoking Alice of the "Brady Bunch" and quoting

Rowlf the Dog on "The Muppet Show." Washington Post writer Maura Judkis assured readers: "If you're an anti-GMO-er about to tee up an objection, know that Sunions are not genetically modified. Instead, they're the result of crossbreeding less-pungent onions…"

Unlike the Roman agrarians who brought us broccoli, the Sunion was supported by a marketing rollout, point-of-sale materials, education for produce managers, social media content and a consumer advertising and public-relations campaign. According to Bayer, while growing in the field, it looks no different from any other onion. "The transition happens in storage," Bayer Senior Crop Sales Manager Lyndon Johnson told National Public Radio. Onions traditionally get more pungent the longer they're stored. The variety developed by Bayer gets sweeter and milder, and tearless, according to Bayer.

The Sunion had the nagging feel of a curiosity — a product on a late-night infomercial promising a solution to an exaggerated problem. After the initial burst of media attention, publicity for the Sunion fell off. Bayer is reported to have introduced 2.4 million pounds of the variety into the market as a handful of growers in Nevada and Washington were permitted to produce them. Bayer says it hopes to ramp up production to 200 million pounds in five years. Since the U.S. onion crop was 6.74 billion pounds in 2016, according to the National Onion Association, Bayer's goal seems modest.

The story of the tearless onion was a timely feel-good story for Leverkusen, Germany-based Bayer as it tries to build public goodwill in the United States prior to its $63 billion plan to devour U.S. agriculture giant Monsanto. During the writing of this book, Bayer closed the deal and immediately killed off the 117-year-old Monsanto name — with its past associations to the Vietnam-era defoliant Agent Orange;

DDT; genetically modified seeds; and glyphosate, the active ingredient in its pesticide Roundup. With the acquisition, Bayer doubled the size of its agriculture business overnight. American grain farmers who claim their fields have been contaminated by Monsanto's proprietary seeds blowing in from neighboring fields will now be up against squads of investigators and attorneys dispatched by a company that is even *larger* than Monsanto – a company based on the other side of the Atlantic no less.

First announced in 2016, Bayer's $63.5 billion takeover of U.S. Monsanto would create the largest seeds and pesticides company on the planet. The transaction makes Bayer the largest supplier of seeds and crop chemicals, surpassing DowDuPont, ChemChina's Syngenta and BASF. Besides dealing a major blow to competition among farmers for seeds, the massively unpopular deal provided something for everyone to dislike: Consumer groups, farmers, environmentalists, natural-food enthusiasts and even national security advocates were mostly opposed to the deal between the German and American companies.

But back to the Sunion. Lest anyone believe old-fashioned cross-breeding is without risk, consider the English bulldog. Centuries of selective breeding have left it so inbred it cannot be restored to health. On the flip side, such staples as broccoli, Brussels sprouts, boysenberries, kohlrabi, grapefruit, Meyer lemons, and a number of apple varieties bear the imprint of human meddling but these cultivars have withstood the test of time. Before human tampering, the banana and corn on the cob were pitiful things. We humans have been cross-breeding plants for centuries and are better off for it. Doing so is in our nature.

The Sunion was developed using such breeding methods. Onions are a biennial crop and take two growing seasons to go from seed to seed. In the case of the Sunion, the lower pungency bulbs were selected from the crop to replant for seed the following year. "We are taking one attribute from a bulb and applying it to grow the next generation. This entire process took 30 years of development in the case of Sunions," said Johnson, a 1986 University of Wyoming grad who has dedicated his career to onions. He started at Bayer in 2008 as a sales specialist in onions and carrots and is now crop sales manager in the NAFTA region, including Central America.

* * *

In California, nearly all onions are grown from seeds. In a couple of corners of the state, farmers plant their fields with transplants. Commercial onion production breaks down into three groups: dehydration onions, storage onions and fresh-market onions. Most of the acreage is for dehydration and storage onions. (Fresh-market onions are generally the purple and sweet onions you find in a hamburger.)

Excluding onions for dehydration, American farmers plant about 125,000 acres of onions annually, producing about 6.74 billion pounds of the bulbs in 2016, according to the National Onion Association. The U.S. accounts for 1.6 percent of the world onion acreage and produces about 4 percent of the world's annual supply. The U.S. dry bulb onion crop value exceeds $1 billion at farmgate and generates $5 billion to $7 billion at the consumer level.

Onions can be enormously labor-intensive since they must be planted and harvested manually. The initial investment for onions is high compared with other field crops. Across the globe, the largest onion-producing countries are China, India, the United States, Turkey and Pakistan, in that order. That American farmers can compete with China and India on any level of onion production is itself astounding given the lopsided labor costs and regulatory pressures in the Unites States.

In the United States, the top three onion-producing regions by acreage are Washington, Idaho-Eastern Oregon and California, according to the National Onion Association.

"Onions are a rotation crop," said Bob Ehn, chief executive and technical manager at the California Garlic and Onion Research Committee. "One year you grow onions and then four to five years you grow something else. Farmers usually rotate into tomatoes or cotton."

What keeps Ehn up at night can be summed up in two words: "white rot." It is a serious fungal disease and the number-one threat worldwide to crops of the onion family. The pathogen wilts the foliage, rots the roots and invades the bulb with white mold. As of this writing, no variety is resistant to it.

The industry term for crops of the onion family – like garlic, shallots, onions, chives and leeks – is "alliums."

"[White rot] can remain in the soil for 20 years. It's selective to alliums. Once it's discovered in soil, that land must be taken out of production for future alliums," said Ehn

Back to the Sunion. A few produce managers say customers are viewing it as a sweet onion. Was the Sunion Bayer's stab at breaking the Vidalia onion's stranglehold on the sweet onion market? Vidalia onions are defined to include only those produced in 13 counties and portions of seven others, all in Georgia, according to the Vidalia Onion Committee. Grow them elsewhere and you risk running afoul of Federal Marketing Order No. 955 as well as Georgia state law.

"Sunions are on the market at a different time of year than the Vidalia onion as [the latter] is a sweet, short-day onion that is available from May to August," said Johnson at Bayer Crop Science. "It has been our experience that along with the flavor experience of Sunion comes a point of distinction with the tearless aspect of the product," he said. "This is an attribute that sets the Sunion apart from all other sweet onions on the market between December and April, when Sunions are available.

"When these two attributes were introduced, the tearless quality stood out as the most unique between the two," said Johnson. "It speaks to the convenience for the consumer and solves an age-old problem of being able to handle an onion in the kitchen without crying." (The next thing Johnson was to write me in an email rocked my foundation. I soon grasped the bald ambition of the Sunion.)

"We believe it will also drive consumption as Sunions can be dipped straight into guacamole and eaten raw," said Johnson. "… dipped straight into guacamole…" The Sunion isn't just a threat to the sweet onion. Good God! This was a charge up shared consumption's Mount Suribachi – a headlong assault not only on the conventionally pungent onion but on the hegemony of the very chip itself. On the very chip itself! "There's a fine line between wrong and visionary," said the character Sheldon Cooper in "The Big Bang Theory," "Unfortunately, you have to be a visionary to see it."

The mega-merger with Monsanto aside, recent findings suggest one of its pesticides is harming a variety of bee species, and there's a connection to the Sunion that was missed by the giddy reporting of the media outlets when the Sunion was first announced. Bayer Crop Science was in the news in 2017 after a study found its neonicotinoid pesticides could be linked to declining honeybee numbers over the past decade. Neonicotinoids, a new class of insecticides, are particularly effective in the battle against sap-feeding insects like aphids.

Chemically related to nicotine, the "neonics" act on certain receptors in the nerve synapse. They're much more toxic to invertebrates, like insects, than they are to mammals, birds and other higher organisms, according to Texas A&M AgriLife Extension. Neonicotinoid insecticides are suspected in the decline of bee colonies when the insecticide occurs at trace levels in the nectar and pollen of crop plants. Because it's water soluble, it can be applied to soil taken up by plants. Soil applications reduce the risks for insecticide drift from the target site, and to some of the beneficial insects that land on plants.

The first neonicotinoid to reach the market was imidacloprid, a common ingredient in Bayer Advanced Vegetable and Garden Insect Spray. It can be sprayed directly on a plant but is often more effective (especially on sucking insects) when applied to the soil, recommends Texas A&M AgriLife.

In 2012, researchers at Lancaster University and the University of Stirling in the United Kingdom exposed colonies of the bumble bee in the laboratory to imidacloprid. They set the exposure levels to those they believed would be expected in the field. They then allowed them to develop naturally under these simulated field conditions.

The researchers found exposed colonies had a significantly reduced growth rate and suffered an 85 percent reduction in new queens compared with control colonies. The U.K. researchers believe the neonicotinoids, given their wide-scale use, may be having a considerably negative impact on wild bumble bee populations across the developed world. Honeybees were affected differently. A group of French researchers reported that exposing honeybees to nonlethal doses of thiamethoxam, also a neonicotinoid, causes homing failure at levels that could put a colony at risk of collapse. Free-ranging foragers were fitted with radio-frequency identification tags. Results showed that homing was impaired by the pesticide after the bees were exposed.

Because they are systemic chemicals, absorbed into the plant, neonicotinoids can be present in pollen and nectar, reports the nonprofit Xerces Society. The potentially long-lasting presence of neonicotinoids in plants, although useful from a pest management standpoint, makes it possible for these chemicals to harm pollinators even when the initial application is made weeks before the bloom period.

In addition, depending on the compound, rate and method of application, neonicotinoids can persist in the soil and be continually taken in by plants for very long periods of time, wrote the nonprofit group.

Beginning in 2008, the U.S. Environmental Protection Agency opened dockets for all the neonicotinoid pesticides. The stated goal of its Pollinator Protection office is to review the pesticides in this class simultaneously, so it can ensure consistency across the class. The EPA is scheduled to complete its risk assessments for the neonicotinoids in 2018.

Studies indicate the levels of neonicotinoids around farms don't wipe out colonies overtly. Instead, they kill insidiously through long-term exposure. The pesticides threaten queens, resulting in lower colony reproductive rates.

* * *

Amro Zayed is an associate professor of biology and a research chair in genomics at Toronto's York University. In lab-speak, Zayed is the "principle investigator." He completed his doctorate in biology at York in 2006, then a postdoctoral fellowship at the University of Illinois Department of Entomology in 2008.

His lab has more than a dozen postdoctoral fellows, research associates and graduate students. Its stated goal is to understand the how's and why's of the evolution of social behavior in insects. Researchers at the lab ask questions about the genetic and molecular bases of social traits and how such traits evolved. If Dr. Zayed's blog is any guide, he's carefully cultivated much collegiality and sense of shared purpose at the lab. In 2017, a lab alumnus, Dr. Brock Harpur, garnered the 2017 George C. Eickwort award from the North American Section of the International Union for the Study of Social Insects. The Eickwort is given annually to a doctoral student or recent graduate who shows the most distinguished record of research and scholarly activity in social insect biology.

The same year, Matt Betti, a Ph.D. in applied mathematics from the University of Western Ontario, joined them to work on mathematical aspects of bee health and evolution. Betti's expertise is the modeling of infection in bee colonies. He has developed a bee-health simulator dubbed "Bee++," a play on the computer programming language C++. (There are countless such jests in the bee research world. When a researcher successfully defended his dissertation and earned his doctoral degree recently, he was dubbed a "Ph. Bee." There are memes floating around referring to researchers "getting the hives" and the like.) Betti turned the bee world into a set of equations and identified patterns. He developed a mathematical model using data from field biologists and discovered that, when something is threatening the colony, forager bees leave the hive at a young age. His simulator looks at the dynamics of the spread of disease within a colony coupled with the underlying demographics of the colony to determine its fate under different scenarios.

His research has been likened to standing on a perch

overlooking Toronto's frenetic Bloor/Young subway station at 5:00 p.m. The riders may appear as one enormous mass during rush hour, but look more closely. Riders toting laptop cases and dressed in business attire tend to head south, while more youthful riders in jeans tend to head west. Betti's new work takes a similar view from the top. By grouping bees by age, he can see patterns among bees at one day old, two days old and onward through their life cycle.

In mid-2017, the lab published a paper in the journal Science examining agricultural chemical use near Canadian cornfields using neonicotinoid-treated seeds over a five-month growing season. The Government of Ontario funded the study. The research team included collaborators from Québec's Université Laval led by Dr. Valérie Fournier and several of Zayed's undergrads.

Researchers looked for traces of neonicotinoids in forager bees, nurse bees, larvae, pollen and nectar. They also examined dead bees for the insecticide. Since neonicotinoids are water-soluble, agricultural runoff containing the chemical enters waterways.

To the surprise of Zayed's team, neonicotinoids were detected in pollen from plants near crop fields. These included clover, willow and wildflowers. Flowers miles away from farms were found to have absorbed the chemicals, which seeped into the stems, leaves, pollen and nectar. It suggests neonicotinoids remain in the environment and are absorbed by wildflowers, exposing bees years after an initial crop use.

Typically, experiments linking neonicotinoids and declining bee health have been criticized for not simulating realistic exposure. With this study, the duration and magnitude of neonicotinoid exposure was pegged to Canada's corn-growing regions. The team's aim was to design realistic experiments to investigate the effect of such insecticides on honeybees. Colonies near cornfields were exposed to neonicotinoids for up to four months — most of the honeybees' active season. Experiments showed neonicotinoids increased worker bee mortality and were associated with declines in social immunity and increased queenlessness over time. The team also reported finding that toxicity of neonicotinoids to honeybees doubles in the presence of a commonly encountered fungicide. The team's work, it contends, demonstrates that field-realistic exposure to "neonics" can reduce honeybee health in corn-growing regions.

The lab's findings were later written about in publications like Forbes, the Los Angeles Times, the Scientist, New Scientist, the Washington Post, the Guardian and Scientific American.

Bayer Crop Science, one of the world's main neonicotinoid producers, says the evidence that the insecticides can harm bees is limited. It asserts it is looking to find solutions to bee health challenges, that its program brings Bayer's extensive bee health experience and knowledge under one coordinated platform. It says it has dedicated 25 years to ensuring the protection of bees.

If the bee researchers in Zayed's lab wielded the odd bee-related pun, Bayer Crop Science's Bee Care Program's U.S. website is brimming with them. The site exudes good cheer and bonhomie but in a "corporate caring" kind of way. No expense (or exclamation mark) was spared in the making of the website. Here, "Buzz-worthy recipes incorporate honey, peaches, cranberries and more delicious foods brought to us by bees and other pollinators!" It's as if to say, Worried about colony collapse? We've gotcha covered! Bayer is also sprinkling around small wads of cash – never a bad thing for a corporate behemoth whose operations meld chemicals and food production. "Feed a Bee's initiative to plant pollinator forage across the country by the end of 2018 is still going strong!" blares a headline on the site with restless exaltation. "In the latest round of funding, 22 new organizations working hard to support bees and other pollinators in their communities were selected to receive awards ranging from $1,000 to $5,000. These diverse projects join the 71 that were awarded in the first two rounds of funding, bringing the total to 93 projects nationwide joining with the Feed a Bee program to promote and protect pollinator health."

Bayer's Bee Care website is a lot like washingtongenerals.com, the site underwritten by the Harlem Globetrotters for their perennially hapless opponent, the Washington Generals.

Caspar Hallmann, a doctoral student at Radboud University in Nijmegen, Holland, authored a study in which dozens of amateur entomologists used traps to collect flying insects from over 60 German nature preserves from 1989 through 2016. The traps were checked at regular intervals following a standardized protocol, and the insects were weighed. The researchers found a 6.1 percent yearly decline in aerial-insect biomass and an overall decline of nearly 77 percent in the 25 years studied. After controlling for seasonal changes and habitat type, researchers found declines were higher in summer months. The data was published in the peer-reviewed journal PLOS One.

The data offered insight into the quantity of insects available to act as herbivores, pollinators and food for other animals. In the United States alone, the ecosystem services provided by wild insects have been estimated at $57 billion annually. The study didn't attempt to pinpoint a cause for the decline in bugs, but the authors say that this voluminous and unexpected loss can't be adequately explained by changes in weather patterns, changes in land use or the loss of habitat. Instead, the researchers and others suspect the biomass in the nature reserves may have been adversely affected by adjacent agricultural areas due to changes in agricultural practices.

"I think it's likely [that] it's how the surrounding land is being managed, because the nature reserves themselves haven't really changed, but the surrounding landscape is full of these big monoculture crops treated with lots of insecticides," Dave Goulson, a co-author of the study, told one publication. Goulson is a biology professor at the University of Sussex in Brighton in the United Kingdom.

Lepidopterists – a dying breed themselves – have chronicled the extinction over the years of certain trophy species of butterfly. They faulted the destruction of habitat. One of the most notable examples was North America's Xerces blue. It flourished in the coastal sand dunes of the Sunset District on the San Francisco Peninsula in California. Urban development in the area caused the loss of the lotus plant, resulting in the last living Xerces blue being spotted in 1941. The Xerces blue lives on but only in the name of the Xerces Society, a non-profit focused on the conservation of invertebrates and their environments.

Loss of habitat may not have been considered a cause in this study, but it does feature prominently in other studies. It has, in fact, been linked to the loss of certain flying insects. In one case, the abandonment of grazing brought about a species' failure.

In Britain, the caterpillar that metamorphoses to the "large blue" requires three weeks amid the flowers of wild thyme or marjoram. The caterpillar then tricks red ants into believing it is one of their own grub. The ants carry it underground into the nest and place it with the ant brood. It then spends the next 10 months feeding on the ant grubs before pupating in the nest the next year and emerging as a butterfly. The thin-soiled grasslands hosting the caterpillar and the requisite ant colonies were abandoned by farmers after they became unproductive. The blues were reintroduced in Britain in the 1980s. Scrub clearance and careful grazing of wildflower-rich grasslands has been key to bringing them back.

But what of the Sunion? Does Bayer Crop Science treat the Sunion seeds with chemicals to inhibit nematodes, onion maggots or other pests or blights that attack alliums? Are any neonicotinoids in the mixture?

"We use a combination of three fungicides and two insecticides to enhance the seed as we do with all of our conventionally grown onions," Bayer Crop Sales Manager Johnson wrote me in an email. "They are not all Bayer chemistries, and our customers order their enhancement to fit their particular growing situation. As a rule, these enhancements protect the seedling against soil-borne diseases (rhizoctonia and pythium, etc.) and insects (onion maggot) until they become established in the field."

A report on new seed treatment options for the onion maggot by Cornell Vegetable Program Specialist Christy Hoepting and Cornell entomologist Brian Nault identifies the neonicotinoids. The Bayer Crop Sciences onion seed treatment Sepresto contains the active ingredients clothianidin and imidacloprid, both neonicotinoids. In fact, many annual field-crop seeds are coated – corn, cotton, soybean, oats, wheat, rye, sunflower, canola. The EPA estimates 30 percent of the 90 million acres of soybeans in the United States are planted with neonicotinoid-coated seeds. That percentage is much greater for corn seed. In fact, neonicotinoids are commonly coated onto seeds rather than sprayed on leaves, so they will guard against soil pests. A piece of policy jiu jitsu regarding "treated articles" has permitted pesticide makers to sell neonicotinoid-coated seeds without the agency questioning any adverse environmental effects.

The onion maggot, says Johnson, attacks seedlings and begins feeding on roots and then into the basal plate – the plant's growth point. Many plants can be destroyed by the larvae as they continue to move down the onion row. Losses can be up to 90 percent if the population of maggots is extreme. The maggots continue to have a new life cycle every couple of weeks. They are a greater problem in the muck soils of the Northeastern United States and Southern Canada, where the cool wet conditions of spring are favorable and the soil has plenty of organic matter. Usually maggots are done feeding and the life cycles are over before the onion is in the late season and bulbing. But by then, the damage has been done.

* * *

Late-season snow in the onion fields of the Northwest usually results in delayed planting. When this happens, production is squeezed into a shorter timeframe, and onions are fewer and smaller. Summer days with heat over 100 degrees also slows growth. The 2016 onion industry in the Northwest was a mess due to a winter like none had seen in decades. The weight of the snow collapsed or heavily damaged buildings, including onion packing and storage sheds, reported the Ontario, Oregon, Argus Observer. "I didn't lose any onions," Grant Kitamura at Murakami Produce told the publication. "[But] it was an expensive winter." Some of his company's buildings were damaged and snow removal costs also piled up. Alexis Taylor, director of Oregon's state Board of Agriculture, toured Malheur County along the Idaho border. "It was overwhelming to see the amount of snow, the destruction, and the lack of infrastructure to deal with snow," she said. Payette-based Partners Produce fared worse. At least 11 of its facilities were damaged, George Rodriguez, Sr., who heads the family-owned operation, told the publication. "Five buildings collapsed completely," he said.

While Oregon's farmers like Kitamura and Rodriguez battle the effects of climate and globalization on their bottom lines, at this moment, they face the prospect of a cap-and-trade bill that would place yet-unknown costs on their fertilizer. They gird their loins.

This and a spate of other state and local taxes and mandates – in place or being debated – have sent some farmers scurrying across the state line into Idaho, but if it someday becomes too expensive to farm this productive onion land, and the costs can't be passed on to consumers due to cheaper onions undercutting them from abroad, the fields will sit fallow while small farmers look for other ways to feed their families, including joining the service economy or re-cropping. Such are the strains on the American onion farmer. When the tipping point is reached and onions become too expensive to produce domestically, don't expect an official announcement from onion farmers. They will fail, sell off their land or re-crop over time and in silence. As Ernest Hemingway wrote of bankruptcy in "The Sun Also Rises," it happens in two ways, "gradually, then suddenly."

But back to the Sunion. How has it fared in stores? Interviews with produce managers at stores where Sunions were marketed ran the gamut. "We had Sunions at the end of the year, then they stopped coming in. Customers liked them a lot," said Andy Cavalier, assistant produce manager at upscale Gelson's market in Calabasas outside Los Angeles. "They moved pretty well. The color was like sweet onions, so customers assumed that's what they were."

In Texas, Sunions were sold at H-E-B, a San Antonio-based supermarket chain. "We had it for a month or so. There wasn't much reaction," said Produce Manager John Jonas at the H-E-B in College Station.

"We didn't have anyone going crazy over them while we had them in stock. People just thought it was a sweet onion," said John Watson, produce manager at H-E-B in Burleson, south of Fort Worth.

"It's been slow. We have a big sign that says 'Tear-Free.' No one has specifically asked me for them. They've been moving slower than the regular yellow onions," said Louie Barbera, produce manager at the H-E-B in Hilltop, south of San Antonio.

Whether the Sunion takes its place in the pantheon of man-made cultivars – like the Brussels sprout and broccoli – or is a meteor shower of non-pungent temporality, it's too soon to say. But if the Sunion enters the onion pantheon, it will perfectly encapsulate what Americans demand of ag: We demand the illusion of pungency without the inconvenience of actual pungency. We want onions, and lots of them, in our shared-consumption foods. We want them available year-round and in perpetuity, so we don't want onion maggots wiping out the crop certain years and making onions expensive and scarce. While you're at it, please do business with only those chemical conglomerates that create pesticides that target the bad insects and spare the beneficial ones. (Also, we don't want to be bothered with the details of how this is done.) Oh, and did I mention that we want farmers to bear all the cost and risk? None of these demands seem unreasonable to us. It's revelatory of what we're asking of ag.

Chapter Three

You Are Now Entering
Santa Clara County

SANTA CLARA COUNTY in Northern California is a one-of-a-kind accretion of fantastical wealth; social malaise; overcrowding; brilliant minds; cratered roads; sky-high living costs; encampments reminiscent of Mumbai slums; winged villas; Superfund cleanup sites and opulent corporate campuses. Amid these extremes, farmers attempt to grow things in some of the nation's most fertile soil. Most of the agriculture, which feels more like a Proustian time warp with each day, takes place in the southern reaches of the county. Like the slumbering – for now – San Andreas Fault, the line separating the two Californias cuts right through Santa Clara County.

But the dystopia that is Santa Clara County cannot be fully understood without first grasping what makes California so genuinely awful for businesses that operate on thin margins and need to employ many people. In 2017, the state garnered the dubious distinction of being ranked 50th for business-friendliness – defined as the freedom from lawsuits and state regulations – in CNBC's scorecard "America's Top States for Business." For housing, food and energy costs, it hardly fared better, ranking 48th. It also ranked a dismal 49th in Cost of Doing Business, which measures the tax climate, utility costs, wages, commercial rents and equipment rental costs.

As it braces for its anticipated "silver tsunami" – when unfunded pension and health-care liabilities for public employees swamp the system as baby boomers retire – the state increasingly seems like a place that has been run for and by government employees. But as irony would have it, even the agencies much responsible for the flight of private-sector jobs in the state and the high cost of everything can no longer afford to do business in wide swaths of the state. As I write this in mid-2018, the California Public Utilities Commission, which regulates the state's electric and natural gas utilities, telecommunications providers, private water companies, railroads and passenger transportation companies, is moving its 1,300 employees from the Bay Area to the Central Valley. Unable to grasp the connection between the vast regulatory state they've helped create and the high cost of living, members of the state's power structure now shrug their shoulders in capitulation: "It's hard to find a place to live in San Francisco on a state employee salary," as the regulator's president, Michael Picker, told the Sacramento Business Journal.

A 2018 study on millionaire migration to the state by Charles Varner and Cristobal Young of Stanford University and Allen Prohofsky of the state's Franchise Tax Board shows, predictably, the wealthy continue to flock to California, despite its high levels of taxation; meanwhile, the U.S. census found from 2007 to 2016, on net, the state lost about 2.5 percent of its population. California is suffering a Warsaw Pact-style brain drain as skilled workers and professionals leave the state. By a wide margin, they are moving to Texas – a low-tax, low-regulation, low-services state.

Nestled in the bosom of this dysfunction is Santa Clara County. Here, the county sales tax is nine cents for every dollar spent. The county seat, San Jose, was until recently home to "the Jungle," a vast huddle of humanity constituting one of the largest homeless encampments in the nation; the poverty rate in the city has risen to 12.9 percent, and the city has allowed its roads to deteriorate to the third-worst in the nation, according to Odometer.com's annual roundup. The county recently notched a $1 billion backlog of deferred maintenance costs for infrastructure.

In stark counterpoint, the county is home to global tech giants and Stanford University. Its northernmost urban areas comprise the Silicon Valley. But even the venerated Silicon Valley has changed. It's a mnemonic triumph to recall the days when innovation, rather than disruption, was the buzzword here. Once completely agricultural, Santa Clara County is now heavily urbanized; only its southern- and easternmost portions remain agricultural and rural.

State and local obstacles – along with relentless anti-growth sentiment – make it largely unfeasible to build new homes in the county. There is much demand for housing due to a steady creation of tech jobs by its corporate titans and the innumerable scrappy startups they attract. Because of the imbalance, the median home price here surpassed $1 million for the first time in early 2018, according to CoreLogic. But what you get in Santa Clara County for $1 million is a starter home, and one just possibly on a Superfund clean-up site.

In Sunnyvale, a 1950s-era starter home of 1,100 square feet was put on the market with a brokerage for $1.1 million in September 2017. It sold in two weeks after multiple parties bid up the price for the three-bedroom, two-bath home to $1.2 million. The home, which is on a plot of land just 6,200 square feet, is in the San Miguel Neighborhood. The neighborhood isn't like any other. It's at the confluence of three underground plumes of toxic solvents containing TCEs, chemicals used to clean silicon wafers during Sunnyvale's chipmaking past. The plumes inspired the EPA to informally, and then formally, dub the area the "Triple Site," one of 24 Superfund sites in north Santa Clara County. Studies have linked TCE exposure to kidney cancers, non-Hodgkin's lymphoma and birth defects. Another midcentury starter home a block away, also atop the Triple Site, sold at about the same time for $1.3 million after spending but eight days on the market. It was bid up from its asking price of $988,000.

As if they were baronial estates, such post-war crackerboxes – contamination and all – are now lovingly handed down from parent to child, so out of reach are starter homes for young families, so dead is the American Dream here.

Next to a Lowe's Home Improvement store is a mound of soil covered with dry grass. It's reported to be ground zero of the contamination. Workers in the local office of the EPA go door-to-door in the San Miguel neighborhood, asking if they can test the air inside homes. Sometimes residents ask them in and allow them to set up monitoring equipment. Other times, residents, some with limited English and an even more limited grasp of underground chemical plumes, shoo them away in distrust. The holy trinity of not-in-my-backyard forces, high development costs and government restrictions is so daunting in at least one corner of Santa Clara County that a starter home atop a contaminated toxic plume now fetches more than $1 million. Meanwhile, in the south of the county, a different reality reigns.

"We are based in Santa Clara County – the same county

as multi-billion-dollar firms like Facebook, Apple and the rest of Silicon Valley," said Ken Christopher, third-generation garlic farmer and scion of U.S. garlic powerhouse Christopher Ranch. "We have some of the toughest regulations in the nation. If we want to invest in new infrastructure, new buildings, new offices, new plants or new equipment, the permitting process is extremely burdensome."

Christopher's characterization of life in the county is epitomized by Mountain View, a city whose name is synonymous with the tech industry. Job creation coupled with the lack of required housing for those new workers has resulted in thousands of squatters living in recreational vehicles on city streets. The city's leadership – lacking the sangfroid to carry out the most basic stewardship of the public roadways – refuses to clear out the squatters. When complaints streamed in of sewage being dumped onto lawns and into sinks in park bathrooms, the city began a pilot program in which police handed out vouchers entitling the "campers" to free honey-wagon services. The city ended the program several months later after it discovered that only one in seven of the new denizens had used their vouchers. It seemed it was more convenient for the interlopers to just dump the sewage onto nearby lawns. The city also learned that more than a few of the squatters were tenants of squatter "landlords," who rented out spaces in broken-down RVs for a profit. Nowadays, people in parts of Mountain View make small talk about scatological discoveries in the same way small-town denizens elsewhere in America discuss the weather.

As I write this, one such wheeled brute disgorged its secrets – a trash bag filled with 20 pounds of human excrement – onto a sidewalk in San Francisco's Tenderloin district. An image quickly found its way to Reddit, then onto a national news outlet. Complaints about human waste around San Francisco increased by 400 percent from 2008 to 2018, according to 311, San Francisco's police app.

The publication Business Insider has pronounced Silicon Valley unaffordable for software engineers, the very talent Silicon Valley attracts. According to Glassdoor.com, the median software developer salary in Silicon Valley was $124,555 in 2018. But according to the mortgage research company HSH.com, based on a 30-year fixed mortgage with an interest rate of 4.20 percent, to purchase a house at the median home price in San Jose of $1,270,000, engineers would require a salary of at least $235,646.

Millennials are being battered by forces they don't understand – forces that are not their doing. Supply and demand are so off kilter in the state that if you had a little over 20 percent more housing, wrote economist Jerry Nickelsburg in a 2017 UCLA Anderson Forecast, home prices would fall by just 10 percent, suggesting the sheer scope of the housing backlog. Applying that to Santa Clara County, where there were 652,000 housing units in 2016, it suggests about 130,500 dwellings would have needed to be built that year just to bring the median home price down from about $988,000 to $889,000. From 2014 through 2016, only about 4,000 units were built.

It's no better in San Jose, where there were 328,000 housing units in the city at the end of 2016. About 65,500 units would have to have been built to work even the modest magic of Nickelsburg's calculation. Only about 2,000 were actually built in the city from 2014 through 2016.

The bright side? California may end up depopulating its way to cheaper housing. Just 11.9 children were born per 1,000 California residents in 2017, according to the Centers for Disease Control and Prevention. That's the lowest birth rate in the state in over 100 years, lower than what was seen during the Great Depression. Net outmigration of about one million residents per decade, as seen from 2006 to 2016, will also help depopulate the state if the trend continues.

In this pressure-cooker of NIMBYism, high taxation and ham-handed regulation, building anything from a fruit stand to farmworker housing to a milking barn is fraught with direct and indirect add-ons – all parties attempt to pass on the bloat to all other parties. The more the costs are passed back and forth, the more hidden and ingrained they become. Nowhere is this more palpable than in so-called soft costs in construction: architect fees, site surveyor fees, structural engineering fees, geotechnical engineering fees, landscape architect fees, Title 24 consultant fees, permit fees, school- and sewer-impact fees, recording fees and utility service hookup fees.

Another driver of housing scarcity in Santa Clara County is its overwrought 316-page zoning ordinance that works in conjunction with a two-volume 532-page general plan. (Compare this with ag-friendly southerly neighbor San Benito County and its 50-page zoning ordinance and its 194-page general plan.) Cities in north Santa Clara County tend to have strong NIMBY movements supercharged by tech-savvy organizers and the confirmation bias of ever-present and ever-vicious social media. There are many ways this county kills its Jeremiahs.

Vanessa Brown Calder, a policy analyst with the Cato Institute, found that increased land-use regulation was linked to rising home prices in 44 states and that increased zoning regulation was associated with rising home prices in 36 states. Blind to the role of taxation and regulation in the crisis – and so many others in California – lawmakers try to bandage the wounds the only way they know how: more taxation and regulation. Wielding these blunt instruments, they act as thought police in the marketplace of ideas. Unlike farmers, other industries can pack a bag and leave. Many have. But farmers – especially the multigenerational ones – are more anchored to the land.

The Christopher Family's presence in Santa Clara County predates Silicon Valley by nearly 100 years. The family began farming a patch of land in the county when it was known by the somewhat hokey moniker Valley of Heart's Delight for its heavy concentration of orchards, flowering trees and plants. Until the 1960s, it was the largest fruit production and packing region in the world with 39 canneries.

During a recent 30-year period, Santa Clara County lost about 21,000 acres of farmland and rangeland. A bastion is the 7,500-acre Coyote Valley between the city limits of San Jose and Morgan Hill. It is primed to be shoveled into the voracious gullet of the Silicon Valley organism. Circling are developers, brokers, buyers, speculators, tenants, planners, investment bankers, bond underwriters, plan-checkers, civil engineers, attorneys, architects, environmental consultants, soils experts, hydrologists and biologists. Meanwhile, the county touts a regional farmland preservation plan that relies on funds from a state cap-and-trade program, which raises operating costs on farmers, ensuring more farm failures.

Today, don't expect to find farmers keynoting conventions in the north county, where cities can't – or don't wish to – unleash the forces that will result in adequate housing to match the explosion in jobs that have so benefited them. Bedroom communities sprout in the south on what was once lovingly enriched soil – perfect farming *terroir*.

"If we were just one [county] further down Highway 25, we'd be in San Benito County and would have a much more agriculture-friendly environment. We'd love to invest more back into our business, which would allow us to produce more items and employ more people, but we're held back by a lot of red tape," intoned Christopher.

(Dear reader: Be assured I tried to draw certain parallels that would allow me to refer to Christopher as the Mark Zuckerberg or Steve Jobs of garlic. But I have too much respect for you, the reader, to resort to such cheap devices.)

The most important thing you need to know about the county Christopher refers to, San Benito County, is that it has a strong right-to-farm law. Such right-to-farm laws can be found in parts of all 50 states. Some are enshrined in state constitutions. They protect farmers against the nuisance lawsuits brought by people with little knowledge of farming. The laws help protect farmers against people who move into agricultural areas and then complain about the smells, noises, clutter and tractors in their newly discovered exurb. The analogy is the person who buys a house under a busy flight path and then complains incessantly about aircraft noise. Right-to-farm laws protect agrarians from those who would litigate (or in some cases legislate) them out of existence. But before officials in California counties like Butte, Colusa, Fresno, Monterey, Napa, San Benito, San Joaquin, Solano, Stanislaus and Yolo hyperextend their shoulders patting themselves on the back over enacting such laws, a far greater threat to farms in the Golden State looms.

Take garlic. All phases of garlic production are done by hand, including harvesting, cleaning, drying and packing – a process that can take about 25 days, depending on the weather. Every bulb needs to be touched by a human hand, so labor costs are a big concern.

California has created new entitlements on the backs of business and agriculture. They function as unfunded mandates, with little risk to the government thought leaders who enact them and all risk passed to those whose operating costs must now absorb them. The state is gradually adding hundreds of thousands of farmworkers to the ranks of those paid overtime after eight hours on the job or 40 hours in a week. Add to this the incremental rise toward the statewide $15-per-hour minimum wage in 2022; labor has put California garlic producers at an even greater disadvantage globally (if that's even possible). The lofty overtime law has begun to lower the threshold by half an hour each year until it reaches the standard eight-hour day by 2022.

Growers will struggle to compete with products out of Mexico where farmworkers make in a week what farmworkers here make in a day, Paul Wenger, president of the California Farm Bureau Federation, told the Los Angeles Times. "And this is not a good day for farmworkers who want to live that California dream of working a lot of hours to buy a home and do things they wouldn't be able to do in Mexico," he said on the day the law was signed. Lost on the Times in its reporting and lost on California's Governor Jerry Brown, who signed the fashionable $15-per-hour minimum wage and farmworker overtime bills, is that many farmers will simply rotate into crops that require less human handling or fallow their fields. Creating an edict that as much as doubles a major operating cost while subjecting farmers to remaining market forces is riding the tiger in a free-market system.

Someone like Christopher is in an impossible predicament. He's heavily branded as a garlic grower. He's tied to the pungent bulb. His company will have to automate to offset the more expensive manhours. Smaller growers who can't afford the required capital investments will be out of luck. "We currently have about 900 employees in Gilroy," said Christopher. "As far as the future is concerned, we are actively looking at adopting some technology to further automate our process. Our goal isn't to replace any labor but to augment our existing workforce with technology that can drive up productivity and help stabilize our costs per pound. Many countries in Europe that have even higher labor costs than [we do] have developed technology like optical scanners, improved aspiration systems and automated sleeve fillers, which may be of benefit to us."

China, with its whole-of-government mercantilism, its cheap labor and an ability to play the long game (as it need not contend with frequent political transitions brought about by pesky practices like democracy) is the world's leading producer and exporter of garlic. It produces nearly 60 million metric tons of it annually. It has been in trade disputes with South Korea, Japan and the United States and has been accused of dumping garlic into U.S. markets.

Most of the U.S. fresh garlic crop is grown in California. In the Golden State, planting takes place from September through November, and harvesting occurs in the summer and early fall.

Imports of garlic into the United States from China have been down in the last few years because the United States has been able to stop China from dumping by enforcing stricter duties and tightening regulations. As of this writing, an episode of the Netflix documentary series "Rotten" had caused a great load of invective to be rained down upon Christopher. The episode purported that Christopher Ranch had been gaming a loophole in anti-dumping restrictions on Chinese garlic.

In the episode, a lawyer, said to be representing aggrieved Chinese garlic dons wrongly barred from the U.S. market for dumping, combs the American outback and finds an artisanal farmer growing garlic and shallots on an acre and a half in the artists enclave of Dixon, New Mexico.

The garlic farmer, who doubles as a new-agey philosopher on the metaphysical properties of the bulb – ideal for the enlightenment-seeking culture of the baby boomers – sells his book (musings on the mystical aura of garlic), along with his piquant bulbs, at a farmer's market in Santa Fe. The farmer-turned-guru agreed to sign his name to a request with the U.S. Department of Commerce to review an anti-dumping order against a Chinese garlic importer. At some point, a purse of $50,000 is transferred to this Jack Kerouac of garlic, along with some shiny new farm equipment, according to the documentary.

Watching from down the road, a New Mexico mom-and-pop farming couple – garlic connoisseurs who identify themselves as "Bernie Sanders people" – agree also to sign on to the anti-dumping review with the understanding that they, too, would receive a payout when all was said and done. They tell the interviewer they believe their share of the haul in the anti-dumping case might be as much as $2.7 million. When only $5,000 changes hands, the pair flips to the other side. Envy, scorn, greed, narcissism, snobbery and class warfare – in short, all the Deadly Sins – have now entered the artisanal garlic world. Such is the allure and transformative potential of the Siberian stink bulb.

The episode also features glimpses of what were said to be Chinese prisoners using their teeth to peel garlic destined for the United States. The episode also details a RICO racketeering lawsuit filed against the New Mexico farmers and other combatants. A picture is painted of a wider agricultural long game by Chinese growers. Perhaps the true intention of the documentary was to show how government safeguards against foreign dumping can be subverted by perpetrator and victim alike. Had the story been submitted as a work of fiction, it would no doubt require the services of a Hollywood script doctor to tie up its loose ends.

Writer Pete Hamill presciently summed up the aim of the modern documentarian in an article for Esquire in 1994: "Even the conflicts of the so-called real world – the non-fiction world of news and society – must be simple, easy to follow through meals and other domestic activities, and preferably violent. Give us good guys and bad guys, white hats and black hats," he wrote.

While the Chinese garlic saga was absent any gunplay and contained just one too many madcap plot twists to feel coherent, the obvious black hat in the whole affair was Christopher Ranch.

"We felt like our reputation [had] been dragged completely through the mud for the sake of entertainment," Christopher told the San Jose Mercury News. On the company's Facebook page, he disputed the show's claims point by point. He denies he exploited anti-dumping loopholes – the central thesis in the documentary. He says his company grows up to 90 million pounds of California garlic a year and that 90 percent of the garlic his company sells to customers is grown in California. He makes a cogent case that his company had been pilloried in the docuseries' storyline for the sake of a good story.

Of course, he didn't help his cause by declining to be interviewed initially. He said he had sensed it was going to be negative, so he elected not to comment. But the silence only made the company the better villain. (One might forgive a garlic grower for lacking in media savvy.) Since the segment aired, he's obviously learned a few things.

"I've personally reached out to the lead investigator and the executive producers of both Zero Point Zero and Netflix to come out to the ranch, to see our fields, our millions of pounds of California garlic inventory, our audits, our production and our completely transparent process," said Christopher. "As Netflix is only 30 minutes or so away from the ranch, it was important for me to show them that their show was extremely biased and was riddled with errors and distortions, and that they're hurting an actual family farm," he said. "To date, I haven't received any correspondence back."

Netflix, a stupendously white-hot mass of expanding global subscribership, is the ideal streaming service for the social media age. Its algorithms gauge the proclivities of its subscribers; it then suggests to them an ever-more predictive menu of tranquilizing mind candy. The company has been in the news lately for its cult-like HR practices, such as encouraging employees to engage in theatrical show-trial confessions in a practice called "sunshining," reports the Wall Street Journal. Middle managers who don't fire enough of their underlings in a rite called the "Keeper Test" risk looking soft. The firings become public spectacles at Netflix.

It's clear Christopher is still fuming over the "Rotten" episode, although he strikes me as too much a gentleman to articulate it. To paraphrase Willie Stark, the fictitious Southern governor in Robert Penn Warren's "All The King's Men," it would be understandable if Christopher wished to fix Netflix CEO Reed Hastings, Jr., in such a way that his unborn great-grandchildren will wet their pants on the show's anniversary and not know why. There are rumors Christopher defenestrated his Roku after watching the episode. But he keeps it classy.

"The biggest threat to allium growers continues to be cheap international imports," said Christopher. "Growing garlic is a very expensive endeavor, and despite our 62 years of expertise in this field, we deal with very high costs of living, high wages, and high food safety standards. It's very hard to compete with countries like China, Mexico and Argentina that don't have the same costs or standards that we do.

"Far too often the California State Assembly and Senate make decisions that benefit populated urban cores versus the Central Valley of California, which is the farming engine of dozens of valuable crops. In particular, when it comes to water allocations, we wish that the legislature would prioritize agriculture," said Christopher.

Christopher isn't looking skyward for extrication from the suffocating effects of California's vast regulatory state or the ignorance or disdain heaped upon ag. Relief won't be the result of a deus ex machina event like the ending of a zombie movie. If it's to regain its rightful role in the state, ag will have to summon the forces by itself.

In 2016, Chinese garlic farmers were brutalized by weather conditions. Eyeing the reduced harvest, farmers in Peru, the Dominican Republic and the Ukraine spotted an opportunity to increase market share and began cultivation. But in 2017, China roared back, increasing its stocks from 196,000 metric tons to 348,000 metric tons.

The crop year for the "war onion" in the United States was not much better. The 2016 crop was also down by as much as 20 percent of normal, also due to inclement weather. Domestic garlic producers tend to say that the "norm" for a garlic crop is being redefined from year to year.

Crop year 2016 was also an interesting year for food fraud detection. A molecular biologist asserts the garlic powder being sold in Canadian grocery stores was being adulterated with chalk or talcum powder. Christopher Elliott, a professor at the Queen's University Belfast in Northern Ireland, aired his concerns in 2017 after analyzing a recent incongruity: garlic sales volume remained steady despite a significant crop loss in China due to bad weather. "Where's all the garlic coming from?" asked Elliott, the director of the school's Institute for Global Food Security. Elliott has a nose for food fraud. He led the United Kingdom's independent review of food systems following the 2013 horse meat scandal. In 2016, Elliott published a study indicating about a quarter of oregano sold in the United Kingdom and Ireland contained other products, including olive and myrtle leaves.

Professor John Spink, director of the Michigan State University Food Fraud Initiative, told the publication Food & Wine that although his team hadn't yet heard of any recent food fraud incidents involving garlic powder, "any type of spice that's ground or blended has a high fraud risk in general."

But back to the other Christopher – Ken Christopher. In fending off assertions made in the Netflix documentary, he says 90 percent of his garlic is grown in the United States. But what of it? What if his company were forced to source half its garlic from China someday? What if his operating costs became so great that he could not afford to grow *any* garlic in California and was forced to convert his fields to a less labor-intensive crop or fallow them or sell his land to developers as the southern edge of Silicon Valley creeps southward toward the garlic fields?

Don't expect state or local thought leaders to alert Christopher and other farmers when the "sweet spot" is about to be lost – when taxation, fees, debt service, payroll and other costs have pushed them irreversibly into the red.

Once farmers battled only the elements and whipsawing crop prices as they tried to stay one step ahead of the bank. They now face a new overlay. State politicians issue dictates, and farmers then adapt or die. Farm failure happens slowly and in silence. But the things these farmers are producing aren't buggy whips. They're food.

Chapter Four

Mandarins in the Garden of Good and Evil

ON THE FIRST day of December 2017, recording artist Taylor Swift took the stage at L.A.'s aging but still venerable Forum and launched into "…Ready for It?" – the pulsating first track on her album "Reputation." Wha … wha … wha … THAP! Wha … wha … wha … THAP! Wha …wha … wha …THAP! "Knew he was a killer first time that I saw him … wondered how many girls he had loved and left haunted."

Here and there, a chaperoning mom could be seen gyrating in the pulsating delirium beside a mortified Kaylee or a Kylee or an Emma or an Abigail. A mom here, eyes closed, hips swiveling in tight arcs, torso heaving, "shoulder-rolling it," "pop, block and dropping it," "piping it up … piping it up … piping it up" to the throbbing beat. Wha … wha … wha … THAP! Wha … wha … wha … THAP! Wha … wha … wha … THAP! Wha … wha … wha … THAP! Wha … wha … wha … THAP!

The song had been released just a month earlier. Later in her set, English pop troubadour Ed Sheeran, in a baseball cap and hiking boots, strutted onto the stage and joined her; the two performed a duet of Swift's "End Game" to the approval of the teens, tweens and whirlybird parental units in attendance.

Backstage, amid the chaos, Sheeran, countryman James Corden, and the perennial hail-fellow-well-met Ryan Seacrest yucked it up for the cameras outside Sheeran's dressing room. The building has nine such dressing rooms, seven built to headliner specs; artists and their entourages chill in the lounge adjacent to the floor seats. Inexplicably that night, three teenage girls in flannel pajamas were horsing around, taking turns pushing each other off one of the lounge's elongated couches under the watchful eye of an enormous bull-necked Samoan bodyguard, his mighty hand stroking his shaved pate in contemplation. With a pinched stare, the giant occasionally tinkered with an elaborate earpiece emerging from an open spread collar. The pajama-attired teens' connection to any of the headliners was unknown, let alone why they were in their PJs. The energy in the private Forum Club that night was an 11 on a scale of 10.

The concert itself was carried live on over 100 iHeartRadio stations and as a live video stream on the official site of the CW Television Network, and within the CW app. Amid the logos of the tour's national sponsors – brands like Absolut, Macy's, Ulta Beauty and the movie "Jumanji: Welcome to the Jungle" – was an unlikely standout for the crowd: Cuties, a brand of seedless mandarin orange marketed by Pasadena, California-based Sun Pacific.

As charter members of that target demographic rollicked to headliners like Swift, Sheeran, the Chainsmokers, Ariana Grande and Demi Lovato, the Cuties logo – with its cartoonish anthropomorphic mandarin sporting a cockeyed smile and emerging from a zippered peel – is never far in the background. The myth-making machinery that has propelled Swift, Sheeran, Grande and Lovato into the consciousness of their young audiences was also helping to lift this little fruit into the rarefied air of such places as the McDonald's Happy Meal, and this tour. The tie-in to the tour was part of Sun Pacific's winter campaign for the Cutie. For the mascot of the meek mandarin hybrid, which I learned later was called "Li'l Zipper," it could hardly get edgier. A mandarin orange could hardly pull more celebrity wattage.

Besides the L.A. date, the tour stopped in Dallas; the Bay Area; Minneapolis; Philadelphia; New York; Boston; Washington, D.C.; Chicago; Atlanta; Tampa; and Miami-Ft. Lauderdale. One hundred and fifty radio stations in the iHeart network advertised the Cuties jingle, with Li'l Zipper gaining exposure on billboards and social media sites.

Like the sensory onslaught that is the modern-day pop stadium extravaganza, the pulsating demand is surging through the gizzards of California's farm patch for new acreage for mandarin plantings, and some of it is coming at the expense of Valencia and navel oranges. In 2010, the number of harvested acres of Valencia and navel oranges was 183,000, while mandarins, tangerines and similar hybrids were at just 30,000 acres, reported California's Department of Food and Agriculture. But by 2015, the number of harvested acres of Valencias and navels had fallen by almost 11 percent to 163,000, while mandarins, tangerines and similar hybrids had grown by 73 percent to 52,000 acres.

"Mandarins lead all citrus categories in dollar sales at retail, representing almost 37 percent of all citrus sales for the past year," Joan Wickham, manager for advertising and public relations at Sunkist Growers, told the publication Produce Business in 2016. Dollar sales were up 17 percent over the prior year. Mandarins also led in per-pound sales, up just over

19 percent, she said.

So, what is the demographic "sweet spot" of Cuties? How did it come to occupy a seasonal spot in the coveted McDonalds Happy Meal? How did Cuties come to sponsor iHeartRadio's annual Jingle Ball Tour? How did Cuties become so ... so ... edgy? Then there are more pressing questions like, Is Li'l Zipper male or female?

* * *

The mandarin is a type of orange that is flatter on both ends with a mild flavor and loose skin. The tangerine and the clementine both fall into the category. Clementines are the smallest member of the mandarin family. The peel is smooth, glossy and deep orange. There are both seeded and seedless varieties, but the seedless varieties fetch a higher price.

The Los Angeles-based Wonderful Co. (formerly Paramount Citrus) owns the competing Halos brand. Both promote their mandarins with extensive advertising campaigns. Valencia, California-based Sunkist Growers recently entered into a deal that doubled its mandarin supply. It sells them under the Delite name. Sunkist, after a hiatus, is actually bringing *back* the Delite, which the company contends is the original California mandarin brand.

"Sun Pacific and Wonderful Citrus are spending millions of dollars promoting Cuties and Halos, and it's been very effective," Miles Fraser-Jones, vice president of AMC Direct in Glassboro, New Jersey, told Produce Business. "They are advertising for kids. They are targeting mothers with small kids looking for healthy snacks."

There are enough types of mandarins adaptable to California growing conditions that many farmers have planted varieties that, when harvested sequentially, allow them to ship fresh fruit almost continuously during a five-month timeframe.

The recent hegemony of just a few companies has spawned creativity by citrus growers. One is SunWest Fruit Company, the Parlier, California, producers of the large, red-fleshed ruby tango – another hybrid mandarin, which is a cross between the blood orange and a clementine bred in Sicily. Some have focused on niche citrus like Japan's coveted dekopon mandarin. A consortium of growers began quietly harvesting the sweet, satisfyingly tactile dekopon in 2011. It is marketed in the United States under the name Sumo. UC Riverside pomologist and self-described "fruit detective" David Karp, who claims he has sampled over 1,000 citrus varieties, pronounced the dekopon the best-tasting citrus fruit he had ever tasted. Hybridized in 1972 at a government fruit research station in Kumamoto Prefecture, Japan, the dekopon is a cross between the ponkan, a large mandarin native to Asia, and the kiyomi tangor, a cross between the satsuma mandarin and an orange.

Budwood branches of the dekopon were somehow smuggled to South Korea and grafted onto citrus rootstock in the 1990s; they then appeared in Brazil and China. A grower in the San Joaquin Valley's citrus belt imported the dekopon budwood from Japan to a plant quarantine station in California, where scientists of the Citrus Clonal Protection Program employed a multiyear technique to rid it of a variety of diseases.

The Citrus Clonal Protection Program is a cooperative among the University of California, Riverside; the California Department of Food and Agriculture; the U.S. Department of Agriculture; and California citrus growers.

With the increased interest in citrus hybrids among growers and hobbyists, there is the well-founded fear that citrus budwood from regions infected with citrus greening disease will be brought into California's Central Valley and then grafted onto native rootstock.

In 2000, authorities raided a rogue orchard of about 1,000 grafted dekopon trees in the loamy clay soils outside Orange Cove, California, in the San Joaquin Valley's citrus belt. It is at the extreme eastern edge of the cultivated Valley floor. The planting was reported to have been infected with severe strains of citrus tristeza virus. Carried by the brown citrus aphid, the virus is deadly to citrus worldwide. The Fresno County Agricultural Commissioner fined the grower, and the trees were piled high and burned.

"People attempt to smuggle illegal budwood here all the time," said Melissa Cregan, quarantine deputy with the Fresno County Agricultural Commissioner's Office. "Many people graft budwood obtained illegally and sell the resulting citrus trees illegally; but that is a different problem from smuggling. Illegal grafting is probably a bigger problem since it's harder to control than smuggling." Nonetheless, her office has many systems in place to thwart such activities. Much effort is put into stemming the flow.

Her biggest fear for the state's citrus is Huanglongbing, the greening disease, and the Asian citrus psyllid, its primary vector. HLB, as it's more commonly known, sends a deep sense of dread into growers here. "I think you're naïve if you don't see HLB as a very serious threat," said Cregan. "It's not something you can just fix with nutrients. All other citrus-growing regions in the United States have this. California is a fresh citrus market. With juicing oranges in Florida, some degree of HLB can be masked. Not so with fresh oranges. You have to control the Asian citrus psyllid to control HLB and you need pesticides to control the psyllid," she said hesitantly, perhaps not wanting to stoke animosities between those in the state's affluent coastal counties — where abstract modifiers like "non-GMO," "free-range" and "organic" add value – and those who live in the state's Central Valley, where the hard realities of agricultural blights, rots, cankers and viruses are felt firsthand and the need for pesticide treatments isn't questioned.

"The majority of the state's HLB is in backyards in Southern California affecting someone's potted tree. All it takes is for someone who grows an infected dwarf citrus tree in a pot in Southern California to move to the Central Valley and there you go," she said.

"A big problem with the disease is by the time you can detect it in a tree, it's been infected for a while and then you have to ask yourself how many others have now been infected. We humans didn't start as farmers. We started as hunter-gatherers," she said. "Farming allowed humans to create communities. There's a human connection to growing things. When you're told you can't do things a certain way, people are going to resist. We see smuggled backyard citrus all the time."

America is a land of immigrants and people want to bring a piece of home with them, and sometimes that piece of home is a tristeza-infested sapling.

"Sometimes, it has cultural significance," said Cregan. "Sometimes they know they're not supposed to do it, sometimes they don't. There's the mentality that it's not going to happen to me."

The effects of citrus diseases are amplified by the long orchard life cycles for citrus trees. Unlike, say, almonds, which growers tend to rip out after about 20 years as yields decline, citrus, like grapes, can be a 50- to 80-year planting.

Another maddening aspect of HLB is figuring out when there's a psyllid infestation. "If we get a [Mediterranean fruit fly], we can put out good traps and good lures and get a pretty good idea of the population quickly. The only thing that attracts the psyllid to the traps is [the color] yellow. Our ability to detect or estimate the size of a psyllid population is limited. It's worrying."

You sense Cregan is dedicated to her work in a profound way. Talking with her instills hope that science, moderation and common sense will prevail and ag will be OK.

"California isn't like Wisconsin or Florida, whose agriculture industries are defined by a single product," she said. "But it can work against [California] because people aren't aware their own state leads the nation in specific crops. They don't have a high level of awareness when it comes to what's at stake."

Meanwhile, new specialty citrus gets introduced onto the valley floor as growers slipstream behind the Cuties-Halos phenom.

* * *

Scene: A crisp winter's morning in a chilly orchard. Jim Churchill and Lisa Brenneis, owners of Churchill Orchard, walk through their 12-acre finca on the outskirts of the town of Ojai, California. Ojai (pronounced "OH-hai"), set in a valley of the same name, is a lush inland enclave in the state's Central Coast region. The town is known for its private boarding schools and spiritual retreats.

Brandishing a handheld refractometer, the couple inspects their seedless kishu tangerines. A cool summer – a rare thing in the notoriously baking summers of the Ojai Valley – left them worried the fruit wouldn't rise to its desired level of sweetness by harvest time. Here in the perfumed air, wood braces support fruit-heavy branches on some of the orchard's trees. The kishu is an ancient golf-ball sized Japanese mandarin. The fruit is small, perishable and harvesting it is labor-intensive. If the kishu were an actress, it would be Mila Kunis – petite and criminally cute.

Kishu budwood arrived at the UC Riverside's Citrus Variety Collection station from Japan in 1983. While it was being quarantined and scrubbed of foreign free riders, it was reported to have been a favorite among scientists and guests at the station.

Churchill, an Ojai native, is a thin, fifty-something man in jeans and a fleece with a frenzy of curly hair compressed under the perennial farmer's ball cap. He fiddles with the handheld device, calibrating it with a small screwdriver and distilled water from a plastic bottle. Backdropped against wispy clouds and Ojai's Topa Topa mountains, a rabbit stirs from a thicket beyond the orchard.

Clipping a specimen off one of his trees, he peels it and squeezes some of its juice onto the refractometer, which looks like a small field glass. "Science. Whew!" erupts Churchill, ironically, feigning excitement. Neil deGrasse Tyson is under no threat of replacement by Churchill. He looks into the eyepiece and aims the device toward the sun. The first fruit pulls a 12.8 on the meter. Churchill nods in approval. The refractometer works on Snell's Law, a formula used to describe the relationship between an angle of incidence and refraction. It's a prism that measures how the sugars in liquid bend light waves. The more sugars in a solution, the more the light will bend, thus the higher the reading.

Another fruit pulls a 14.8. This time, Churchill doesn't feign excitement; he *is* excited (to the extent a laid-back specialty citrus man in mid-life can get excited).

Churchill Orchard, the first to plant the seedless kishu cultivar commercially, has been at it since the late 1990s. By 2010, the couple had 780 trees, and at least five other growers in the area had kishu plantings.

When Churchill, whom one would not be wrong to call

a "tangerine *artiste*," is without his refractometer, his testing of the satsumas, pages and pixies for ripeness is less prolix, more left to one's interpretation of a series of grunts, a brief flaring of nostrils, and occasional nods, punctuated by the spewing of fruit meats onto the ground.

"We grow pixie tangerines for the schools," said Brenneis. "We have about 1,000 pixie tangerine trees," said Churchill "and [we harvest] about 150 pounds to 250 pounds per tree."

Growers in the Ojai Valley hold to the narrative that the kishu, pixie, page and satsuma cultivars reach an ideal sugar balance only in the unique growing conditions of the Ojai Valley. They speak about the Ojai Valley's *terroir*. The pixie is a leading cultivar in the Ojai Valley.

"Kids love [pixies]. You don't have that tang you have from minneolas and navels. They're just super-sweet," said fifth-generation Ojai farmer Emily Thacher Ayala of Friend's Ranches. "They're like candy." Growers tend to ship the pixies only after they ripen on the tree. Friend's aim is to get its fruit on store shelves within 10 days of being picked. "Pixie tangerines can be grown everywhere in the world but they're not going to develop good flavor everywhere in the world," she told America's Heartland. "Much like wine grapes taste better if grown in Napa versus Stockton."

The Ojai Pixie Growers association is an eclectic group of full-time and part-time citrus farmers in the Ojai Valley. "We both looked at the fact that there were all these other people who had tangerines coming on and we thought it would be better if all the other tangerine growers worked together," said Churchill.

New Pixie plantings take four years before they're ready to bear their first commercial crop. They're alternate-bearing, which means heavy harvests occur only every other year.

Churchill and Thacher Ayala are on a mission to satisfy the seemingly insatiable demand for the ambrosial, easy-to-peel fruit.

* * *

Omaha-based Bailey Lauerman is the niche ad firm handling the Cuties account. Fruit packers tend to be privately held companies. They keep their cards close to their chest. But Bailey Lauerman was an ad agency. The firm prides itself in having its finger on the pulse of the Heartland. "From our office in Omaha," the firm's website reads, "we have developed an understanding of a large segment of the population between the coasts that is often overlooked by marketers. Misunderstood. Ignored. We call it The Everything In Between. Through that understanding, we develop work that is smart, respectful, and clever."

This seemed like the perfect match for an ag product. I had many questions for this McCann on the Missouri, this Ogilvy of Omaha, this corn-fed Sterling Cooper, and I had hoped the answers would penetrate the expected ad-world tropes. I didn't want to talk about "touchstones," "cultural infusion" or "messaging strategies." What were the creatives *really* thinking when they decided Li'l Zipper had become a Taylor Swift fan? Whose brainchild was it? How did it come about?

I emailed Bailey Lauerman my questions. The firm assigned Senior Public Relations Strategist Mel Dohmen to deal with me. According to Mel's company bio, she holds a master's in marketing from the University of Nebraska-Lincoln and designs kitchenware on the side. Her Twitter page described her as a "marketer, storyteller, brand enthusiast and proud Midwesterner." She is a "serial nester," and, if her Twitter page is to be believed, a "lover of all things vintage/modern."

After an initial period of silence, she got back to me. "I am wondering if you can provide a little more context as to what the overall book is about," she asked. Then it took an oddly collegial turn. "Have you already spoken to contacts at Halos or Sunkist?"

Part of her questioning was the familiar size-up. Any reporter who must deal with public-relations people on a regular basis will recognize it – having to explain oneself, provide certain signals as to the direction of a piece and, sometimes, to grovel for table scraps. I tell her I'm a certified real estate appraiser in California and I write about land-use issues. One of my focus areas is agriculture. My book will be about the changing face of agriculture. I tell her I've been tracking the number of acres planted to mandarins and mandarin hybrids in California's Central Valley.

No, I hadn't yet approached anyone at Wonderful or Sunkist, I told her. But what of it? I thought. Her question left an unpleasant metallic aftertaste that seemed to ask, What information can you share about my client's competitors?

I tell her Cuties seems like the more interesting story (not all flattery) – The Cuties brand came first, and its main competitor, Halos, seems more focused on a younger demographic and its branding more one-dimensional. "Cuties seems to be focused on a teen or tween demographic and strikes me as somehow edgier (at least for a mandarin). Am I wrong?" I ask Dohmen.

She emailed more weed-out questions. Over time, I felt I'd been fobbed off on a combination of the Hooterville telephone operator and an information-age bouncer peering through a speakeasy door grate asking for a code word. I once read about a writer for a major magazine having to negotiate with publicists at ABC for five months to interview Diane

Sawyer, who herself is a journalist.

* * *

Like fund managers trying to time cycles in the stock market, farm managers try to time the droughts. During a drought, tree-nut and citrus farmers find it advantageous to push down older, less productive trees and plant anew. They use the opportunity to rotate into a different variety or a different crop altogether. New plantings use much less water.

"A lot of the new trees are Mandarins," Jim Marderosian, owner of Bee Sweet Citrus, in Fowler, California, told Produce Business. In fact, tens of thousands of citrus trees were replanted during the 2011 to 2017 drought in California. Much of that new acreage was in mandarin trees that will begin yielding even larger crops in coming years. In 2016, there were nearly 50,000 acres of mandarins and mandarin hybrids planted in the loam soils of Tulare, Kern and Fresno counties, the three largest counties for the variety. In those three counties, according to the California Department of Food and Agriculture, 8,300 acres, or nearly 17 percent, were non-bearing acres in the pipeline.

"When they're new, price drives it, and high production per acre," said Marderosian. "Some of the older citrus trees were only getting 15 to 20 bins per acre during the drought. Mandarins can handle the drought a little better. With the higher water costs, people look at crops that support less water."

Mandarins are typically hand-harvested by pickers with satchel-style picking bags, ladders and hand clippers. The fruit is emptied into special bins, that, when full, are hauled to a fruit-packing house, sometimes called a "fruit-packing shed." In the ag world, no matter how big a building, it's still usually called a "shed."

Once in the clatter of the packing shed, fruit is often placed in a cell where it's gassed with ethylene, a naturally occurring hormone and de-greening agent. It helps turn the peel from green to orange and promote natural ripening until the fruit itself starts producing its own ethylene. A mandarin can be harvested green and ripened like a banana.

Many restaurant and convenience store chains are trying to meet the needs of health-conscious customers seeking "better-for-you" options. The trend has been good for mandarin growers. In a "U.S. Restaurant Outlook" survey of 1,008 adults published in April 2017 by AlixPartners global consulting firm, 91 percent of respondents said the availability of healthy menu options is at least somewhat important to them. That number is higher than the still-high 86 percent recorded the year before. The trend has been decades in the making. Consumers have wanted healthier food. The demand has forced menu changes at fast-food and fast-casual restaurants.

In a nod to millennial parents, who tend to be more quality- and health-conscious than previous generations, McDonald's tweaked the Happy Meal, eliminating cheeseburgers, downsizing French fry servings, adding bottled water as a beverage option and reformulating its chocolate milk to reduce sugar. In 2014, it added Cuties as an alternative to fries in the Happy Meal. It became an alternative to apple slices, which the company began adding to Happy Meals in 2012 at participating locations. Since 2014, the fast food chain has served more than 38 million Cuties in Happy Meals, though this is still dwarfed by the 850 million bags of apple slices it has served.

Cuties rose from the ashes of a 1990 freeze that damaged citrus in California. A variety of clementine was planted for its ability to endure more extreme weather. Sun Pacific partnered with Paramount Citrus to grow equal amounts of seedless clementines and sell them under a single brand name.

Halos, a spinoff of Cuties after a legal break-up between Sun Pacific and Paramount – Paramount later changed its name to Wonderful – is part of a farming empire owned by Beverly Hills billionaires Stewart and Lynda Resnick. The Resnicks, who have become magnates of the healthy snack, also own Fiji Water, POM Wonderful, and the world's largest pistachio and almond growing operations. During California's recent drought, urbanists in places like Santa Monica, West Los Angeles and San Francisco's Marina district found a convenient foil in the couple.

"The Resnicks have amassed [an] empire by following a simple agricultural precept: Crops need water," Josh Harkinson wrote in Mother Jones in 2016. "Having shrewdly maneuvered the backroom politics of California's Byzantine water rules, they are now thought to consume more of the state's water than any other family, farm or company. They control more of it in some years than what's used by the residents of Los Angeles and the entire San Francisco Bay Area combined," he wrote.

As much as the Resnicks have been suspected of Machiavellian dealings in smoke-filled backrooms – something they deny – they've also been mythologized.

Besides being the world's biggest producers of pistachios and almonds, they own vast groves of mandarins, lemons, grapefruit and navel oranges. In Mexico, they own lime groves. It is believed their closely held company is America's second-largest produce company. Their net worth in early 2018, according to Forbes, was $3.9 billion.

The couple owns Teleflora, the nation's largest clearinghouse for processing floral orders worldwide; Fiji Water, a high-end bottled water shipped from an artesian aquifer in Fiji; Pom Wonderful, the pomegranate juice brand; and Wonderful Pistachios, known by its iconic "Get Crackin'" ad campaign. Wonderful also owns the Halos brand.

In 2015, "America's nuttiest billionaire couple" (as Forbes magazine called them for their considerable almond and pistachio holdings), rebranded all their holdings as the Wonderful Company to emphasize the company's healthy products and philanthropy. The couple owned 32,000 acres of California citrus in 2016, according to Forbes.

With a single donor check in the $2 million range, either could have bought the embassy in, say, Wellington or Madrid during the Obama or Trump presidencies and gone quietly into that velvety, emissarial good night, selling their holdings to a private-equity or pension fund and trading their Beverly Hills digs for an ambassador's residence and the grand salons of Andorra or Auckland. Instead, this force of nature chose food production. It's admirable.

Cuties and Halos both use varying types of mandarins, depending on the time of year. They are not always the clementine variety. In fact, clementines are only available during the beginning of the citrus season (from November to January). The other mandarin variety commonly used is the W. Murcott. Often Grocery stores mislabel Murcotts as clementines because the name sells better.

In California, nearly 12,000 bearing acres were planted to clementine mandarins in 2016 with the W. Murcott the second-most commonly grown mandarin variety at a little over 10,000 bearing acres. A close third was the tango.

"Cuties" and "Halos" are strictly marketing names. They are not actual varieties. The Cuties and Halo brands are not sold in stores year-round. By spring, usually in May, some years early June, they disappear until the following fall. Sunkist has joined – or rejoined – the fray, shipping Murcotts under the aforementioned Delite name. Sunkist, according to The Packer, has aimed to differentiate the Delite brand by focusing on the quality of the fruit over ease of use and appeal to kids.

The Agriculture Department estimated that California would produce 21 million boxes of tangerines and mandarins in 2018, down from 23.9 million in 2017. Florida would likely add 860,000 boxes, down from 1.62 million the year before, with the plunge the result of Hurricane Irma and citrus greening disease. Irma, a mayhem factory of the Category 5 variety, alone knocked 50 percent to 90 percent of the Sunshine State's citrus fruit to the ground in some areas, according to the state's agriculture commissioner, Adam Putnam.

Sales of mandarins have been growing at the expense of navel oranges. "It has eroded (navel) sales," Randy Jacobsen, sales manager at Orange Cove, California-based Cecelia Packing Corporation, told the publication The Packer. "The mandarins have become the driver of the citrus category, whereas navels were a decade ago." Still, navels remain the core of citrus in Arizona and California.

Still, the seedless mandarin's ascension did not occur without controversy.

The first sign of trouble came in late 2007 with the enactment of Assembly Bill 771. It authorized something called "The Seedless Mandarin and Honey Bee Coexistence Working Group." Then, in early 2008, an item in the Western Farm Press detailed a public hearing in Fresno aimed at resolving what were at first called "differences" between mandarin orange growers in four California counties and beekeepers.

Normally, seedless cultivars like tangerines, navel oranges and clementines are self-pollinating. They fail to set seeds when they're planted in orchards of identical plants, known as "clones." They will fail to set seeds so long as the flowers never come into contact with pollen from seeded varieties of citrus. When this does happen, presto – seeds!

A major vector of that undesirable seeded pollen is the honeybee. The degree of seediness of a mandarin often comes down to how many other varieties of citrus are within a bee's flying distance from that tree.

At the meeting, an initial veneer of civility quickly wore thin. The state's bejowled mandarin dons claimed bees were defiling their trees, causing seediness in their fruit. The peripatetic bee men countered solicitously that their pollinators were being unfairly banned from whole swaths of citrus land. The men stared daggers at one another in a tableau of suspicion, each side primed to sniff out the mendacity of the other. Fangs were bared. The tension would slacken briefly only to ramp up again. When individuals spoke, it was in gaseous monologues. Puffs of spittle aerosolized in rat-a-tat-tat eruptions of invective. Partisans looked to co-belligerents for validation of the righteousness of their cause. Adrenaline, that most powerful of human intoxicants, thumped through veins. The mandarin growers demanded bee-free zones with buffers two miles around their plantings; beekeepers demanded their historical access to the citrus groves for the health and well-being of their colonies, and for the honey.

There was a Wild West feel about this Mexican standoff; it felt a lot like an apian-citrus version of the sheep and cattle wars fought over grazing rights in Texas. About 80 people attended the Fresno meeting and about 25 spoke. The three hours of testimony and comments only divided the voluble mandarin men and beekeepers further, according to reports.

The Los Angeles Times ran a story with the headline "Tangerine growers tell beekeepers to buzz off." (A rich vein of puns was mined that day. Words like "seedy" and "abuzz" were stretched to their limits by journalists looking for the easy lede.)

In high dudgeon, Paramount Citrus had sent letters to beekeepers near its groves of clementines in Kern County. The letters promised to seek "compensation for any and all damages caused to its crops, as well as punitive damages," if pips developed in the otherwise seedless fruit.

Although nothing new to the mandarin growers themselves, a 2005 University of California, Riverside, study found that seedless mandarins commanded three to four times as much revenue as the seeded ones. (In 2010, it was reported by the Western Farm Press that netted W. Murcotts – the variety that produces unwanted seeds when pollinated by bees – achieved the best prices because buyers were assured a seedless fruit. Unnetted Murcotts lost about half their value, growers said, due to the taint of seediness, whether the pips were real or merely suspected.)

Another factor in seediness is the weather during the pollination period, since bees are less effective pollinators during cold, wet and windy days. Some citrus-producing countries have adopted citrus-protection zones to limit cross-pollination losses. Otherwise, the citrus and beekeeping industries have had a long history of cooperation. Traditionally, citrus growers allowed beekeepers to place hives in their groves during the bloom. Beekeepers positioned their hives in or near citrus groves for their bees to forage. The resources provided by the citrus bloom are key for beekeepers and the rejuvenation of their hives. New bee colonies are produced in the groves, and citrus nectar is a necessary source for the coveted orange-blossom honey.

In many cases, a beekeeper makes arrangements with grove owners to place hives within the grove during the citrus bloom. Sometimes signals get crossed and hives are placed in groves without permission.

Mandarin acreage had already grown from 24,000 in 2005 to more than 31,000 by 2008. Suddenly, citrus growers were indeed telling beekeepers to buzz off.

Meanwhile, almond trees in the Valley need plenty of bees to pollinate them. During the almond pollination season, beekeepers from around the country converge on California's Central Valley with their hives in tow. This triumph of man and beast is the largest annual staged pollination in the world. The rule of thumb is it takes two healthy hives to pollinate an acre of almonds trees. At most recent count, the pollination required around 1.7 million hives. The almond men, never far in the background, were keeping a close eye on the beekeeper-citrus donnybrook.

* * *

Under a radiantly blue sky, a black Labrador lollygags in the shade of someone's porch in downtown Wasco. Two young boys take turns flinging an old sneaker at one another in a fenced front yard. The barrel-chested creature makes a couple perfunctory circles on the porch and then lies down, haunches first, in a display of utter boredom and indolence. In proximity to this lazy little operetta playing itself out on a side street in Wasco, population 25,000, is Teresa's, a place for anyone hunting the jungles of the almond-sphere (or just looking for a plate of chili verde). It is an unpretentious corner restaurant in north Kern County. There are booths along the windows that look out over F Street, which is largely empty this day.

Wasco is ground zero of Kern County's almond country, and at Teresa's a daily lunchtime cavalcade files in and out – growers, consultants, orchard chippers, agronomists, equipment salesmen, shellers, appraisers, ag journalists and members of the local gendarmerie. If you cock an ear, you will sometimes hear earthy and unwarped men in short-sleeved shirts, paunches extending over their belt buckles, discussing the merits of nematode-resistant rootstocks or micro-sprinkler irrigation systems. They arrive in platoons and rise weakly after eating heavy meals. They sometimes hover like yard gnomes around pick-up trucks in Teresa's parking lot, examining salsa spots on their shirts and discussing the plan of action for the afternoon.

The scene is evocative of all of almond country. If you camped out at a table at Teresa's, you would likely encounter every important person in the almond industry in the San Joaquin Valley, including the occasional institutional investor from away. During February, you would see a great many beekeepers come and go.

In a 2015 interview with National Public Radio, Gene Brandi, a California beekeeper and vice president of the American Beekeeping Federation, estimated about 85 percent of all available commercial hives in the United States converge on the Central Valley of California. Others put it at a "mere" 70 percent.

As almond blossoms begin to fall in late March, some beekeepers relocate hives to make orange blossom honey before heading to the Midwest for spring clover season. The almond men are generally aligned with the beekeepers and are all in favor of a strong bee industry. Naturally, they sympathize with the beekeepers, who want only to rest their hives in or near the citrus groves.

Other beekeepers immediately truck their hives north to pollinate the apple orchards of Eastern Washington. From there, some head west to Whatcom County, north of Seattle, to pollinate the blueberry and red raspberry crops.

Some stay on the pollination circuit and take their hives

to Montana for canola seeds; some go to alfalfa fields, and some go to bee yards. Most income for major beekeeping operations these days comes from pollination services, not honey sales. The aggrieved citrus men were unsympathetic.

"We've coexisted with them, but we don't need them," Joel Nelson, executive director of California Citrus Mutual, a trade association, told the Associated Press in 2009. "Now we're trying to adapt to changing consumer demands and we're hamstrung."

Beekeepers fulminated that they were being squeezed into shrinking areas in which to feed and rest their bees.

"Our winter losses are increasing [because of colony collapse], and part of the problem is finding places to put bees where they have access to natural food, and citrus is part of that," said beekeeper Brandi.

Colony collapse disorder, which at the time of the feud was thought to pose a greater long-term threat to bees than what is now known, is the phenomenon that occurs when worker bees in a colony disappear and leave behind food and a few nurse bees to care for the remaining immature bees and the queen.

According to the EPA in early 2018, reported cases of the phenomenon have declined substantially over the last five years. The number of hives that do not survive over the winter months – the overall indicator for bee health – has maintained an average of about 29 percent since 2007 but dropped to 23 percent for the 2014-2015 winter. While winter losses remain high, the number of those losses attributed to colony collapse disorder has dropped from roughly 60 percent of total hives lost in 2008 to 31 percent in 2013. (No doubt 31 percent is still a shocking and unacceptable number.)

The honeybee industry has been credited with pollinating about $6 billion in California crops. During the impasse, lawmakers – and the interests lobbying them with ferocity – made it clear that any best management practice must not affect the pollination process of almonds, avocados, peaches, plums, nectarines, seed crops or other commodities during the blooming cycle in the Central Valley.

Chris Lange, a grower from Woodlake in Tulare County, told the Associated Press in January 2009 that he had converted some of his 1,600 acres of citrus groves to the more profitable mandarins, which he would be harvesting at the end of that month. "We already have an idea of where we'll find the seeds," said Lange, lamenting that most of his crop could wind up as juice. "You can't grow the crop for the juice market. You have to grow for the premium crop [market] or you won't recover your costs."

Joe Traynor, a Bakersfield bee broker representing the California Beekeepers Association, charged mandarin growers with poor land management. "Mandarin growers with seed problems did not properly isolate their plantings from other pollen sources," he said at a hearing and was later quoted in the Western Farm Press.

At that hearing, Traynor submitted a copy of a letter from Ray Copeland, an Exeter, California-based citrus consultant. It was addressed to the secretary of the California Department of Food and Agriculture and others. Copeland, a larger-than-life figure in the mandarin world – Indiana Jones meets Luther Burbank – died in 2016. Copeland had been a pioneer in the introduction of seedless varieties from Spain and Morocco.

Copeland's letter stated that he had emphasized to California growers the importance of clementines and other seedless varieties being isolated from other pollen sources, but some growers planted trees in high-density bee areas, "knowing full well that [pollination] would be a problem and now want to see all of the bees excluded without paying the price of the exclusion."

During the impasse, beekeepers suggested mandarin growers net their crops to keep out bees. Growers wanted beekeepers to reduce hive density, so bees didn't have to fly so far to compete for food. Neither side was willing to yield. "The ag industry is being forced to weigh which side should have a stronger case," said a state agriculture official, "and that's a difficult thing for us to decide. We're just not going to make anyone happy."

Representing California Citrus Mutual, an advocacy group for the state's citrus growers, attorney Louie A. Brown, Jr., of Sacramento-based Kahn, Soares and Conway, said there was no intent to force out bee operations originating in the four-county area. He said there had been an influx of imported bees not in the area 10 to 20 years earlier.

Brown, who has a youthful mien and cuts a rakish figure, possesses stellar bona fides for his role, including a bachelor's degree in ag business from Cal Poly San Luis Obispo – one of the state's two preeminent life science schools (UC Davis being the other). He holds a law degree from the University of the Pacific's McGeorge School of Law. He also had a point. Etienne Rabe, technical director of Sun Pacific, referred to the influx of pollinators from across the United States as a "supersaturation" of bees. He said growers were overwhelmed.

Before the dust had settled, growers had sued beekeepers, were patrolling their groves with helicopters and were protecting trees from bee pollination with nets. It was even rumored that some had resorted to insecticides against the honeybees. It was a dark period.

Harley Phillips, a septuagenarian citrus farmer whose off-farm job involves demolishing orchards when they've reached the end of their life cycle, said the tango – a mandarin variety bred to be seedless even when pollinated by bees that have visited seeded trees – has slaked some of the mutual vexation.

"The beekeepers have smartened up, too, and are now paying the citrus guys. That wasn't the case before, even though they were charging the almond guys through the teeth. They need the citrus [bloom] to build their hives back up, so each side is getting something out of it."

One navel orange grower in Kern County said beekeepers no longer approach him about resting their hives in his groves because they know he will be unable to accommodate their requests to postpone spraying his trees early in the season. The resting of the bees in citrus orchards can't occur during spraying without the bees being harmed.

Phillips reported in 2018 seeing many acres of Valencia trees coming out and being replaced with the seed-proof tango variety.

Then another crisis hit. In early February 2016, social media users had begun sharing posts warning that specific brands of produce, some of it citrus, were being grown in wastewater that was a byproduct of fracking.

The posts were linked to a February 10, 2016, piece on the blog EcoWatch that recapped the second episode of a Web documentary series titled "Spotlight California" in which it was suggested that farmers in a specific irrigation district were "so desperate for water" that they used oil wastewater produced by Chevron to grow food crops (including tangerines). The post quoted a retired almond farmer who purported the irrigation water being used in that area was toxic.

Besides producing much of California's agriculture, the San Joaquin Valley, namely the southern part of it, is a major oil producing area. Beneath it is the Kern River Oil Field, the fifth-largest oilfield in the United States. In 2013, about 150 million barrels of oil were brought to the surface, along with nearly 2 billion barrels of water.

Much of the recycled water originates in the oilfield in the lower Sierra foothills northeast of Bakersfield. The biggest product of the U.S. petroleum industry isn't oil or gas but water. To extract a single barrel of crude from the ground, oil companies must use between 10 and 100 barrels of water.

Much of the so-called "produced water" is recycled for use in the oilfields during enhanced oil recovery efforts (steam injection and water flooding). The remaining produced water is typically disposed of in permitted underground injection wells or surface disposal ponds. A portion of the produced water is recycled for irrigation of crops.

The NBC Bay Area affiliate broke a story in November 2014 revealing that California officials had allowed oil and gas companies to pump nearly three billion gallons of wastewater into aquifers that could have been used for drinking water or irrigation.

California Department of Conservation Chief Deputy Director Jason Marshall told NBC Bay Area, "In multiple different places of the permitting process an error could have been made. There have been past [instances] where permits were issued to operators who shouldn't be injecting into those zones and so we're fixing that," he told the news outlet, saying that oil companies will often re-inject wastewater deep underground where the oil was originally extracted. But other times, he said, the wastewater is re-injected into shallower aquifers. For those injections, the liquid is supposed to go into so-called "exempt aquifers" that are considered off-limits for humans to drink or use.

But officials admitted in a letter to the EPA that in at

least nine wastewater injection sites, the wastewater was emptied into "non-exempt," or clean, aquifers containing high-quality water.

In March 2015, state lawmakers took turns rebuking the heads of California's Division of Oil, Gas and Geothermal Resources – known more commonly by its tough-sounding acronym "DOGGR" – and the State Water Resources Control Board, for allowing the dumping of water containing high levels of benzene, a carcinogen, into hundreds of wells in protected aquifers, a violation of federal law.

"Shocking" was the word one federal EPA official used about the state's lack of oversight and said California's oilfield wastewater injection program didn't comply with the federal Safe Drinking Water Act. After scrutiny it was shown that California, that great laboratory of the green revolution and tenacious environmental regulation, had, *comme ça*, allowed 2,500 oil wastewater injection wells to operate in aquifers that, under federal standards, contained clean water.

Two months after the hearing, the Los Angeles Times reported that Chevron was recycling 21 million gallons of water each day and selling it to growers, who used it on about 45,000 acres of crops, about 10 percent of farmland in California's citrus- and almond-heavy Kern County. To no one's surprise, growers check their crops for pests and disease but they don't test for contamination from waterborne chemicals. They rely instead on supervision and testing by state and local water authorities. It was unknown whether citrus, nuts or field crops irrigated with the oilfield water had been contaminated.

Oil producers were notified of new, broader testing requirements and ordered to begin checking for chemicals covered under California's new fracking disclosure regulations. Until that time, authorities had required only limited testing of the recycled irrigation water for only naturally occurring toxins like salts and arsenic, not for the array of chemicals used in modern oil extraction.

Oil companies like Chevron had been providing half the water that went to the 45,000 acres of farmland in Kern County's Cawelo Water District, up about 35 percent from 2011, the year before the most recent drought, as reported by the publication Mother Jones.

The Cawelo Water District, which has been around for a half-century, is located just north of Bakersfield at the southern end of the Valley. The district provides irrigation water to citrus orchards, nut orchards, vineyards and other crop land.

"I admit that [some oilfield contaminants] are in there," David Ansolabehere, the General Manager of the Cawelo Water District told the publication in 2015, "but they are at such a low level, I wouldn't think they are doing any harm. But we are looking into that to make sure there isn't any harm being done," he said.

"It's a very good resource to have, especially during droughts," Ansolabehere (pronounced "an-SOH-la-beer") told CBS's Bay Area affiliate 5KPIX. "It's enabled our farmers to continue farming when some of the other farming companies have had very reduced supplies."

A study commissioned by the Cawelo Water District and made public in late 2016 found concentrations of 70 chemicals of concern to be below or equal to minimum drinking water standards. Toxicologist Heriberto Robles of the environmental risk assessment firm Enviro-Tox Services concluded the initial results showed the water met standards for irrigation of agriculture.

Robles reported there was no difference in the chemicals present in samples of almonds, grapes and pistachios collected from areas in the Cawelo district and those in a control group from fields not supported by Cawelo. For mandarins, oranges and lemons, Robles explained, samples were collected from test fields in Cawelo, and a control group was created with the same varieties. Compounds detected in the water included acetone, benzene, toluene, ethylbenzene, xylenes, acenaphthene, fluorene, naphthalene and phenanthrene. He clarified the lab team found acetone in both the test field samples and control group, concluding acetone is naturally occurring.

Since two out of three test samples showed phenanthrene in oranges, Robles retested those samples. He went back and tested the oranges and the dust from surfaces around the test fields because he had reason to believe phenanthrene was sourced from nearby dust. Results showed no phenanthrene in the three repeat samples. In carrots and potatoes, samples showed low levels of acetone in both test and control groups, leading the study team similarly to conclude that acetone was naturally occurring.

Going mano a mano with the Cawelo Water District was Bill Allayaud, a policy director for the non-profit group Environmental Working Group and former planner with the California Coastal Commission. "These are quick and dirty studies. You need to do long-term sampling," he told the CBS affiliate.

Safety consultants hired by the state took a hard-line approach. "Current water district requirements for testing such waters before they are used for irrigation are not sufficient to guarantee that [well] stimulation chemicals are removed, although some local treatment plants do use appropriate protocols," read the state-commissioned fracking report released in 2015 by the California Council on Science and Technology. "If produced water used in irrigation contains well stimulation and other chemicals, this would provide a possible exposure pathway for farmworkers and animals and could lead to exposure through the food," said the report.

Billions of gallons of produced water contain dissolved salts, grease and even naturally occurring radioactive matter. The produced water is filtered through tanks containing crushed walnut shells. The oil adheres to the crushed shells. The water then flows to special ponds where oil is skimmed from the surface. If necessary, it's cycled through the filtration process again before the Cawelo Water District blends the oil wastewater with water from other sources, such as snowmelt from the Kern River, before sending it to about 90 farms outside Bakersfield.

The water district and the oil companies test the water. They assure farmers the water is safe. Area farmers use more than 20 million gallons daily. Crops grown with the produced water are distributed throughout the nation. A study released by PSE Healthy Energy, a non-profit energy science and policy research institute; Berkeley National Lab; and the University of the Pacific found that nearly 40 percent of the chemicals used by the companies providing oil wastewater to the districts are classified as trade secrets or couldn't otherwise be identified.

Of the known chemicals, a total of 10 from the list were classified as either carcinogenic or possibly carcinogenic in humans by IARC, the International Agency for Research on Cancer, a branch of the World Health Organization. But this is fraught with its own problems. The organization made news in 2018 for adding acrylamide to its list of carcinogenic and probably carcinogenic substances. Acrylamide is a naturally occurring byproduct of coffee roasting; it also occurs in overcooked foods and roasted starchy foods like potato chips,

French fries and toast. The acrylamide pronouncement was said to have been based on studies that dosed rodents at levels between 1,000 and 10,000 times levels humans might be exposed to. In the past, the IARC has reported processed meat as a Group 1 carcinogen and red meat as a Group 2A carcinogen. (The 2A classification denotes it is probably carcinogenic to humans.) Critics of the IARC claim the group is susceptible to industry influence and that it lacks transparency. A 2017 investigation by Reuters found that when the IARC assessed the weed killer glyphosate, it had dismissed or manipulated findings in its draft report that were at odds with its final conclusion that the chemical probably causes cancer. The agency wouldn't say who made the changes or why.

Four water districts receive the oilfield-produced water in California's Central Valley. They are the Cawelo Water District, the North Kern Water District, the Jasmin Mutual Water District, and the Kern-Tulare Water District. All are located within the Tulare Lake Basin, a massive freshwater aquifer with residual wetlands and marshes. The districts use produced water to supplement imported surface water and pumped groundwater to irrigate crops grown within their districts. Together, the four districts receive up to 50,000 acre-feet per year of produced water, helping to irrigate 95,000 acres of cropland.

"We need to make sure we fully understand what goes into the wastewater," Clay Rodgers, assistant executive officer of the Central Valley Water Quality Control Board, told the Los Angeles Times.

* * *

Thick as bream are the environmental consultants, lawyers, policy analysts, toxicology experts and the various other nabobs who gravitate to water-quality controversies. Things can get fractious and combative quickly. Portentous assertions are made – sometimes in shrill tones, sometimes *basso profondo* – into microphones at hearings, panel discussions, symposiums and broadcast studios. Jaws jut. Eyebrows arch. Lips purse. Brows furrow. Eyelids sometimes retract widely and freeze theatrically in mock amazement as if the listener has just been poleaxed in the back of the head.

In this roiling pool of testosterone, sallow-skinned personages harrumph, tut and crack wise. Middle-aged thoroughbreds whose taste runs to the "architect rig" – blue blazer, regimental "repp" tie, luxury serge pleated wool trousers and the occasional Salvatore Ferragamo moccasins or Stefano Ricci loafers – duck out of hearing rooms to relieve their coffee- and orange-juice-filled bladders, and make phone calls. Muffled yawps of collegial laughter erupt.

Variants of the species, in shirt sleeves and rolled-up shirt cuffs, dutifully roll bulging bankers boxes on wheeled contraptions from hearing room to conference room to court room, all a study in *sprezzatura* – that ephemeral, difficult-to-define Italian fashion quality denoting just the right amount of studied carelessness. They toil deep in the weeds – in the *weeds* within the weeds.

Scott Smith, chief scientist for the advocacy group Water Defense, which was founded by the actor-turned-activist Mark Ruffalo, collected samples of the water the Cawelo Water District purchased from Chevron over a two-year period. Laboratory analysis of those samples found compounds that are toxic to humans, including the industrial solvents acetone and methylene chloride, along with oil.

A separate 2016 water-quality assessment commissioned by Cawelo pointed out that acetone is a naturally occurring compound produced by humans, animals, plants and algae.

"Acetone is so ubiquitous in the environment," the report pointed out, "that it would, in fact, be surprising not to find it in the analyzed water samples." The study concluded that the presence of acetone was not related to the produced water.

None of the water samples collected at the Cawelo ponds in the 2016 study contained detectable concentrations of methylene chloride or any other chlorinated volatile organic compound.

Sarah Oktay, a water-testing expert and director of the Nantucket field station of the University of Massachusetts, Boston, reviewed Smith's methods and the laboratory analysis of the water he sampled. "I wouldn't necessarily panic," she told the Times, "but I would certainly think I would rather not have that," she said, referring to the chemicals identified in the water samples. "My next step would be most likely to look and make sure the crop is healthy."

The CBS San Francisco television affiliate KPIX5 broadcast a series of special reports on the use of oilfield wastewater on crops in 2016. The broadcast called out the Halos brand by name.

"It was a well-kept secret," local almond farmer Tom Frantz told a reporter. He said he had learned the water's unusual source a few years earlier after getting curious about a stench and a strange-looking pond filled with steaming hot water just a few miles from his orchard. "The smell, it's like rotten eggs, sulfur [and] asphalt."

Quick to bale the political fescue, state Senator Fran Pavley, representing a district in an affluent coastal county far from the Central Valley (though, to be fair, in a district in which her constituents were certainly eating nuts and fruits) sponsored legislation that would require expanded testing of water produced in oil operations. It's obviously unacceptable, said Pavley, that oil contaminants are found in irrigation water.

"Anyone would be extremely concerned." In the Golden State, water issues are always politicized.

Certain people are very strong on the term "powerful industrial solvent" for its shock value when describing chemicals found in drinking water, even when they are at trace levels or have not been found to cause harm in humans. A biomedical engineer reminded a reporter that water is a powerful industrial solvent, indeed the most powerful of all industrial solvents. "Water can even be given the scientific name 'oxidane,' which makes it sound pretty bad," he said. All too often, the thing degenerates into a molasses of oozing circumlocution, leaving observers to locate reports and scour footnotes to identify the short bursts of meaning and context.

Sadly, the degree to which waterborne chemicals at toxic concentrations are affecting crops – or people – has come down to much breast-beating and urinational sparring among attention-seeking elected officials, political appointees to assorted boards and commissions, and members of the priesthood of paid consiglieri and obscurants, all selectively interpreting the findings and methods of studies to suit their needs and those of their patrons. Entire cottage industries have sprung up around the Federal Clean Water Act and, in the Golden State, around the California Environmental Quality Act. Lawyers, lobbyists, environmentalists and representatives of the state's suppurating bureaucracies discuss obtuse corners of these laws like medieval priests debating how many angels can dance on the head of a pin. The public is no better off after any of it. Farmers deeply mistrust these people and believe they want to regulate every rut and puddle on their farms or deprive them of irrigation water.

Millennials are forming future battalions of environmental lawyers and consultants. And what better generation to begin populating the professions than the one that grew up on "Harry Potter," with its alchemy, mythology, potions, spells, talismans and wizardry. As members of this priesthood interpret and debate state and federal canons with confreres at well-catered roundtables, panel discussions and symposiums, hapless Muggles are left scratching their heads and directly or indirectly footing the bill. The carefully couched and footnoted conclusions of reports are always political, but only sometimes reliable.

It comes down to a certain down-home truth of one non-Harry Potter alchemist, Paracelsus, who famously said: "Only the dose makes the poison."

* * *

On the main page of Bailey Lauerman's website, in a section titled "How we think," the firm touts its knack for "trimming the unnecessary and delivering results most efficiently. We try to live in an abbreviated world," it reads. A photo of a large, cubicle-free work space revealed about a dozen millennials, ostensibly creatives or account executives, at Bailey Lauerman, doing ad-agency stuff – some lounging with feet elevated, some sitting upright, some interacting with their technology. One old guy in the photo – maybe a fellow in his 40s – seems to be tapping out a text on his smartphone.

Senior Public Relations Strategist Mel Dohmen went dark from her Delphic perch after email exchanges lasting a couple months in early 2018. Then, out of the blue in late April, she sent me an email informing me the firm had a policy of not responding on behalf of client work.

If I'd ever had any chance of gaining entry to the sanctum sanctorum of the fruit and its mythic transformation, it now seemed out the door. Maybe the high priests at Bailey Lauerman believed I was writing a pulpy novella that would bring discredit to Li'l Zipper. For now, on the periphery of an orange, I'd been sized up and trimmed away as unnecessary to the effort. I understand now I'd had about as much chance of getting inside the Cuties marketing machinery as Justin Bieber being invited to Clarence House for an evening of card games with Chuck and Camilla. I, the fool, had failed to grasp some essential protocol of deference between peon and star. I accepted the failure as my own.

It didn't diminish my admiration for Cuties and the marketing genius behind the brand. It did elicit sympathy for the writer who'd spent half a year trying to get an interview with Sawyer. It also struck me that the story of getting big-timed by a fruit had probably become more interesting than whatever insights the creatives at Bailey Lauerman might have provided about the Cuties tour de force. We'll never know.

Chapter Five

The World's Nuthouse

IT WAS THE heyday of the Red Delicious apple in the United States. During the 1980s, the variety had come to represent three-quarters of the apple harvest in Washington State. But behind the scenes, a cafeteria lunch lady – a Wanda, a Dottie or a Roz – scratched the scalp under her netted bouffant in bewilderment, wondering why the variety, with its chewy, bitter skin encasing a sugary, mushy flesh, came to dominate the apple market over the previous 70 years.

By 2000, as consumers discovered the Fuji and Gala varieties, Red Delicious had declined to less than half the state's production. It had clearly fallen from favor among consumers, putting Washington's apple industry at the verge of collapse. The Red Delicious had become "the largest compost-maker in the country," as shoppers routinely bought the apples and threw them away, Tom Burford, author of "Apples of North America," told the Atlantic's Sarah Yager in a 2014 piece titled "The Awful Reign of the Red Delicious: How the worst apple took over the United States, and continues to spread."

Congress approved a bill to bail out the apple industry in 2000. President Clinton signed it after apple growers had lost a combined $760 million.

"About 100,000 acres of Red Delicious [was] turned into firewood," wrote James McCandless, head of global real estate, farmland at UBS AgriVest in the pages of the publication Institutional Investor.

As the Red Delicious swan dive illustrates, orchards and vineyards come with higher risk and higher opportunity cost than field crops. Orchards require years to mature and can't be fallowed when conditions change. This makes them hard to adapt to quick reversals. Demand can fall on a whim, but supply isn't so easily adjusted.

* * *

Owners of vast swaths of California's Central Valley, where fields of cotton and vegetables once stretched as far as the eye could see, have succumbed to the great siren call of the almond monocrop. In 2000, an already eyebrow-raising 500,000 acres in the Valley were planted to almonds. By 2017, the number had doubled to over a million.

But orchard efficiency also increased. During a 10-year period prior to 2004, the average almond yield per acre was about 1,500 pounds, according to the Agriculture Department. But ten years later, that had risen to more than 2,100 pounds an acre. So, as planted acreage doubled, output increased by 40 percent per acre.

Almonds have become one of California's most lucrative crops, valued at about $5.2 billion in 2016, according to Agriculture Department figures. The value of the total crop in 1995 was a paltry $880 million. Almond production increased nearly 500 percent in that time with growth far outpacing other popular nuts. Shipments to China alone were up nearly

1,000 percent in 2011 compared with almond exports to China a decade earlier, according to the Oakland Institute.

In 2015, about 44 percent of California's almond crop was exported to Asia, according to the Almond Board of California. As of this writing in 2018, China had clamped duties on about 80 fruit and nut products from the United States, including California almonds and pistachios, as the United States placed tariffs on $250 billion in Chinese goods. Almonds are most popular in China during autumn and winter, especially during the Chinese New Year. Tariffs now make them pricier for the Chinese consumer.

Increasingly etched across almonds, as hedge funds, pension funds and university endowments pile headlong into the orchards, is a label reading "self-destruct."

Generally, an almond orchard doesn't bear fruit during the first three to four years after planting. Also, almond trees are alternate-bearing – a large crop one year is often followed by a lighter crop the next. The yield plateau typically ends at around 15 years, after which time it begins to slowly decline. The life cycle for almond orchards is generally 25 to 30 years, but in California's Central Valley trees are getting pushed down far earlier. By about 20 years, the decline in production can be precipitous enough to warrant demolition.

The state of California will soon work its own brand of magic on almonds. It will soon regulate the extraction of groundwater. During the worst of the recent drought, almond orchards in the Central Valley lived or died by the availability of groundwater, as most of the irrigation water districts had stopped delivery of surface water. There just wasn't enough snowmelt off the western slope of the Sierra. A 2015 jeremiad in the New York Times reminded readers that each almond they ate required about a gallon of water to produce. The American taxpayer should brace for a Red Delicious-style bailout of almonds if the two pincers – tariffs and regulation – exert sufficient pressure on the nut.

* * *

Lactose has emerged as one of the leading ingredients consumers actively avoid. This has helped spur sales of plant-based milk beverages. In the pantheon of such "milks," soy milk is believed to have been the first. It was later supplanted by almond milk. This was followed by a cavalcade of other plant-based elixirs – oat milk, rice milk, peanut milk, pea milk, hemp milk, cashew milk and quinoa milk.

Sales of almond milk alone exploded 250 percent between 2011 and 2016. Meanwhile, dairy milk consumption has fallen by 37 percent since the 1970s, according to the Agriculture Department.

* * *

California has done little to encourage crop diversification in its fertile Central Valley, one of the world's most productive agricultural regions. In fact, it's just the opposite. Elites representing densely populated and affluent coastal corridors have enacted generous wage floors, overtime pay, taxes and environmental restrictions that have unwittingly spurred crop consolidation and uniformity.

Governor Jerry Brown, pen in hand and about to sign the state's one-size-fits-all $15 minimum wage law in Los Angeles in 2016, was quoted by the Sacramento Bee as saying, "Economically, minimum wages may not make sense." The governor, like many officeholders in the state, lacked the sangfroid to oppose it. He simply questioned its rationale, shrugged and signed on the line that was dotted. The state had already begun adding hundreds of thousands of farmworkers to the ranks of those paid overtime after eight hours or 40 hours in a week. The law lowered the 10-hour-day threshold for overtime by half an hour each year until it reaches the standard eight-hour day by 2022. It also phases in a 40-hour standard workweek for seasonal pickers. In so doing, the state has created distortions that drive farmers into crops that can be machine-harvested with great efficiency, like almonds.

Other distortions farmers have brought on themselves. Undocumented workers make up at least half the agriculture workforce, according to industry estimates. This means feasibility for planting certain crops has always been based on a wink and nod. With the price pressures created by globalization, it was never feasible to grow these crops while having to fuss with such matters as a legal workforce. Agriculture, small and large, has been living a lie in the United States, which has not exactly ingratiated it to nonfarmers or instilled confidence inside or outside the farm patch. Increased deportations under the Obama administration, and later under the Trump administration, have depleted the labor pool, further laying bare the longstanding fiction behind the business model for hand-harvested crops and much of America's meatpacking industry. Much of the labor has "fallen off the back of a truck," as a member of the Cosa Nostra might put it. Less charitable critics of the extralegal labor arrangement might call it racketeering.

Regardless, farmers who once produced a wide variety of hand-harvested crops profitably are now being drawn by the seductive song of the almond monoculture.

Jeff Klein, a fourth-generation Stockton, California, farmer, told the Los Angeles Times in 2016 that he would be spending the coming five years replacing his 1,000 acres of grapevines with almond and olive trees, which require less human contact to grow. Five years earlier, said Klein, he could afford a crew of 100 workers to prune, tie and sucker his vines.

Wineries paid $700 for a ton of grapes, and Klein could clear a profit by paying $8 an hour, the minimum wage at that time. Those times are gone, so it's now almonds and olives.

As Big Labor succeeds in forcing abrupt hikes in labor inputs in Western ag states, America's working poor – including some of the very same farmworkers furloughed by the flight to machine-harvested crops – will be eating more corn-syrup-infused sugar bombs, more fast food, more starches, more cereal grains and fewer fruits and vegetables as farmers who once grew carrots, broccoli, apricots, turnips, peaches, asparagus and onions now pile into mechanically harvested crops like tree nuts. Also, expect California cotton and cut flowers to be further undercut by foreign competitors. The trend of officeholders in the Western ag states pandering to their densely populated, voter-rich regions to the detriment of agriculture began long before the $15 wage fiat but has only intensified since. The ease with which these state lawmakers have succeeded in erasing a complex market mechanism and creating an arbitrary benchmark with the stroke of a pen have left farmers in ag regions gobsmacked but not without options. Not only are these state lawmakers being hoist by their own petard, but they're taking every American along for the increasingly unhealthy ride.

* * *

The brute heaves and bellows. It looks like a cross between a street sweeper, a Humvee and a velociraptor. The operator sits inside a protected cabin and operates a massive hydraulic arm and a circular broom. The machine delivers an ear-splitting din and throws voluminous quantities of almonds into the air as it drives down each row between the trees.

Almonds on the tree are made up of three parts: an elastic hull, a hard shell and a nut. In California, each tree averages about 5,000 nuts a year. Each year, the trees produce one harvest, which takes place during the late summer.

About a week after being mechanically shaken from their trees, after the almonds have been sitting on the orchard floor and drying out, another machine – this one looks something like a hovercraft – is called in. Generating a mighty baritone rumble and thick clouds of dust, it sweeps the almonds to the center of each row. The dust is a necessary evil. Farmers purposely stop irrigation prior to the harvest to reduce the risk of mold as nuts sit on the orchard floor.

Next, a machine that looks something like a wood chipper is pulled through the orchard by a tractor. It vacuums the rows of nuts left on the orchard floor by earlier machines. Conveyer belts, Archimedes screws and hydraulic actuators jiggle, vibrate and comb through the haul to pull out twigs and leaves.

When the nuts are on the trees, some farmers call them "AHL-monds" with a short "a" as in the word "awe." Once they're off the tree, growers and processors start calling them "A-munds" no longer pronouncing the "l" and giving the "a" the same open sound as in "apple." No one seems to be able to explain this phenomenon.

The almond monocrop is a vast thing. And it brings monolithic risk. Themis Michailides, a UC Davis plant pathologist based at the Kearney Agricultural Research and Extension Center in tiny Parlier, California, recently told California Ag Today that almond band canker is back and becoming a big problem. "This was a very old disease, and almost forgotten, but now we have major problems, particularly in the young orchards," Michailides told the publication in late 2017. It's a fungal pathogen caused by a group of Botryosphaeria fungi that are common in major orchard crops like grapes, almonds, pistachios, walnuts, avocados and citrus. Another point of vulnerability is the outsized demand for bees. Here, a stressed and decreasing number of bee colonies are trucked in from across the United States in February and March to pollinate the proliferating almonds. It's been called the largest controlled pollination in the world. The going rental rate in 2017 was $200 a hive, as mentioned in the previous chapter. Two hives are typically required per acre of trees.

Another emerging threat is the prospect of a glut caused by sheer numbers alone. According to a prediction by the Almond Board of California, production of almonds in the state is estimated to rise from 2.25 billion pounds in 2017 to 3 billion pounds by 2021. Even dairy farmers are hopping aboard the almond band wagon. They've been planting almonds on land they once used to grow forage crops.

Speaking to media outlet Foodnavigator USA, Almond Board of California CEO Richard Waycott explained dairy farmers "might have traditionally planted x-number of acres of corn or silage for their dairy herds but are now sourcing that from out of state and diversifying into almonds." The plant-based milk industry is predicted to be worth $35 billion by 2024.

Amid the strains of an average combined sales tax of 8.25 percent, average individual income tax of 13.3 percent, a per-gallon gas tax of $0.58, a state corporate tax of 8.84 percent and an $11 an hour minimum wage rising by a dollar a year until it reaches $15, California almond farmers have held their own. But Sacramento has now turned its eyes beadily not to the monocrop enveloping the state's Central Valley but to the water underneath it.

The state's new concerns were manifested in the Sustainable Groundwater Management Act, known to most farmers by its acronym "SGMA" (given the grand-sounding pronunciation "sigma"). It will change the face of ag in the San Joaquin Valley, since it will limit the groundwater farmers can pump to the surface to irrigate their crops. The state has never before regulated groundwater like this. Plans must be put into place by 2020 and 2022, and sustainability nirvana must be reached by 2040 or else. SGMA has fueled speculation over how water shortfalls will affect existing orchards. New consiglieri, intermediaries and hand-holders are now being minted.

The dryly worded legislation contains playoff-caliber vagueness. It "requires the creation of local agencies to develop and implement plans to manage their groundwater basins sustainably within 20 years. Sustainable groundwater management is defined as the management and use of groundwater in a manner that can be maintained … without causing undesirable results, which are defined in the legislation as unreasonable depletion of the aquifer, land subsidence, seawater intrusion, degraded water quality, and surface water impacts."

The groundwater situation has, in fact, become perilous but state officeholders are blind to the regulations and buried costs that have driven farmers into water-intensive tree nuts in the first place. Wells have been drilled to unheard of depths—2,000 feet or more—requiring powerful pumps to bring the water up.

Onion man Bob Ehn said he recently began hearing rumors of growers spending upwards of $1 million to drill a well on the Valley's arid west side. "That million-dollar mark would be for something like a 2,000 foot well," said Ken Williams, owner and president of Willitts Pump Co. in Exeter, California. "You get past 1,100 to 1,200 feet, you might see costs as high as $400 a foot. It takes a massive rig with a big crew – seven or eight guys."

For that million-dollar well, the driller accepts no risk, said Williams. "We have a pretty good idea where the water is, but [the risk is] on the property owner. There are other risk factors. We could hit oil and gas. That can add costs."

Ag broker Ken Macklin of Visalia, California-based H.R. Macklin & Sons, Inc., said he recently got a bid for what is now a relatively shallow well – a mere 400 feet – for $150 a foot. "I drilled a well 25 years ago. It cost me $200,000. I couldn't believe it. The cost at the time was mind-blowing," said Macklin. It's only gotten more expensive, he said.

The water that comes up from a 2,000-foot well will likely be mineral-laden and will have to be heavily filtered. As shallow farm and domestic wells go dry, only growers who can afford to dig deep can stay in the game. Some big growers have purchased their own drilling rigs from places like Texas.

If an almond glut – like the Red Delicious glut in Washington – develops, things could get interesting as getting out of almonds might involve more than cutting down trees and replacing them with row crops. This kind of waste can't be easily processed in the Central Valley, because many contracts between biomass power plants and utility companies have expired. Any wholesale demolition of orchards would leave mounds of dead trees or wood chips on the land itself, making it unusable for other crops. Harley Phillips, a citrus farmer who demolishes orchards as his off-farm job, said it has been increasingly difficult to dispose of the wood chips with closures of cogeneration plants (also known as "biomass plants") across the Central Valley. "[The utility] is not renewing the contracts as they come up for renewal; they're having to shut down. I have a long-term contract, but many don't."

With little past experience with the practice, growers in the southern Valley have begun plowing wood chips from demolished trees deep into the ground before replanting their orchards. "Last year was the first year anyone in Kern County had spread the chips back on the ground," said Phillips in 2018. "It can be as much as 60 tons of woodchips to the acre." The smaller the chips, the faster they'll break down, and growers work them as deep into the ground as they can. "Up north, it's reported to be having positive effects, adding nutrients to the soil, but here in the south, where the soil is drier, we just don't know," he said. "How could it not attract bacteria, nematodes and termites? We're advising people to pour liquid nitrogen on the soil to promote the breakdown of the wood chips."

In counterpoint to the faceless institutional investors and Wall Street firms piling into almond land as of late are the Resnicks of Beverly Hills, written about in the previous chapter. The billionaire couple, Stewart and Lynda Resnick, own about 70,000 acres of almonds and pistachios in the Valley. It's the biggest chunk of their $4 billion Wonderful Co., the largest grower and processor of pistachios and almonds in the world.

Octogenarian Stewart Resnick, something of a Blake Carrington type, is the all-business side of the power couple; Lynda Resnick, a former child actress who founded an advertising agency at the tender age of 19, is nothing short of a marketing maestra. She is credited with having developed the Halos brand of mandarin, as well as Fiji Water and POM Wonderful.

Lynda Resnick is also credited as the mastermind of the memorable "Get Crackin" ad campaign. In the wake of the state's largest ever pistachio crop, Wonderful launched a $55 million campaign in 2016 featuring Ernie the Elephant, a pistachio-loving computer-generated spokes-pachyderm voiced by WWE star John Cena. Later, Seattle Seahawks player Richard Sherman would be featured in digital videos and two "Get Crackin'" commercials during the football season. In 2018, the company hosted a media tour to extol its position as the top pistachio producer in the world (no doubt it also touted its status as the world's top supplier of pomegranates, mandarins, lemons and Texas grapefruit, and the top importer of limes).

The Resnicks' massive holdings require the use of at least 120 billion gallons of water a year, two-thirds on nuts, enough to supply San Francisco's 852,000 residents for a decade, reported Forbes in 2015. By owning a majority of seats on Dudley Ridge Water District and the private Westside Mutual Water Company, the duo is able to exercise control of the Kern Water Bank, one of the largest underground water storage banks in the nation. It can store 500 billion gallons of water during wet years for use during dry ones. It is a vast system of wells, pipelines and subterranean cisterns spanning 20,000 acres in the southern San Joaquin Valley along the Kern River. It was developed as a critical reservoir by the state of California in the late 1980s. The sandy, alluvial ground is ideal for storing water underground.

The Monterey Amendment, a controversial 1994 pact between California's Department of Water Resources and State Water Project contractors, transferred ownership and operation of the Kern Water Bank from the state to the Kern County Water Agency, which is effectively controlled by the Resnicks. Like many water deals in the Golden State, the Monterey Amendment has resulted in a delirium of legal challenges that have taken decades to sort through, resulting in court-ordered environmental reviews, settlements and appeals. In 2016, it was reported that the Resnicks had enough water to sell some back to the state for a cool $30 million. The couple – known also for their philanthropy – spent at least

$35 million during the 2011-2017 California drought, according to Forbes, snapping up more water rights from nearby districts. "The Resnicks saw the value of water very early on and spent considerable time and money securing various water rights, from riparian to groundwater, all over the Valley," said Lois Henry, the former columnist for the Bakersfield Californian.

"They were the first to see the value in groundwater banking. Some say the Kern Water Bank was a 'gift of public resources' but the Resnicks put the money in to make the [Kern Water Bank] a viable facility," said Henry, who grew up in Fresno, attended Fresno State University and penned a twice-weekly column for the Californian for 27 years.

The anti-Resnick camp unites an array of diverse bedfellows. Some fear the Resnicks' agricultural empire is a cover crop – literally – to mask the pair's true intention, which, they believe, is to pull water from the California Water Project and resell it to the highest bidder. They bristle at the couple's ownership rights to the Kern Water Bank, accusing them of nefarious behavior. Some of the more censorious types were featured in director and Fresno-native Marina Zenovich's 2017 documentary for National Geographic "Water & Power: A California Heist."

"I love the underdog, I love the fight – fighting corporate power, fighting big money – water loss, especially in California, is an absolute nightmare," Adam Keats, an environmental lawyer for the Center for Food Safety, told the documentarian. Keats told Josh Harkinson of Mother Jones that the transfer of the water bank to the Resnicks and other farmers was "an unconstitutional rip-off."

"I don't know if [the Resnicks] are villains," said Henry, "but one family in control of that much water does give me pause." While some who follow water rights in the state do project their rage and phobias onto the Resnicks, Henry's concern seems legitimate. Critics seem to jeer at the Resnicks for the purposes of stoking class envy, likening them to Gilded Age oligarchs and deploying terms like "water baron" to whip up indignation, hoping to still the duo's dark talents for selling fruits and nuts to unsuspecting persons. The detractors clearly don't like the size of the couple's land holdings and control of the water required to irrigate them. Lost Hills, population 2,400, is the base of operations for the Resnicks' Wonderful Pistachio and Almond production. Generally, just a handful of skilled drivers can harvest thousands of trees in a few hours from the cabs of their chundering shakers and harvesters. The removal of the husks and shells is also largely an automated affair. In fact, the almond and pistachio orchards always seem eerily devoid of humans.

The Resnicks have been able "to extract millions and millions of pounds and tens of millions of dollars off the fields of Lost Hills, and you wonder how much of that is going back to the workers," asked former L.A. Times reporter Mark Arax in Zenovich's documentary. "What I'm trying to do," said Arax, "is get all these big guys and lift the veil on what they're doing."

Later in the documentary, Arax stumbles upon a crew demolishing an almond orchard with heavy equipment. Mike Wallace-style, he walks up and questions the operator of a track excavator. Because the trees are still alive, the documentary implies some Rubicon has been crossed or some skullduggery is afoot – maybe the "heist" in the documentary's title. (Omitted from the narrative was that during droughts, growers often decide to push over older trees that are in declining production and plant new ones, since the newly planted trees use less water when water is scarce. Some growers summarily demolish their orchards after 20 years and replant. In those cases, yes, the trees they push down are still green and alive.) But Arax's warning on the unsustainable groundwater-only irrigation in the Valley during droughts is cogent.

The Resnicks deny allegations of nefarious dealings; they maintain they're legally and morally in the right. "I don't even know what these [lawsuits] are about, because my view is we're going to win," the otherwise publicity-shy Stewart Resnick told Forbes. "We've been sued over the same thing over and over and continue to win."

The shame campaign and lawsuits midwifed by assorted environmental groups, water-rights obscurants, rage *artistes* and agents of endarkenment haven't made the duo go gentle into that great good night. There are signs the couple, perhaps tired of being easy quarry for their detractors, have been waging a charm offensive, and it may be working.

Two years after his muck-raking interviews in Zenovich's documentary, even the sharp-elbowed Arax seems to have softened a little. In a 2018 interview with Joe Moore of Valley Public Radio, he praised the couple for their philanthropy. Gone was the Edward R. Murrow officiousness from the documentary. Gone, the redistribution rhetoric. Gone, the lines of questioning about the Lost Hills drinking water.

"The philanthropy they do is extraordinary," he told Moore in dulcet tones. "All that marketing, from the pomegranate juice to the Wonderful pistachios and almonds to the Fiji Water ... a lot of it started with Lynda. She's got a crew now ... but she's still very hands-on," he said with a reverence just short of what one might reserve for a discussion about Joan of Arc. "They're really this extraordinary, interesting, quirky couple ... they're breaking the mold in *so* many ways."

So, what do the long-suffering residents of Lost Hills portrayed in Zenovich's film now think?

"They really like the boss lady," said Arax. In fact, Lost Hills may be a tad *too* utopian these days. "There is some pushback to some of the health-[related] things they're trying. There's a gym there and if you lose a certain amount of weight you get money. There's a little pushback on that. They feel it's too coercive."

So, has any San Joaquin Valley ag water – specifically snowmelt off the western slope of the Sierra Nevada – actually been used to flush toilets in L.A.? In fact, yes.

The Arvin-Edison Water Storage District south of Bakersfield has rights to water delivered from the diminutive Millerton Lake above the pastoral town of Friant, population 550. The lake, dammed in 1942, impounds snowmelt off the western slope for irrigation. The water is distributed by the Madera and Friant-Kern canals to many parts of the San Joaquin Valley. One problem is there isn't much storage space in the lake; it's one of the smallest reservoirs in California, and to make good on the total Friant contracts of 2.2 million acre-feet, Millerton would need to fill and drain about five times during an average season (or 10 times during a season of heavy snowmelt), according to Jeevan Muhar, an affable engineer and manager with the Arvin-Edison Water Storage District. (He tells people that the easiest way to remember and pronounce his first name is it rhymes with "Steven.")

"In wetter periods, the snowmelt runoff can come in short duration and high flows," he said. "That means it's coming down fast and furious." For about 20 years, Arvin-Edison Water Storage District has had a water management program with the Metropolitan Water District of Southern California, which is eyed with suspicion by Valley farmers, since Metropolitan supplies member agencies in the state's heavily urbanized south. (By way of full disclosure, the author has worked for firms involved in Metropolitan Water District projects.)

"Typical snowmelt occurs in the spring when irrigation demand is low," said Muhar, "and, assuming Metropolitan has available storage, they can take delivery and then return the water to Arvin during the summer when irrigation demand is at its highest." Arvin is the only Friant district in the Valley that has a long-term program with the Metropolitan Water District, he said. Arvin received much criticism over the exchange; there was suspicion the deal would be Owens Valley 2.0, said Muhar, referring to Los Angeles sending land agents hundreds of miles north to buy up land with water rights to snowmelt off the Sierra Nevada's eastern slope. Acts of violence and sabotage wracked the Owens Valley in the 1920s as 300,000 acres – some of it luxuriant grazing and farmland – and the enormous Owens Lake wasted away to scrubland and a dry lakebed.

During wet periods, Arvin can make deposits with the Metropolitan Water District and get the water back later, allowing flexibility in Arvin's scheduling of water deliveries to farmers. The Metropolitan Water District likes the quality of the Friant water, and why wouldn't it? It's pure snowmelt. The water the Arvin district gets back can be up to 10 times higher in salinity, but still acceptable for irrigation, said Muhar.

But seizing on Arvin-Edison's purported "deal with the enemy" or the Resnicks' quest to control ample water to irrigate 70,000 acres of tree nuts is missing the point. Assorted policy geeks, environmental-justice crusaders, urban sophisticates, regional rights advocates and documentarians are asking the wrong questions.

Amid the invective leveled at the Resnicks, more than

ten times the couple's land holdings have been planted to almonds in the Central Valley, much of it by the dead hand of institutional investors influenced by groupthink and confirmation bias as they chased returns in a low-return environment.

Hancock Agricultural Investment Group manages 325,000 acres of prime farmland in North America and Australia. As of the close of 2017, almonds made up 20 percent of its global portfolio, and pistachios, an additional 18 percent. The publication Mother Jones reported in 2014 that Hancock controlled on behalf of its clients 24,000 acres, making it the second-largest nut producer behind the Resnicks. TIAA-CREF, a large retirement and investment fund, owns 37,000 acres of California farmland. It buys the land and then leases it back to farmers, reports the publication Institutional Investor. In 2010, the fund, which bills itself as one of the five largest holdings of almond acreage in the world, bought a controlling stake in Champaign, Illinois-based Westchester Agriculture Asset Management. With the trees and vines it owns, TIAA-CREF keeps all interests and has Westchester manage them. UBS AgriVest has piled into trees and vines, too. The fund is reported to be leasing all its holdings back to farmers, though the lease structure involves a percentage of gross income.

In the Central Valley, row-crop land is increasingly seen as the necessary raw material for conversion to trees and vines – mostly trees and, of that, mostly almonds where soil quality permits. The market increasingly sees such land through the prism of conversion rather than on its own merits.

That's where the big boys have the advantage. A small farmer may be able to buy on credit or lease 180 acres to grow, say, black beans or peppers, but the farmer isn't likely to have the upfront capital to develop the land to tree nuts – buy the land, upgrade the well, install an irrigation system, plant the trees and then wait multiple years for the crop to come in. Hedge funds, endowments and pension funds have the wherewithal to foot the upfront costs and ride out the first few years.

And it's not just in California – home of 80 percent of the world's almond crop. Swiss fund of funds Adveq joined with the Municipal Employees' Retirement System of Michigan and Danish fund Danica Pension in 2014 to snap up 50 percent of Australia's almond-producing acreage in an 18-year leaseback arrangement with the seller.

After enduring criticism for not investing enough in domestic agriculture, the Australian pension fund First State Super made a $150 million acquisition of 10,000 acres of almonds Down Under in 2015. The advisor to the state pension fund in the deal caught the attention of the publication AgFundernews.com, which noticed PPB Advisory, a firm more commonly associated with corporate restructuring, had recast itself as an ag advisor. The publication also pointed out that accountancy firms Deloitte and BDO have been building teams to play a role in this market. This may be the classic sell signal – the equivalent of hearing your grandma discuss taking up a position in commercial-backed mortgage securities. Heather Davis, a senior managing director of global private markets for global investment manager Nuveen, unwittingly captured this *idée fixe* among institutional investors in a 2015 assessment:

"The challenge producers face is a scarcity of available land that's conducive to growing almonds, part of a global trend in which urbanization, water scarcity and environmental factors are pressuring the amount of arable acreage."

While Davis was right that urbanization has accounted for a loss of land in California – nearly 1.1 million acres of farmland between 1984 and 2010, according to the state's Department of Conservation – much of the loss has occurred on the outskirts of the state's two big urban centers: San Francisco and Los Angeles.

In the Central Valley, the scarcity of land Davis laments is the result of the monocrop itself, not single-family homes and shopping centers. The California Department of Food and Agriculture estimated for 2017, the most recent figures at this writing, that over one million acres were planted to bearing almond trees with as many as 300,000 non-bearing acres in the pipeline.

As if planned by committee, 750,000 acres of row-crop land was converted to the monocrop from 2004 to 2017. That's nearly 1,200 square miles, or an area twice the size of the city of Houston, in new almond plantings during the period. That's one square mile every four days in new almonds. Davis' "vanishing land" is as much due to almond-orchard development devouring row-crop land as it is due to urbanization. In fairness to Davis, though, urbanization tends to permanently remove land from agricultural use whereas conversion from field crops to trees is a 20-year proposition and it's still an ag use. (But from the perspective of institutional investors looking to hop on the almond bandwagon with new orchard development, the land already converted to the tree nut has "vanished" for them.)

The almond craze among institutional investors may be the classic case of FOMO – fear of missing out. Pension funds, endowments and other institutional investors see their cohorts piling into permanent crops and they, too, want in. Advisory firms are only too glad to tell them what they want to hear.

"I'm concerned by how many new, unsustainable acres were opened up for almonds, pistachios and pomegranates on the west side of the Valley," said the former columnist Lois Henry. "Those areas, especially in the southern San Joaquin, have little to no usable ground water so they are totally dependent on surface water out of the Sacramento Delta." Some of the areas Henry refers to looked like outdoor ashtrays in the early 2000s. Now they're orchards.

"Given problems in the Delta ecosystem, I don't see how those farming operations can continue, and increased wages are driving farmers to greater mechanization.

"The Valley has always been a place of extremes," she said. "Yes, we used to grow more cotton and alfalfa, *lots* more. So much so that many environmentalists wagged their fingers at us for growing low-value crops with high-value water, which was true. Well, now we grow high-value crops with high-value water. The real question is whether we will have enough water to sustain all the ag we currently have, and I think the answer is no."

Globalization has become embedded in California's almond monocrop. As tariffs begin to bite in Asia and Europe, almond consumption will slacken there. Expect to see a surplus of cheap almonds flooding into all manner of domestic nut products and used as thickening agents and additives in processed foods. Around the coffee table this Christmas, expect to see Grandma cracking many more almond than filberts and Brazil nuts. It's not inconceivable that the hedge funds, pension funds and endowments that piled headlong into almonds a decade ago will be lined up, hat in hand, seeking federal relief in the next farm bill.

While the creature – now 1.3 million acres and growing – creeps into every nook and cranny of the Central Valley, the nation will need to come to grips with a hard fact: One of its key sources of fruits, vegetables and cotton is becoming the world's nuthouse.

Chapter Six

The Guac Is My Copilot

IN 2018, MEXICAN officials discovered 7.4 acres of illegal avocado plantings in a monarch butterfly preserve west of Mexico City, reported Mark Stevenson of the Associated Press.

Deforestation to make room for avocados has been rumored for a while with the belief that mom-and-pop growers in the avocado-growing state of Michoacán have been cutting down sections of pine forest to clear the way for new plantings. But this incursion was different. Now the growers had encroached into sacred ground: An area frequented by *gabachos* in L.L. Bean tropic-weight cargo shorts, tufts of gray chest hair cascading from the collars of cane-cutter shirts, slinging Filson rugged twill backpacks and toting Wood & Faulk hardwood and bridle leather collapsible stools *comme il faut*. A middle-school principal from Phoenix here; a retired investment banker from Bergen County, New Jersey, there – with liver-spotted pates, sloped shoulders, leathery wattles and three-day stubble, their slow-footed second and third wives, with ortho-perfect teeth, complaining bitterly about the humidity. These AARP-card-toting eco-tourists *Yanquis* – with a few Euro-travelers mixed in – are willing to spend substantial wads of cash to be surrounded by swarms of the gossamer-winged monarchs. The meaning of the avocado incursion into the protected butterfly preserve was not lost on the tour operators.

The illegal orchard was believed to be the first such encroachment into the preserve. The creatures are fussy. They won't perch on avocado trees. They will only roost on pine, fir and cedar trees; they cluster in the needles. Clustering protects them from the cold. The monarch itself isn't endangered, but its perplexing multi-generational 3,400-mile north-south migration is a mystery, and it could be compromised by avocado plantings.

Avocados are considered one of the most lucrative crops in Mexico – "green gold." The avocado trade employs about 100,000 people in the state of Michoacán alone. Rising supplies of avocados from Mexico have whetted demand in the United States. Now, the Chinese consumer is gaining a taste for the avocado, promising big future pressure on the Mexican forests and an expanding monocrop.

The eastern population of North America's monarchs overwinters in the same dozen or so mountain areas in the states of Mexico and Michoacán from October to late March. If the exalted creatures get cold, they have to use their fat reserves. The humidity in this part of Mexico assures the monarchs won't dry out, allowing them to conserve their energy. Mexico's environmental protection office reported a man had been taken into custody on weapons charges in connection with the encroachment. In April 2017, police found a 91-acre stand of pine trees had been chopped down in the Valle de Bravo nature reserve to the east.

An NGO known as Gira had already claimed in 2016

that half of all orchards planted in forestland were bought via dubious legal means and that avocado-driven deforestation was growing in Mexico at a rate of 2.5 percent annually. It has been previously speculated that Michoacán – where part of the reserve is located – loses about 15,000 to 20,000 acres of forestland annually to avocado plantations.

Ramon Paz, the spokesman for Mexico's Association of Avocado Export Packers and Producers, told the Associated Press that almost all avocados are grown on land that was *not* deforested to make way for plantations. "We have been accused a lot of deforestation, but according to the information we have ... between 85 percent and 90 percent of the area planted with avocado trees was previously occupied for other agricultural uses," Paz said, adding they were usually corn fields. He said his group, known as APEAM, was concerned about conserving forests. "We don't want our product to be perceived as one that results from deforestation."

Deforestation or not, many of the new orchards are in the mountains and chemicals used in production are reported to be showing up as runoff in the groundwater and in streams and highland lakes. Some believe it is causing illnesses in humans who rely on this water for their drinking supply. In Michoacán, about 80 percent of the state's 23,000 avocado growers are reported to be on orchards of 12 acres and smaller. There is a gold rush mentality as small growers flock to the region in search of land, seeking to hitch their wagon to the great avocado mule train.

The New Zealand Herald advised its readers to stop eating avocados. In Michoacán there is hardly any forest left as the state gets filled with avocado trees to meet demand, it wrote in an editorial in its Lifestyle section.

* * *

It is viewed as the Original Sin by U.S. avocado growers. In 1997, the Agriculture Department opened the door to the largest avocado market in the world by rescinding an 83-year-old ban on the importation of Mexican avocados into the Lower 48 States.

The California Avocado Commission had spearheaded the resistance to lifting the ban. There was already friction from a small number of avocados coming in from Chile at the time. It turned out to be the first leak in a soon-to-burst dike.

Just two decades later, Mexico would not only come to dominate the U.S. market, but the relaxation would lead to the Agriculture Department dangling the promise of the "Mexican Miracle" to other would-be avocado strongholds, like growers in the hinterlands of post-conflict Colombia, as Colombia that year was granted access to the U.S. market. It marked a new era for growers there.

Importation from Mexico had been banned since U.S. agriculture officials first identified avocado seed weevils in Mexican orchards as threats to U.S. crops in the early 20th century. Adult weevils feed on a tree's foliage, which stresses trees, but the adult weevil is not the main problem. The true damage is caused by the larvae, which feed on the pits within the fruit. In doing so, they damage the fruit, and it leads to premature fruit drop.

In 1997, California growers believed cheaper imports from Mexico would spawn a black market promoting the smuggling of avocados into California, putting the domestic crop at risk. (Importation had already been happening for more than three years: Mexican avocados were being allowed to enter Alaska, but subject to restrictions.) At the time, the Agriculture Department ruled that only Hass avocados from the Mexican state of Michoacán met U.S. import requirements. California farmers were growing more than 90 percent of the 300 million pounds of avocados eaten by Americans annually at the time. These were halcyon days for the California avocado.

But U.S. trade negotiators were in a quandary. The ban on the Mexican fruit had always been a source of friction in negotiations. If Mexican avocados remained banned from the U.S. market, Mexico City might retaliate by throttling importation of more valuable U.S. farm products into Mexico. California avocado farmers feared they'd be sacrificed at the altar so their brethren in the Farm Belt could prosper.

Those fears proved well-founded. Two decades later, Mexico had become the third-biggest destination for exported big-ticket U.S farm products ranging from corn and wheat to dairy foods and high-fructose corn syrup. The total value of the U.S. avocado crop was just $316 million in 2016, while the value of U.S. corn exports alone to Mexico rose to nearly $18 billion.

When the avocado floodgates were thrown open, free-trade advocates estimated American consumers would benefit from the competition. Analysts estimated at the time that Mexican avocado imports would drive down U.S. prices by as much as 17 percent by 2010. The United States quickly became a net importer of avocados, with Mexico producing most of the avocados imported into the United States, followed by Chile.

The increase in supply not only sated the appetite for avocados in the United States but also whetted it. U.S. consumption of avocados soared from about 1.1 pounds per capita in 1989 to seven pounds per capita by 2014. About the time U.S. per capita consumption hit seven pounds, the Internet became absurdly obsessed with avocados. The mania likely began when actress and lifestyle-monger Gwyneth

Paltrow made avocado toast a pillar of her 2013 bestselling cookbook "It's All Good."

"It's the holy trinity of Vegenaise, avocado and salt that makes this like a favorite pair of jeans — so reliable and easy and always just what you want," she wrote about avocado toast. The inclusion of avocado toast as a "dish" in the cookbook left some waiting for Paltrow to invent toast and jam or the PBJ. Some complained that avo-toast should not have been in the cookbook, since it requires zero cooking. Others believe it is something akin to a secret handshake between Paltrow and her minions or a conceptual inside joke with hints of self-mockery. In July 2015, twerk queen and newly converted vegan Miley Cyrus solidified her own bond with the avocado by getting an avocado tattooed on her left triceps.

The credit-card processing company Square reported in 2017 that Americans were spending nearly $900,000 a month on avocado toast. That's a stupendous increase from what the company reported for 2014, when its clients turned over just $17,000 of the avo-toast monthly. It was reported that 3 million new pictures of avocados were being posted on Instagram daily.

* * *

In the early 20th century, avocados were called "alligator pears." Before that, the Aztecs are said to have called them "ahuacacuahatl," meaning "fruit from the testicle tree." If ever there was justification for a sophisticated rebranding rollout, that was it. The Incas of modern-day Peru buried avocados with mummies as early as 750 B.C., and there is evidence that avocados were cultivated in Mexico as early as 500 B.C.

Fast forward to 1871, when Judge R.B. Ord of Santa Barbara, California, purchased three saplings in Mexico and a few weeks later planted them on a small patch at the corner of his property in what is now the coastal enclave's downtown. They were the first known avocado trees in the United States. One died, but the two surviving trees bore fruit for many years and created interest in further plantings.

By the early 1900s, growers had spotted a commercial growing opportunity. The avocado of the early 20th century was still called the "alligator pear." Some of the first guacamole recipes were published in the 1940s. Guacamole is a combination of the words for "avocado" and "sauce" in the Nahuatl language.

Now eclipsed by Mexico's massive avocado juggernaut, California is still the leading U.S. producer, growing about 90 percent of the domestic crop. Most are harvested on about 50,000 acres in the coastal counties from San Luis Obispo to San Diego by nearly 5,000 growers. (San Diego County, which produces 60 percent of all California avocados, is ground zero of the smoldering remains of U.S. avocado production in the aftermath of the Mexican onslaught.)

As a surge in supply and lower prices have whetted appetites in the United States, the same is being seen with Chinese avocado consumption. It is exploding. "It appears to just double every year, from what we've seen," Steve Barnard, president of Oxnard, California-based Mission Produce, the world's largest distributor of avocados, told CNBC in 2018. A decade earlier, not a single avocado was known to have been imported to China. By 2017, Latin American countries had shipped 76 million pounds of the fruit to China. This is still a fraction of the 1.8 billion pounds of avocados Mexico shipped to the United States in the 2018 season, but if Chinese demand doubles annually a modest pipeline is turning into a big fat artery before our eyes. It's only a matter of time before demand outpaces current supply. While it's been speculated that China could begin producing enough of its own avocados to cut into imports, few believe this will happen any time soon.

* * *

Cinco de Mayo, which marks the Mexican army's victory over the French in 1862, has become the second-biggest event for avocado sales in the United States – outdone only by the Super Bowl. Cinco de Mayo tends to be celebrated with greater fanfare in the United States than in Mexico. If it falls on a Friday, Saturday or Sunday, it can mean increased restaurant purchases and increased pressures on avocado supplies.

Avocados are alternate-bearing. So-called off-crop yields can range from 60 percent to 100 percent less than on-crop yields.

When Cinco de Mayo or the Super Bowl falls on an off-crop year, prices spike. It takes 14 to 18 months to grow a single avocado. Some industry savants believe Mexico reached "peak avocado" in 2015. Between 2015 and 2016, Mexico exported one million tons of avocados – 800,000 tons more than its closest competitor, Indonesia.

* * *

The town of Tancítaro sits at the base of the majestic Pico de Tancítaro, a 12,615-foot volcanic peak – the highest point in Michoacán state. Tancítaro is a farming town of about 30,000. It is also a global center of avocado production at the heart of Michoacán, Mexico's leading state for avocados. The state produced about 80 percent of Mexico's avocados in 2016. Avocado exports earned Mexico more than $1.5 billion that year. Tancítaro alone ships more than $1 million of avocados daily. But the local industry has been as much of a bane as a blessing. It has been two years since the outskirts of Tancítaro saw skirmishes between vigilantes and cartel gunmen. The families whose orchards had been seized, whose members had been kidnapped for ransom, were now running their farms again.

The run-up to NAFTA not only triggered new thinking about exports at the highest levels in the Mexican government but it also led to new thinking at the highest levels of Mexico's drug cartels. Beginning in the 1990s, Mexico's Jalisco New Generation Cartel and the Cuinis criminal group began pioneering the extortion and kidnapping of wealthy avocado farmers to fund their expansion, according to a report from the National Center for Planning, Analysis and Information for Combating Crime.

Avocado production evolved with NAFTA as Mexican growers were able to sell into the U.S. market and undercut California growers. In lockstep with this process, the criminal groups launched a hostile takeover – literally – of Tancítaro, levying a tax on growers and packers under the threat of kidnapping, murder or both.

The extortion turned large-scale avocado producers into "parallel financial sources" that supplemented income from drug trafficking, according to a 2017 InSight Crime Report. There was no Robin Hood element to the gangs. Rich and poor alike were at risk. Worse, it was suspected that the syndicates had developed an intelligence network in Mexico's Agriculture Secretariat. With the information gleaned from government records, the cartels were better able to target the country's newly affluent avocado farmers.

The narco-syndicates parlayed their proceeds to tighten their grip. Murders in Michoacán, according to the official count, numbered 8,258 between 2006 and 2015. As Mexico's drug wars erupted, Michoacán's growers understood they needed not only to mind their avocado groves, but they needed to cultivate a farmer's militia. In 2013, growers and packers, tired of being victimized, did just that in Michoacán. A self-defense force formed in Tancítaro.

A headline in NPR's online service blared, "Blood Avocados No More: Mexican Farm Town Says It's Kicked Out Cartels" Carrie Kahn, NPR's international correspondent, visited the town before the 2018 Super Bowl, as avocado production ramped up.

"We know when it's Super Bowl time," Hugo Naranjo, the manager at the Frutas Finas packing plant, told her. "Our production jumps."

Although a fascinating glimpse into the hard realities behind avocado production in Mexico, Kahn's story seemed to imply that not only was the seemingly insatiable appetite for illegal drugs north of the border fueling organized crime in Mexico, but now an appetite for cheap guacamole had added to the victimization in this idyllic town.

"By early 2014, they had 80 residents trained and ready to go," she wrote. "The new force is equipped with armored patrol trucks, and each officer wears full combat gear, including bullet-proof vest, helmet and high-powered rifle — all provided by the state police. Their salaries come in part from local avocado growers and packers, who wield much power and influence over the town. The other half comes from city coffers."

Not everyone was painting the same picture as NPR. Among them was a researcher with an aristocratic name, Frenchman Romain Le Cour Grandmaison, who studies Central American security issues and is co-director at the Paris-based think tank Noria Research. "From one village to another, their behavior, their motivations, and their scale of organization differ," wrote Le Cour Grandmaison about the militias. Le Cour Grandmaison is a doctoral candidate in political science at the Sorbonne in Paris. His research deals with the relationship between criminal organizations and local politics in Michoacán.

"[Some of the vigilantes] are heavily armed groups – the origin and mode of acquisition of the arsenal not being clearly determined – while others are limited to surveillance rounds without having a real coercion capacity," he wrote.

"It's very hard to believe that Tancítaro is just this island of peace and perfect transparency in Michoacán," Le Cour Grandmaison told the New York Times in January 2018. Falko Ernst, his colleague at the think tank, added, "You have an armed group acting on behalf of the real political authority, the grower's council" — a body of wealthy orchard owners — "doing the cleansing in their name and in their interests."

The 2015 documentary "Cartel Land," directed by Dartmouth-educated filmmaker Matthew Heineman, deals with the Mexican Drug War. In particular, Heineman examines the vigilante groups. These are the same groups Le Cour Grandmaison studies. In "Cartel Land," one is led by larger-than-life militia leaders who might have stepped from the pages of a Hemingway novel, like the impossibly bearded "Papa Smurf" and the dashing, mustachioed ladies' man Dr. Jose Manuel Mireles.

But critics charge that the self-defense forces have overstepped and devolved into warlordism. Any aficionado of the post-apocalyptic AMC series "The Walking Dead" will instantly recognize the fine line between the utopian and dystopian in groups formed ad hoc to fight a common enemy. The casual observer will see the avocado police dispensing justice, extracting intelligence and handling prisoners. It's not pretty and it's an old story. If cattle and sheep were swapped for avocados and meth, it's the range wars of the American West in which the hired militias of cattle barons dispensed frontier justice to rustlers, trespassers, sheep herders and other mountebanks.

The situation also attracts its share of romantics and social-engineering types. Community organizer Cinthia Garcia Nieves moved to the Mexican state to try to help build institutions. She told the New York Times of her efforts to create community justice mechanisms and citizens councils. She'd hoped they would turn into something resembling a justice system. But efforts stalled, she told the Times; power still rested with the militias. "Authority has become blurred, in a way. So, then who gets legitimized? Who is really an authority?" She pondered.

As of this writing in 2018, the Michoacán self-defense groups have either disbanded, been infiltrated by the cartels or their members have begrudgingly enlisted in the state government's volunteer and professional police.

As Mexico approaches "peak avocado," having cultivated a monocrop of its own as a more lucrative alternative to corn and beans, the cartels are certain to see more opportunities to exact tributes from the farmers. Meanwhile, the aforementioned Chinese consumers are doubling their consumption of avocados annually, and the cartels are watching.

Peruvian growers, observing the action up north, are hoping to replicate the Mexican Miracle. They have now increased plantings to help meet global demand.

Meanwhile, several factors hit the U.S. crop hard in 2017. At 200 million pounds, California production was half of 2016's crop. Industry veteran Avi Crane calculated a 46-million-pound avocado shortfall that year. "The supply will not reach the 460 million pounds required" for the previous year's Cinco de Mayo holiday, Crane wrote in Fresh Fruit Portal in mid-April. As supplies dwindled that year, demand didn't. "We always say demand is increasing 15 percent a year, and volume out of Mexico has increased 12 percent to 15 percent a year," said one industry insider. "This year, (supply) declined, so it set everything a little bit off kilter."

Reefer rates were also up in the United States in 2017. "Reefer rates" refers to the cost of hauling refrigerated perishables in special containers that have stand-alone cooling systems, called "reefers." June is the annual zenith for reefer rates. The average national rate was $1.87 per mile leading up to Easter and Cinco de Mayo in 2017. By midyear 2018, the rate to haul perishables like avocados from the border at McAllen, Texas, was as high as $2.64.

Trucking capacity has been tight, running close to 100 percent, and no more so than in the major reefer markets. Rates have been near record highs since the beginning of 2018. The market would otherwise be set for fleet expansion but there is a driver shortage. Carriers are turning down loads, shippers are paying double in some markets, and "we've heard stories of freight sitting on the docks," Todd Amen, president and chief executive officer of ATBS, a trucking financial services provider, told Linda Longton of the Commercial Carrier Journal in March 2018.

Gordon Klemp, president of the National Transportation Institute, cites regulation-driven productivity losses as a factor in trucking's underlying labor problem. The American Trucking Associations estimates the industry is short about 50,000 drivers, a shortfall it says could grow to 174,000 over the next decade. Nearly half of drivers are projected to retire over the next decade. Meanwhile, freight volumes continue to climb.

Foretelling indigestion at 2017's marking of the Mexican victory at Puebla were the prices themselves. The Agriculture Department reported the terminal market price in Chicago on April 14, 2017 for a two-layer carton of Haas avocados from

Mexico at $54 to $57. A year earlier, the range was just $23 to $25.

Meanwhile, warring cartels continue to branch out and infiltrate the rich, volcanic growing regions of Michoacán. Mexico's National Public Security System logged nearly 600 intentional homicides in the state in the first half of 2018. The two most powerful criminal organizations that operate in the state — the Jalisco New Generation Cartel and Los Viagra — are locked in a turf war, according to security authorities. Alarm and indignation at the inability of law enforcement to tackle the problem have resulted in the re-formation of several self-defense groups that have taken up arms and vowed to protect their towns until the threat dissipates. The emergence of the groups may be a prelude for new chaos in the orchards.

Chapter Seven

Wings over America

"AHEAD OF SUPER BOWL, poll shows NFL is losing its core audience," the headline of the Wall Street Journal's online edition trumpeted just 48 hours before Super Bowl LII between the New England Patriots and the Philadelphia Eagles.

By the Journal's own polling, together with NBC News, the number of adults who reported following the NFL closely had dropped by 9 percent since 2014, and by 2018, just 51 percent of men aged 18 to 49 said they followed the NFL closely, down from 75 percent just four years earlier. That was bad news for the advertisers who shelled out over $5 million each for a 30-second Super Bowl spot that year.

When viewers lose interest in the NFL, it can also send chicken wings into a tailspin. That's one theory behind a purported falloff in wing sales.

Normally, the chicken wing market is cyclical. The U.S. wing-eating season ratchets up in the fall with the beginning of football season and continues through the end of March Madness.

The Take a Knee movement clearly upset many viewers, who took it out on the NFL and its sponsors, among which were purveyors of chicken wings and one vocal pizza man.

Professional football has also been marred by revelations of player violence against women and findings of the long-term effects of traumatic brain injury. But at least a few NFL sponsors are learning that fans don't wish to be reminded of these issues while knocking back beers, eating wings and watching football. Until the Take a Knee movement, NFL fans didn't much contemplate the national anthem. It had become football's most predictable non-event.

San Francisco 49ers quarterback Colin Kaepernick began the movement when he knelt during the anthem of a pre-season game in 2016. Soon, protests were seen at every NFL game held in the United States. By the 2017 season, it had coalesced into a national movement and a new era of "total protest." Even the Russian trolls were getting into the act, using the controversy to stir up emotion on both sides of the issue, according to Senator James Lankford of Oklahoma.

By 2017, Take a Knee had crossed the Pond. As an American opera singer, an African-American, sang the "Star-Spangled Banner" at an NFL game held at London's Wembley Stadium – the U.K.'s largest sports venue – some American athletes took a knee. The Philadelphia Eagles were the first reigning Super Bowl champions to play on British soil when they played the Jacksonville Jaguars. It didn't go unnoticed that the players who had taken a knee for the "Star-Spangled Banner" rose for "God Save the Queen" a few minutes later. Stateside, players also demonstrated during the anthem that Sunday. Following the NFL's edict in 2018 that players would have to stand and show respect for the anthem, the U.K. newspaper The Guardian spoke with experts in non-violent protest to ask how players might express resistance in view of the new NFL edict. The British public suddenly has an interest in the knee-taking.

"They have a number of options," Adolphus Belk, a political science professor at Winthrop University in South Carolina, told the Guardian. "They can continue to kneel, raise their fists and dare the league to enforce this policy. Or they can engage in some other kind of demonstration: bowing their heads during the anthem or adopting a position of prayer." Some speculate the alienation between fans and players will get worse. As more feathers are plucked off the NFL golden goose, the lowly chicken wing may be the collateral damage.

The Take a Knee fallout aside, one of the first questions to ask in understanding the wing market is, what is the trend in the wholesale price of wings under normal conditions? The cycle usually looks like this: The wing-eating season takes off with the start of college and professional football in late August and continues through about April 1st, the end of March Madness. During the chicken wing "off-season," wholesalers stock their freezers as prices typically drop.

Worth mentioning upfront is an insidious interloper that is mucking up the analytical henhouse. This *arriviste* is the so-called boneless wing, which is not a wing at all. In 2017, Delaney Strunk, a writer with the site BuzzFeed, correctly identified boneless wings as "glorified chicken nuggets." After the $1.9 billion "pink slime" defamation lawsuit against ABC in 2012 and the 1998 cattlemen's $10.3 million lawsuit against Oprah in the maligning of beef, the media is running scared when it comes to potential meat defamation. In America, you can't be held liable for defaming a dead *person*, but you might be taken to court by a large, vertically integrated corporation or a trade association for defaming a dead animal part or piece of plant matter. The media tiptoes around terms like "almond milk," "vegan cheese" and "boneless wings." The latter, of course, necessitated a second nonsensical term for actual chicken wings, which are now called "bone-in" wings. Business columnist Matt Kempner, a reporter with the Journal-Constitution, took Strunk's pronouncement a step further and called boneless wings flat-out fraudulent. (Atlanta, by the way, is home to Roark Capital Group, a private-equity firm that controls Arby's and other brands. It acquired Buffalo Wild Wings for $2.9 billion in 2017. The Journal-Constitution has since taken the mantle of the paper of record for the chicken wing.)

Increasing substitution of the so-called boneless wings is also taking a bite out of wing demand, Sanderson said. Buffalo Wild Wings announced cost-cutting efforts that included selling more boneless wings to dodge the escalation in the price of real chicken wings.

Wing Zone CEO Matt Friedman told the Constitution-Journal in late 2017 that wing costs had recently shot up to $100 a case. A case holds about 300 wings. Global information provider NPD published a seminal study titled "The Chicken Wing Dilemma." It examined the purchase patterns of wing buyers and how restaurant operators react to fluctuating wing prices. The data provider also tracks the volume and price of the average wing order at full-service restaurant chains.

Aside from the Take a Knee blowback — real or perceived — Americans' taste for wings overall has exploded. Buffalo Wild Wings had fewer than 500 locations in 2006. It has more than doubled its stores to 1,238 since. Competitor Wingstop opened its 1,000th location just outside Atlanta in early 2017. A hundred of those locations had come on line in just the previous year. Other food sellers have been watching the wing upsurge and taking notes. Wings can now be found in grocery store chains, pizza joints, gas stations and fast-food restaurants.

The popularity of wings is tied to primordial human cravings for salt, sugar and fat. Wings, the perfect delivery vehicle for this holy trinity, switches on the brain's opiate receptors; neural networks throb with endorphins.

"You start off with the fatty part of the chicken, usually fried in the manufacturing plant first. That pushes a lot of fat into that chicken wing," Dr. David Kessler, the former commissioner of the U.S. Food and Drug Administration, told author Michael Pollan in a PBS documentary based on the latter's 2008 bestselling book "In Defense of Food: An Eater's Manifesto."

"It's fried usually again in the restaurant. That pushes more fat into that wing. That red sauce: what is it? Sugar and salt. That white creamy sauce on the side? Fat, sugar and salt. What are we eating? We're eating fat on fat, on fat on sugar, on fat, sugar and salt."

Kessler's own 2009 book, "The End of Overeating," became a New York Times bestseller. In it, he details the amount of fat, salt and sugar in the typical American's food intake. He contends that restaurant and processed foods condition us to eat more in a way that rewires our brains, and that children may develop a pattern of overeating and obesity lasting a lifetime. He believes this outcome isn't genetic but purely environmental. The degree to which wing eating has reinforced the trend is an open question.

But the NFL fan who wears his favorite player's jersey on Sundays during football season tends to take the day off from worrying about such trifling matters as morbidity. At least, such might have been the case during the run-up to the 2017 football season.

A heedless wing-eating bacchanal took off in August of that year with jumbo chicken wing prices rising like a telethon tote board until prices reached record highs as inventories were depleted, according to market research firm Urner Barry. When bone-in wing prices soar, the aforementioned boneless wings are more heavily promoted. Regardless, things looked promising. It looked like business as usual for the red-hot wings market. Laurel, Mississippi-based Sanderson, the third-largest U.S. chicken processor, reported a 40 percent increase in jumbo wing prices during the quarter. The spike exceeded analysts' average profit and sales projections during the company's fiscal third quarter.

But spot prices fell in September, October and November of 2017, reported Sanderson, and by December, they were 14 percent lower than the same period in 2016. CEO Joe Sanderson, Jr., faulted the NFL dispute, telling Bloomberg it was unclear where prices were headed from here. In September of that season, President Trump had poured gasoline onto the fire by tweeting that NFL players should be either fired or suspended if they failed to stand for the anthem. Following the presidential tweets, some NFL teams joined ranks as if to protest Trump as much as police brutality. At least one team stayed in the locker room during the playing of the anthem. The only stakeholders seemingly left outside the drama were the fans, who reacted angrily toward the players, the NFL and, if banter from earnings calls is to be believed, by throwing down their chicken wings and pizza slices in disgust.

During the 2017 season, a gaggle of A-, B- and C-list celebrities emerged from the woodwork, some for and some against the protest movement. Actor James Woods, singer Joy Villa and comedienne Roseanne Barr, along with civil rights activist Jim Brown, came out publicly in opposition to the Take a Knee movement. Siding with the movement were music legend Stevie Wonder, rapper Diddy, talk show host

Ellen DeGeneres, actress Uzo Aduba and the entire cast of "Grey's Anatomy." Former NYPD officer and whistleblower Frank Serpico, as if emerging from a Proustian wormhole from the early '70s, gave a speech on Facebook Live and stood with police officers on the banks of the East River at the base of the Brooklyn Bridge to support Kaepernick.

Meanwhile, the movement's effects on wing sales and food sellers' revenue became muddied with conflicting reports. Papa John's International claimed the dust-up had stymied pizza sales, while Wingstop reported it had seen no connection to declining NFL viewership or the protests. There was much head-scratching.

"The only thing puzzling me right now is wings," Sanderson said in a late 2017 call to discuss earnings. He speculated NFL protests that involve players taking a knee had turned off fans, who no longer flocked to sports bars to devour chicken wings. "The NFL has hurt the wing stores. There's not as much traffic going through some of the wing places we service. It's just been reported to us that some of our customers think their traffic is down because of the demonstrations by some of the NFL players," he later told Bloomberg.

Papa John's, a high-profile NFL sponsor and advertiser, reported that protests by NFL players had cooled the public's appetite for pizza, causing sales to dwindle. "The NFL was eighth of the top 10 primetime shows, so it's experiencing a significant decline, which is leading us to have to look at other investments to create that consumer preference of our brand," Brandon Rhoten, chief marketing officer with Papa John's, said in an earnings call.

In an interview in the Waco Tribune-Herald, Mike Cockrell, Sanderson Farms' chief financial officer, said food-service providers, including powerhouse Sysco, had been telling him that wing sales were lighter than normal. "Wing prices usually go up during football season, but that has not been the case this year."

Bonnie Riggs is a restaurant industry analyst and wings oracle. Riggs has written a report called the "Chicken Wing Dilemma." It has become the magnum opus of modern chicken wing thought in early 21st century America, making her something of a female Samuel Johnson of chicken wings. To those who ascend the mountain in search of her Delphic wisdom, she reminds seekers that just a few years ago, chicken producers couldn't give wings away. Now, they are the most expensive part of the bird. Perhaps the wings phenom isn't old enough to draw a baseline for what is a "normal" cycle.

At the retail level, the sauces and spices are a key differentiator for winning wing loyalty, Riggs told the Journal-Constitution. Blackened Voodoo, Mango Fire, Lemon Zinger, Buffalo Bliss and ten other sauce flavors are in the offing at Wing Zone. Buffalo Wild Wings reports in at 21 sauces and seasonings, from Desert Heat to Asian Zing.

Buffalo Wild Wings runs specials on boneless wings multiple times a week, but customers' acceptance of boneless wings is still an open question – terra incognita. In her report, Riggs asks the supremely important questions: Will consumers accept the boneless wing? Will they pay the higher price of the bone-in wing? How will all of this affect the demand for chicken wings at restaurants?"

Smelling blood in the water over a weakened wings market, People for the Ethical Treatment of Animals is circling the demoralized but still largely carnivorous carcass of the NFL fan base. It bought airtime during the 2018 Super Bowl and aired a spot with actor and longtime PETA supporter James Cromwell. In it, Cromwell plays a priest refusing to forgive a man who tells the padre he's a meat marketer. "No Hail Mary can absolve someone for duping consumers into feeling good about buying 'humane' meat, a myth exploded by countless undercover exposés inside the businesses that produce it," said PETA Senior Vice President Lisa Lange in a statement. "PETA's Super Bowl spot encourages meat-eaters to seek redemption by choosing the only truly humane meals." She mentions vegan wings. It was unclear who PETA was trying to offend more, Roman Catholics or carnivores.

One more storm cloud on the horizon for the wing is the #MeToo movement, which can only be eyeing professional athletes, agents and front-office personnel as a potential treasure trove. Running out of red meat in Tinseltown, Washington and the state capitals, activists have turned an eye toward sports. As of this writing, NFL cheerleaders had begun filing lawsuits against teams, alleging their jobs required enduring fan concupiscence as just another part of the job. The New York Times reported in April 2018 that cheerleaders were required to attend pregame tailgates, visit luxury suites or even go into the stands, where they were expected to pose with sometimes blotto members of the fan base, setting the stage for rogue stirrings and lubricious fumbling forays by anonymous drunken meat hooks.

Unwilling to vamp it up with fans when duty calls, cheerleaders from two NFL teams have filed gender discrimination complaints. Members of the legal profession are looking into the nondisclosure agreements they're required to sign. Opening up additional avenues for bad behavior, the Los Angeles Rams and the New Orleans Saints announced they would field male cheerleaders on their squads for the first time. The males would not be doing stunts and lifts, that is, serving as traditional yell leaders. Instead, they would be dancing alongside their female counterparts – and doing identical dance moves. (Most NFL cheer squads have morphed into choreographed dance teams.) The announcement meant males would be doing the types of moves one Dallas Cowboys choreographer has coined "sexy hips," "shimmer-down with toe pop" and "party wave." The sports news site SB Nation covered one such rollout – a preseason game between the Arizona Cardinals and the New Orleans Saints at the Mercedes-Benz Superdome. The outlet reported a good number of Saints fans disapproving, rankled by the Broadway-style head snaps, the come-hither phrasings of the arms, hands and fingers; the *chassé* glides; the wide pelvic arcs; and the cabaret chorus-line high kicks. Most Saints fans had probably never much contemplated these moves, that is, until a dude in a high pompadour fade – known in certain trendy locales as a "Santa Barbara batting helmet" – started executing the moves alongside the Saints' female dancers. The change proved too much for many fans, causing a great cloudburst of invective to be rained down upon the Saints organization. Some fans brayed malevolently across that modern paragon of civic virtue, Facebook, reported SB Nation.

A handful of cynics immediately speculated the introduction of male dancers was not a sign from on High of a new, ultra-progressive National Football League or the beginning of an epoch of meritocracy in football pep but rather window-dressing should the NFL and individual teams be hit with a class-action lawsuit for maintaining a double standard all these years regarding expected player behavior (read "male employee behavior") and that of the cheerleaders (read "female employee behavior").

If these issues bleed over to the on-field product – which seems to be slowly happening – stay tuned for more potential disruption to the wing market. Suppliers are on tenterhooks.

Chapter Eight

Doritos Throwdown

ARCHIBALD CLARK "ARCH" West was born to Scottish immigrants James and Jessie West on September 8, 1914, in Indianapolis. A graduate of Franklin College, West became a naval officer and served in the Pacific during World War II. His story bears a vague likeness to that of the fictitious Don Draper in the AMC series "Mad Men." West, an impeccable dresser, became a marketer on Madison Avenue during the early days of the Kennedy administration.

After success on the J-E-L-L-O campaign, he landed a job as vice-president of marketing for Frito-Lay. In 1961, during a trip with his family to San Diego, West came across a snack shack that sold corn chips. Jana Hacker, his daughter, described the chance encounter to the Toronto Star after his death in 2011. And thus Doritos entered the canon of shared-consumption mythology.

He liked the way the chip he'd tasted differed from the Frito, the company's eponymous corn chip, an extruded and deep-fried cornmeal affair Frito-Lay had been cranking out since 1959. When he returned from California, he tried to develop the tortilla chip but encountered stiff resistance at Frito-Lay. He diverted money from other budgets and covertly developed the chip, along with doing the necessary market research, Hacker, who lives in Texas, told the Star.

Having handed Frito-Lay a fait accompli, West rolled out "Doritos" coast to coast in 1966. It was the first tortilla chip to go national in the United States. The first flavors were corn and taco. West, who also oversaw the marketing of Pace salsas and picante sauces, angled for grocers to display the salsas with the Doritos.

West preferred the plain Doritos. His daughter said he was disgusted by the exotic flavors that evolved over time, like the cheeseburger-flavored Doritos. When West died in 2011, mourners honored his legacy by tossing Doritos into his grave as his coffin was lowered into the ground. "He would think it was hilarious," said Hacker at the time.

Doritos was an icon of the cool, minimalist mid-1960s. They were the junk-food equivalent of bottle-green stovepipe pants. The cut of the Doritos evoked the angularity of the age. It was the Chrysler tail fin in a chip. A 1966 Doritos commercial shows a clean-cut teenage surf band practicing while a mom and sis keep the trio supplied with plenty of soft drinks, sandwiches and bowls of Doritos. An off-screen narrator calls them "the biggest news since the big beat! The new beat in things to eat – thin, crisp wedges of toasted tortilla with a lightly salted buttery taste. Doritos are a swinging Latin sort of snack."

It was no stretch to envisage Steve McQueen eating them behind darkened aviators at Newport with the jazz-flute stylizations of Herbie Mann in the background, or the 1968 black-leather "Comeback Elvis" compulsively eating Doritos in his NBC dressing room before the taping of "Lawdy Miss Clawdy." But by the 1980s, the Dorito had been somewhat usurped in the shared-consumption space by the Tostito.

In his book, "This Is What You Just Put in Your Mouth?: From Eggnog to Beef Jerky, the Surprising Secrets," Wired magazine columnist and author Patrick Di Justo, puts each Dorito chip at nearly 29 percent fat by weight, and almost all of that is corn oil, sunflower oil or soybean oil. Doritos contains simple pasteurized cow's milk, used as the basis for the cheddar and Swiss cheese cultures. The cheese cultures are "usually Lactococcus lactis cremoris bacteria," writes Di Justo. "They're injected into the milk during the cheese-making process, and their enzymes break down milk proteins into various smelly [and] tasty compounds. Those bubble holes in Swiss cheese? The acne sores on your face? They're both the result of gas and acids given off by members of the propionibacterium family, which have been distilled into these chips," Di Justo observes.

* * *

America's Corn Belt is concentrated in the Heartland. At just under 100 million acres – or roughly the size of California – it extends across Iowa, Illinois, Indiana, southern Michigan, western Ohio, eastern Nebraska, eastern Kansas, southern Minnesota and parts of Missouri. It can be spotted from space. No other single manmade undertaking matches it in sheer geographic size.

For the past decade, U.S. corn production has plateaued between about 11 billion and 15 billion bushels, according to the Agriculture Department. Iowa led the states with production of 2.7 billion bushels in 2016. Average yield per acre topped out that year at about 175 bushels. A bushel is equal to eight gallons of dry product. Corn is America's primary feed grain, accounting for more than 95 percent of total feed grain in the United States. It is one of the major world feed grains, along with sorghum, barley and oats.

* * *

The blunt, bumptious and, at times, openly bigoted Earl "Rusty" Butz served as agriculture secretary under presidents Richard Nixon and Gerald Ford. He shepherded in the era of corporate farming and plowed under Depression-era programs that propped up small farmers. As secretary of agriculture, the Indiana native, who'd been dean of the College of Agriculture at Purdue University from 1957 to 1967, ended a program that paid corn farmers to fallow their land. Under the slogan "get big or get out," his free-market vision of hyperproduction in the Farm Belt involved sowing commodity crops like corn and soybean "from fencerow to fencerow." His tenure set the stage for the emergence of Big Ag in the decades to come.

The Purdue alum, who grew up on a farm in Albion, Indiana, also had a fondness for barnyard humor. He kept a wood carving in a cabinet behind his desk. It portrayed two elephants copulating. He would glory in any opportunity to show it off to visitors. It had been given to him by a fellow Hoosier. Cackling in delight, the obstreperous Butz would tell visitors the fornicating pachyderms symbolized his goal of multiplying farm votes for the GOP.

Before Butz, much of the nation's ag policy was still tethered to the dark days of the Great Depression, to a period of massive farm failures, grain surpluses and endemic hunger. The New Dealers set up market controls designed to smooth out the peaks and troughs by manipulating supply. As such, the policies promoted discipline and moderation. Farmers would not get rich during the good times, but they wouldn't go broke and lose the farm during the bad times.

Butz blew up many of these restraints and ushered in the

Great American Farm Revolution. During his five years as agriculture secretary, net farm income more than doubled and exports tripled. In 1972, he orchestrated a grain sale to the Soviets in which the United States essentially sold off the U.S. grain reserve. Some view Butz as the nation's greatest secretary of agriculture. He's credited with restoring pride among grain farmers as they demonstrated their full production potential. Congressional Democrats denounced him as the voice of corporate agriculture and a foe of the small farmer and consumer. Peanut farmer Jimmy Carter campaigned on the promise he would jettison Butz if elected.

Butz took the brashness of Eisenhower's secretary of agriculture, Ezra Taft Benson, to a whole new level. Benson, an Idaho farmer, a Mormon apostle and an outspoken supporter of the John Birch Society, argued that government price supports amounted to socialism. (He wasn't wrong.) He published a pamphlet in 1966 entitled "Civil Rights, Tool of Communist Deception." (There, he was mostly wrong.) Ike appointed Benson in 1958 as a member of the Eisenhower Ten, a secret continuity-of-government group made up of three federal officials and six captains of industry who would serve as federal administrators in the event of a nuclear attack or other national emergency. Like Butz, Benson could be crass. When marine biologist Rachel Carson attacked Benson by name in her 1962 bestselling book "Silent Spring" – most remembered for its indictment of the pesticide DDT – Benson reportedly asked why a "spinster was so worried about genetics." But Butz, considered the architect of the modern farm bill, was less the ideologue than Benson. Both chafed at the federal government's manipulation of agricultural markets though.

A legacy of Butz's tenure is the flab now hanging over the average American's belt buckle. Makers of calorie-dense processed foods and the emerging fast-food industry were favored by his policies. As the corn crop shattered production records, high-fructose corn syrup replaced cane sugar in processed foods and drinks. Although sweetness itself is not a determinant of calories, liquid sugar produced from corn starch is six times sweeter than cane sugar. Butz also championed extensive importation of artery-hardening palm oil. Nicknamed "tree lard," it was cheaper than other commercial fats. It entered the national diet on his watch. According to Greg Critser, author of "Fat Land: How Americans Became the Fattest People in the World," his policies allowed ever-larger portions to be offered by fast-food outlets and soft drink makers, helping make America the world's fattest nation.

But many aging farmers fondly remember the early boom years under Butz, describing it as the lifting of an enormous burden and a breath of fresh air. He promoted the American farmer and had faith in the power of the markets. He was said to have had the admiration of Secretary of State Henry Kissinger, Secretary of the Treasury Bill Simon and then-Chairman of the Council of Economic Advisers Alan Greenspan.

In "King Corn," a 2007 feature-length documentary set in the cornfields of Iowa, documentarians Aaron Woolf and Curt Ellis calculated that every acre of corn at the time of the documentary's filming would have lost $19.92 but became profitable with a government subsidy of $28. Woolf and Ellis paid Butz a visit a year before his death with the intention of "taking him down." They found the 98-year-old Butz in a nursing home in the Hoosier State still very much coherent. "It's our secret weapon," Butz said of corn. "We feed ourselves with only 16 or 17 percent of our take-home pay. That is marvelous." The documentarians had to agree.

Butz was felled during the 1976 presidential race by a fatal slur: an obscenity-laced racial remark that might have made President Donald "Grab 'em by the 'P.'" Trump or former Senator Al "Mr. Grabby-Hands" Franken blush a deep crimson. It was told to Rolling Stone reporter John Dean — yes, that John Dean — the former White House counsel and turncoat witness jailed in the Watergate scandal. Dean, released from prison, decided he wanted to become a journalist. Rolling Stone gave him an assignment to cover the Republican National Convention in Kansas City. In the piece, Dean recounted a remark Butz had made to him and singer Pat Boone. His exact words are unfit for print, and many newspapers at the time wrote around the comment. When the issue of Rolling Stone hit newsstands, it touched off a conflagration. Soon after, Butz resigned. In 1981, he pleaded guilty to income tax evasion. A decade later, he endowed a million-dollar chair at Purdue. He died in 2008. His name lives on in other ways. In Jane Smiley's academic farce "Moo," a prized 700-pound pure white hog is named Earl Butz. He left his mark on agriculture in the 21st century.

* * *

Across the heartland, spikes in the price of corn, wheat and other farm commodities in 2008 and again in 2010 prompted growers to double-down on their plantings, some using credit to finance their seed and fertilizer. It was partly due to a jump in biofuel crops to the detriment of food crops.

The spikes caused food riots in places like Indonesia. Local news channels in the United States ran footage of shoppers at big box stores like Costco and Sam's Club emptying shelves of Basmati rice. Survivalist bulletin boards were blowing up with projections of the End of Days.

It quickly led to a multiyear slump in commodity prices

brought about by a global grain glut in reaction to the shortages, pushing many farmers further into debt. Some have speculated that the next several years will see a round of farm closures not witnessed since the early 1980s. The U.S. share of the global grain market by 2018 was less than half of what it was in the 1970s. Without the spectacularly awful agricultural policies of the Soviet Union and Mao's China to compare itself with, U.S. agriculture has failed to dominate. According to the Agriculture Department, net farm income slid from nearly $124 billion in 2013 to what will be about $60 billion for 2018. Meanwhile, according to research by Adjunct Professor of Agronomy Don Duvick at Iowa State University, corn yields have risen nationwide since the early 1970s at the rate of about 2 bushels per acre per year. About half that increase is due to plant breeding. The other half, improved crop-management practices.

But expenses have steadily risen, too. The two key costs for any grain crop are seed and fertilizer. Any creditable scrutiny of life in the farm patch needs to include these. For an average corn farmer, the cost for an acre's worth of seeds has nearly quadrupled in the past 20 years, while fertilizer has more than doubled, and the price received for the sale of a bushel of corn had fallen 54 percent as of early 2018 off the commodity's most recent high in 2012. "If you look at ag commodity prices over time, they haven't kept up with inflation," Vice President of CoBank's Knowledge Exchange Division Dan Kowalski told the Wall Street Journal in 2018. "Farmers need to produce more from their land, which they have. But in many cases, that's not enough." Another key cog in the survival of the family farm is health care.

The national health-care debates have not dealt with how exploding health-care costs fit into U.S. agriculture. (Short answer: They don't.) A 2015 survey found that 65 percent of commercial farmers identified the cost of health insurance as the most serious threat to their farm, more significant than the cost of land, inputs, market conditions or development pressure, according to research published by the Agricultural & Applied Economics Association.

"Many producers, many farmers, either the husband or the wife are looking for off-farm employment to obtain affordable health insurance. It takes them off the farm," Iowa Farm Bureau President Craig Hill told the Quad-City Times in February 2018.

Those considerations aside, just a small portion of the corn produced in the United States goes to feeding anyone directly. Of that, much of it is from high-fructose corn syrup. About 40 percent of the U.S. corn crop goes to make ethanol and about 36 percent of U.S. corn feeds livestock. Much of the rest is exported. Over the past three decades, high-fructose corn syrup has also replaced sugar as the sweetener in soft drinks and processed foods.

The reasons high-fructose corn syrup has oozed into our daily lives are many: The U.S. Congress enacted the first tariff against foreign-produced sugar in 1789. Since then, the U.S. government has continuously provided trade support and protection for its domestic sugar industry, making table sugar a costly proposition for food processors and bottlers. At the same time, Uncle Sam subsidizes U.S. corn production.

These two mechanisms raise the price of table sugar and lower the price of high-fructose corn syrup, making it the cheapest of many sweeteners in the United States. The relative sweetness of so-called HFCS 55 – high-fructose corn syrup that contains 55 percent fructose – resembles that of sucrose. The Agriculture Department estimates that Americans consumed an average of about 27 pounds of high-fructose corn syrup per man, woman and child in 2014.

Besides its low cost, the food industry likes HFCS 55 because it browns when heated, providing color in baked foods; it feeds yeasts and helps in the baking process; it thickens processed food; and it prolongs shelf life.

In 2010, researchers at Princeton University demonstrated that all sweeteners aren't equal when it comes to weight gain: They found that rats fed high-fructose corn syrup gained significantly more weight than those with access to table sugar, even when their overall caloric intake was the same. Besides causing significant weight gain in lab animals, long-term consumption of high-fructose corn syrup also led to abnormal increases in body fat, especially in the abdomen, and a rise in circulating blood fats known as triglycerides. The researchers say the work sheds light on the factors contributing to obesity in the United States.

A 2012 UCLA rat study suggests how a diet high in fructose slows the brain, hampering memory and learning. It also found that omega-3 fatty acids can counteract the disruption. The peer-reviewed Journal of Physiology published the findings. "Our findings illustrate that what you eat affects how you think," said Fernando Gomez-Pinilla, a professor of neurosurgery at the David Geffen School of Medicine at UCLA and a professor of integrative biology and physiology in the UCLA College of Letters and Science.

"Eating a high-fructose diet over the long term alters your brain's ability to learn and remember information. But adding omega-3 fatty acids to your meals can help minimize the damage." Another rat study by UCLA life scientists found in 2016 that hundreds of genes can be damaged by fructose in a way that could lead to diabetes, cardiovascular disease, Alzheimer's disease and attention-deficit hyperactivity disorder.

The United States is a major player in the world corn

trade market, with between 10 percent and 20 percent of the corn crop exported.

And some of that corn is ground to make corn chips and found in products like Nacho Cheese Doritos. Steven A. Witherly, Ph.D., is a food scientist and the author of "Why Humans Like Junk Food." He believes foods like Nacho Cheese Doritos are archetypes of addictive processed foods. Witherly has developed what he calls the food-pleasure equation: Pleasure = Sensation + Calories. When humans eat a combination of sugar, fat and salt, he told the New York Times in 2011, they get an enormous synergistic bang.

Doritos have been engineered in a way that make you feel like you've never eaten enough. The payoff starts in pleasure-seeking parts of the brain. It continues in the gut, which detects and responds more favorably to the high calories in sugar and fat. It's caveman stuff, going back to when we learned to identify big-calorie foods to survive, Witherly told the Times. The chips have what he calls "long hang-time flavors" like garlic, that create a lingering smell that stimulates memories.

Two acids – lactic and citric – get the saliva flowing and trigger the impulse to eat. Citric acid is also often used to keep foods like Doritos fresh, even if they've been sitting on the shelves for months at a time. Next, foods with a dominant flavor make you feel full faster. The Doritos Nacho Cheese recipe carefully balances flavors in such a way that no single taste dominates. By balancing the flavors in this way, the recipe steers clear of what food scientists call "sensory-specific satiety" — a phenomenon that results in declining satisfaction generated by the consumption of one type of food or one flavor. This, too, is likely to be a survival mechanism hard-wired into us. It would have encouraged early man to diversify his diet and may have also prevented poisonings. So, if you were to eat chips dominated by a single flavor, like onion or basil or oregano, you would stop eating them sooner. Not so with Nacho Cheese Doritos.

The foods humans perceive as most palatable are those that are both energy-dense and high in fat content. To maximize cravability, the goal is to deliver half the calories through fat, and Nacho Cheese Doritos hits this mark precisely, Witherly told the Times.

It's not well-understood but scientists say fat is experienced not as a taste, like sweetness or bitterness, but as a sensation; it contributes to the texture, flavor and aroma of many foods. When fat-laden snacks melt in the mouth, according to Witherly, the brain thinks the calories have disappeared, too, in what food scientists call "vanishing caloric density." This tends to delay the feeling of fullness.

Dorito dust has even more effect if you lick it without the chip to dilute it. Like artificial flavors, artificial colors are also the product of considerable research. Like hatchery trout and fruit flies, consumers are attracted to certain bright colors. Doritos has three artificial colorings found to be the optimal attractant: two different yellows and a red.

The Dorito underwent a minor flavor reformulation in 1992 and a major redesign in 1994. With the earlier tweak, Frito-Lay altered the nacho cheese variety's recipe to make it "cheesier." In 1994, PepsiCo invested a reported $50 million in what the New York Times called "the costliest redesign in Frito-Lay's history." At the time, the Doritos line accounted for 80 percent of all flavored tortilla chip sales and 10 percent of the entire salty snack category, which includes popcorn, pretzels, potato chips, multigrain chips and tortilla chips.

The redesigned Dorito now had a stronger flavor; each chip was 15 percent thinner and 20 percent larger. The new chip also had rounded corners "It's easier to eat them, without the sharp corners. And a lot of the scrap in the bottom of the bag was from the corners," Frito-Lay director of corn products Jerry Vogel told the Times.

The redesign was commemorated with a 60-second Super Bowl ad in 1995 featuring a pair of newly defeated Democratic governors: New York Governor Mario Cuomo and Texas Governor Ann Richards. "Change can be exciting," Cuomo tells Richards as he helps her pack up her office as Auld Lang Syne plays in the background. Naturally, Cuomo was referring to the new Doritos shape and bag design, not the fact that both had been turned out of office by Republicans.

*　*　*

Indra Nooyi, the CEO of PepsiCo, told the Freakonomics podcast following Super Bowl LII in 2018 that Frito-Lay would release a "low-crunch" female-friendly version of Doritos because, she said, women prefer to eat politely in public.

Men "lick their fingers with great glee" after eating Doritos chips, she said. "And when they reach the bottom of the bag, they pour the little broken pieces into their mouth, because they don't want to lose that taste of the flavor, and the broken chips in the bottom," she said.

Women "would love to do the same," she said, attempting to sum up the distaff unease, but they choose not to because "they don't like to crunch too loudly in public. They don't lick their fingers generously and they don't like to pour the little broken pieces and the flavor into their mouth."

Certainly, Sarah Porter of Ms. Porter's Finishing School for Young Ladies or author Emily Post must have written, "a well-mannered young woman never licks her fingers generously and pours the flavor into her mouth." When asked whether Frito-Lay was looking to create male and female versions of Doritos, Nooyi said that "it's not a male and female" thing, but added: "Are there snacks for women that can be designed and packaged differently? The answer is yes, according to Nooyi, and the company is preparing to launch chips for women that will be "low-crunch" with a "full taste profile" that will "not have so much of the flavor stick on the fingers."

To some, it seemed like Nooyi was commenting on the way she views the eating habits of the unbathed masses — namely men, possibly just American men. Her words reflected a hauteur that was hard to reconcile with her position as chief hawker of such extruded delicacies as XXtra Flamin' Hot Cheetos and corn syrup-laced caffeine-and-sugar grenades like Mountain Dew Kickstart Fruit Punch.

Her comments didn't seem to recognize that perhaps some men don't eat Doritos out of small bags, but perhaps only begrudgingly from a chip bowl after all the bacon-wrapped stuffed dates have been cleaned out. Nooyi may also be surprised to learn that some men don't blow their noses into their hands or spit tobacco into their waistcoat pockets, either.

"How often do I eat chips?" mockingly asked Washington Post columnist Maura Judkis. "Well, I only eat them when I am alone, laugh-crying while wearing fuzzy slippers and watching 'The Bachelor,' and there are no men nearby to see my shame. I sure wish I could eat chips more often, but it's so difficult to avoid the embarrassment of being a Lady who eats chips. I know I'm only supposed to eat salad, but the Doritos tempt me so. Now you know my terrible secret."

Others chimed in on the prospect of gendered Doritos.

"I feel it's a great time to be a woman," said comedian

and television host Ellen DeGeneres. "This is what our mothers and grandmothers marched for. When men get to the bottom of a bag of chips, they get all the broken pieces and put them in their mouth and lick their fingers with tremendous glee. This is one of the reasons I don't have a husband."

One would be forgiven for wondering at what point in Nooyi's impressive corporate career she hung out with men "licking their fingers with great glee." Certainly not at late-night bull sessions over bags of "Jacked Spicy Street Taco" Doritos with the party animals on the Foundation Board of the World Economic Forum where Nooyi is a trustee.

There was also no small amount of wishful thinking to her comments – that the flavoring compounds now sprinkled on, say, the Dinamita Chile Limón Doritos are finger-licking good. (See the passage earlier in this chapter on why Doritos wants you licking the dust off your fingers or, better still, pouring the flavor granules directly onto your taste receptors.)

Regardless, PepsiCo has since denied that it is manufacturing gendered Doritos. "The reporting on a specific Doritos product for female consumers is inaccurate," a company spokeswoman told Forbes the day after Nooyi's comments. "We already have Doritos for women – they're called Doritos, and they're enjoyed by millions of people every day." In a way, PepsiCo is denying the company has placed any special encumbrance on men of having to lick excessive male-targeted finger residue or subjected males to overly explosive crunchiness in the mouth.

The difference between these items and Nooyi's Lady Doritos, Jill Avery, a senior lecturer at Harvard Business School, told Forbes, comes down to utility. "Consumers are generally open to gendered products and brands when they can perceive real, meaningful differences in how men and women consume a product," she said.

"For example, women love Gillette's Venus razor because they perceive a significant difference between the way women and men shave – both in terms of the areas of the body that are shaved [and] the technique used to shave them (men use short strokes to shave their faces, while women use longer, more sweeping strokes to shave their legs). Venus is specially designed to address these significant differences and to offer women a product that meets their (very real) needs."

Items deserving a place on the pointlessly gendered ash heap include "Mansize" Kleenex tissues, female energy drinks, men's toothpaste, men's hand sanitizer and investment books for women (the money doesn't know who is investing it, and good investment advice for a woman is certainly good advice for a man).

When gendered products fail – like the idea of "Lady Doritos" did, or as "Bic Pens for Her" did a few years ago – it's because women see the changes made to the female-focused item as trivial or even demeaning, said Avery. It would be no less demeaning than Nooyi's blanket characterization of male eating habits.

Chapter Nine

Cork-ucopia

THE CORK FOLKS are nice enough. If you're a writer based in North America and you email an inquiry to the Portuguese Cork Association, you will no doubt get routed to Michael Colangelo, who represents the trade group in the United States. APCOR, as it is called, works closely with the Cork Quality Council in Napa, California, a nonprofit that promotes the use of cork wine stoppers in the United States.

If you broach the topic of a potential global cork shortage, you may get an answer like this:

"No, there is not a shortage of cork, and there cannot be in the same way that there can be a shortage of other types of wood or trees, as cork is a fully sustainable and renewable natural resource. The cork oak is truly the gift that keeps on giving; its bark is harvested without damage to the tree, only to grow back to be harvested again after nine years."

Fair enough. The bark of trees is stripped away to harvest the cork; the tree isn't felled like a Douglas fir. Cork is one of the few tree varieties that can be stripped of its bark without harming the tree. But once the bark is harvested, it takes nine to 12 years before a re-harvest can occur. That harvest cycle is a dilemma from a supply-and-demand standpoint. Demand for cork stoppers has increased much faster than cork supply. In the past decade, the supply has grown by only 3 percent (the Portuguese cork forest is now said to be undergoing a period of expansion). António Rios de Amorim, chairman of the eponymous cork company Corticeira Amorim, described a pressing need to expand the global supply of cork. He told the publication Drinks Business he's trying to encourage more landowners to consider cork oaks as a source of income. But the return on cork isn't enticing planters because of the long wait time before growers can harvest the bark. The experimental use of drip irrigation shows promise and could speed up the time to maturity for the first harvest from 25 years to between 8 and 10 years, but there are many open questions. It can take as many as three harvests before a young tree's bark is suitable for production of wine corks.

What follows is my back-of-the-envelope supply-and-demand calculation: If the average cork oak yields 4,000 corks at harvest and cork oak woodlands have an average of 40.49 trees per acre and if corks are harvested on a nine-year harvest cycle and trees younger than 25 years can't be touched, that's 4.12 trees per acre that are harvestable on any given year (being charitable), equating to 16,500 cork stoppers per acre annually. According to the Portuguese Cork Association, 1.8 million acres of land in Portugal is planted to cork oak. This implies 29.7 billion corks are – or could be – harvested annually in Portugal alone. Since about 70 percent of the 36 billion bottles of wine produced each year worldwide are stopped with a natural cork, it appears supply from Portugal alone is capable of meeting a big chunk of the current global demand with a few million acres of cork trees in reserve around the Mediterranean for the world's fishing-rod handles, drink coasters, bulletin boards and vegan boating shoes.

Wine consumption is surging in China. Ninety-seven percent of Chinese consumers say they believe natural cork is beneficial to wine quality, and 85 percent prefer to buy wines with a cork, as Colangelo reports. The reserve could evaporate as the Chinese pile into wine. A decades-long cork shortage could ensue while forest managers nurture young trees during the requisite 25 year wait time to the first harvest. (Remember, young trees don't hit their production stride until the third harvest, so that wait time is really about 40 years.) Wineries in Australia, where the screw cap has dominated for the past quarter-century, are reported to be switching back to cork, putting added pressure on cork suppliers.

* * *

They resemble Viking battle axes but are smaller. These hatchets have broad heads with corners that flair out. Harvesters, who've passed the needed skills down from father to son for centuries, know exactly how to wield them; they sink them into the trees deep enough to cut through the cork bark but not so deep that they injure the tree flesh beneath.

At ground level and with the aid of ladders, they make short work of each tree, cleanly stripping it of its bark, the sweet perfume of cork explodes into the air. The more times a cork oak has been harvested of its bark, the better the quality of its cork. Cork oaks can live up to 300 years.

Each year, from mid-May to mid-August, cork is harvested like this in the cork forests of Portugal. Teams of men descend on the trees as they've done commercially since the 1700s and noncommercially since the Greeks and Romans ruled the Mediterranean. Once harvested, each denuded tree is painted with a number designating when it can next be harvested. Portugal has a combination of low rainfall and high humidity, which makes it ideal for the cork oak – a protected tree in Portugal. All aspects of the harvest are enshrined in Portuguese law, including how high the bark may be stripped from a given tree.

Cork has traditionally been used for wine bottle closures, but growers have faced competition in the closure market with screw caps, synthetic cork, the Zork (a combination closure and pull-off capsule) and glass stoppers (known most commonly by the brand name Vinolok). By many accounts, the wine closure market has become something of a knife fight in a telephone booth.

Founded in 1870, Portugal-based Corticeira Amorim bills itself as the world's biggest cork producer. Cork contains many insulating and fire-retardant properties. The bark is made up of tiny chambers. Viewed under a microscope, each is a 14-sided polyhedron. The inner chambers are entirely filled with air. The properties of the cork make it ideally suited to seal a bottle.

After harvest, the cork is "rested" – aged outdoors in yards where it is exposed to the wind, rain and sun. During this period, chemical transformations occur. It is then boiled to sterilize it.

Americans like their bottles stopped with a cork. They expect it. Cork was viewed as an indicator of wine quality by as many as 97 percent of U.S. respondents, according to a joint study conducted by U.S. wine market research company Wine Opinions, the Portuguese Cork Association and the California-based Cork Quality Council. The polling also revealed that natural cork is the closure of choice for wine purchased at a restaurant (91 percent), wine purchased as a gift (93 percent), and wine purchased to bring to a dinner party (86 percent). Similar findings compiled by the research company Wine Intelligence indicate that natural cork remains dominant in the U.S., China and Germany, where a combined 60 percent of survey respondents chose it as their closure of choice. The research, conducted in 2016 and 2017, relied on surveys of 1,000 adults who were regular wine drinkers. Of all cork-preferring nations, China was found to be most skeptical toward the screwcap. Almost one in three surveyed responded they did not like buying wine with this closure.

Contributing to the stress on supply, a condition known as "cork taint" can contaminate a certain amount of it. It is caused by a chemical known as trichloroanisole, or, more commonly, TCA, a natural compound that at higher concentrations can imbue wines with a certain mustiness that some have described as "wet dog smell." Others have likened the aroma to cardboard, damp cement or a gym towel that's remained wet for a couple of days. At its worst, it makes the wine undrinkable.

In 2005, the publication Wine Spectator tested 42,800 bottles; seven percent were found to be contaminated with TCA. The cork industry has managed to get TCA levels down through better forestry practices and by culling bad corks using technology that screens them individually and in a nondestructive way.

There are differing grades of cork, but no industrywide system for grading them. Champagne corks are a composite made of extruded chopped corks and glue. It's why Champagne corks never feel quite natural – and never go back in the bottle. Importing cork from the Mediterranean is expensive, especially for wineries in Australia and New Zealand. Most switched to screw-caps prior to 2010. That trend appears to be reversing.

So, what does this mean for cork supply and demand? It means supply is largely at a standstill due to the elephantine process of bringing new cork forests into production.

Meanwhile demand seems to be rapidly rising.

Chinese consumers are developing a taste for wine. The bulge in demand promises to do to corks what the American baby boomers did for the Hula Hoop, the Harley and, now, hearing aids. In 2014, China overtook France as the biggest consumer of reds; it's set to become the second-biggest consumer of wine in the world by 2020, drinking 6.1 billion liters, worth $21.7 billion, which is up nearly 40 percent from 2016, according to International Wine & Spirit Research. Chinese investors have acquired vineyards in France, Chile and Australia, and elsewhere.

The Chinese are drinking more wine, and the way the Chinese drink it is also changing. At one point in the not-too-distant past, they didn't drink wine at home; this is no longer the case. While reds still dominate the Chinese market, white and sparkling wines are growing in popularity. China's capacity to produce enough good-quality wine domestically is dubious. In the north-central autonomous region of Ningxia, the neighboring Shaanxi province and the Uyghur autonomous region of Xinjiang, the summers are warm and dry, but fall and winter can be cold. Growers in these regions sometimes harvest the grapes early, before they've developed adequate sugars. Also, winter freezes pose a severe threat to vines, which means growers must bury them in mounds of soil or mulch to keep them alive.

On the Shandong Peninsula, the problem is flipped. The winters are mild, but summer and fall comprise the rainy season, which means grapes are abjectly vulnerable to all the many nasties that fill the nightmares of grape farmers – mildew, black rot, mold and fungus.

As of this writing, Chinese wine consumers are generally millennials, but their ranks will swell as the millennials grow older. This has been the case in other developing countries, according to research by analysts Liao Xufa and Lincoln Kong as reported in the English-language South China Morning Post.

Traditionally, Chinese drinkers imbibed a white spirit, called baijiu, which is made from grain, but the two researchers forecast total consumption volume of grape-based alcohol in China will rise at a compound annual rate of about 6 percent through 2025. The duo also forecast imported wine brands will capture more market share from domestic labels, since wines from recognized wine-growing regions have stronger appeal in China.

"Future wine industry revenue growth in China will be mainly driven by imported wine, a 145 percent rise from 2016 to 2025," Xufa and Kong wrote. "Imported wine revenue share will increase from 40 percent in 2016 to 63 percent by 2025." This was before the Trumpian era trade wars. Still, the demand – whether pent-up or freely exercised – is there.

The cruel and whimsical realities of consumer preference – triggered no doubt by the aspirational qualities of wine in China – will put big pressure on global supply. Domestic Chinese wines with names like Great Wall and Dynasty, much of it made by a company called Changyu, and imported wines from California, France and Australia are steadily being normalized in China. The cork industry can't have it both ways. It can't have abundant, affordable cork supplies and at the same time, an enormous, emerging demand from China when it takes at least a quarter-century to develop new cork forests. Expect big pressure on cork prices and growing scarcity, at least until the lumbering ship of cork production can be turned to meet new demand.

Chapter Ten

Agave Blues

A PROFICIENT *JIMADOR* wielding his *coa* – a spade-like cutting tool – can reduce a chest-high spiny blue agave to its 150-pound starchy heart in three to six minutes. It's mesmerizing. The word *jimador* means "harvester" and stems from Nahuatl, the language spoken by the Aztecs. The agave harvest is done completely by hand (at least to the point humans heave the massive hearts into the buckets of wheel loaders to be lifted onto truck beds). The process hasn't changed much since tequila was invented by the conquistadors in the 17th century.

But while a good *jimador* can make quick work of a blue agave at harvest time, it takes a grower at least seven years – sometimes longer – to bring a single plant to maturity. Once the heart is harvested and separated from its root, the plant is gone. In contrast to an almond harvested from a tree or a grape from a vine, the agave provides a one-time use only.

That's a problem, since global demand for tequila has exploded in recent years. As a result, there is now an agave shortage in Mexico. Given the grow-out period for the blue agave – otherwise known as the Agave tequilana – growers and producers need always to be looking a decade into the future. The lead time seems so absurdly distant as not to warrant further analysis. But there are plenty of people trying to do this.

Meanwhile, volume sales of tequila in the United States have grown about 6 percent per year since 2002, according to the Distilled Council of America.

Once these agave hearts – also known as *piñas* – are harvested, they're split in half, sometimes into quarters, and pushed into ovens for roasting. This process triggers a chemical change in the hearts, transforming starches into a fibrous pulp high in fermentable sugars.

Shortages are projected through at least 2021, portending bleak years ahead for penurious drinkers of the distillate. As a result of the imbalance, the value of the succulent has risen six-fold over the past two years. According to the Tequila Regulatory Council and the National Tequila Industry Chamber, just 17.7 million agave plants, first planted in 2011, were available for harvest in 2018. Juxtapose this against an anticipated demand in 2018 of 42 million plants.

Certain to amplify future shortages was the rumored use of immature plants in crop year 2017 to compensate for the shortage of mature plants. "They are using four-year-old plants because there aren't any others. I can guarantee it because I have sold them," Marco Polo Magdaleno told Reuters in early 2018. Magdaleno is a grower in the state of Guanajuato. Some producers report that more farmers are having to deal with stolen agave plants, which are then sold on the gray market. The situation harkens back to a similar shortfall in the 1990s.

Native New Yorker Grover Sanschagrin and his wife, Scarlet, live in Tlaquepaque in the state of Jalisco. Grover, a photojournalist turned Internet entrepreneur, received formal *catador* training in the evaluation of tequila from the pulchritudinous Maestra Tequilera Ana Maria Romero Mena, and passed the official test administered by the Tequila Regulatory Council, earning an "Award T" certificate. (Incidentally, any tequila-drinking straight male seeking proof of the existence of God need only look at Ana Maria Romero Mena, whose immense regal beauty is only possibly – *possibly* – outmatched by her encyclopedic knowledge of tequila.)

"We're right in the middle of the agave action. It has been an interesting experience," said Sanschagrin, who grasps the convulsive nature of the blue agave crop but believes most U.S. drinkers have only a vague understanding of it. "I think tequila consumers generally understand that the agave plant takes time to get to maturity, but they may not understand the circumstances behind the supply at any given time in the cycle," he said.

"There has been a lot of press around the 'agave shortage,' and some even go as far as to say the crop is nearing extinction. The truth is that we are currently at the high point of a regularly occurring cycle of boom and bust. As a result, agave growers can get extremely high prices for their crop (about 22 Mexican pesos per kilo right now.) But, check back in seven years and you'll see the value of agave near the one-peso price point," he said.

He believes there is plenty of available supply today, enough to satisfy market demand, but tequila makers need to pay more for it. "The future supply of agave will be oversupply, which will discourage many farmers, who will then write off their crop as a loss, and plant corn instead, setting the stage for the shortage that comes eight years later," said Sanschagrin.

The heartland of the tequila industry is Mexico's state of

Jalisco. Tequila is only permitted to be produced in this state and in limited municipalities in the states of Guanajuato, Michoacán, Nayarit and Tamaulipas. Agave tequilana is a key economic product of Jalisco, where the rich reddish clay and volcanic silica soil is credited for crops that distill into the best liquor.

The plant itself is physically dangerous, with needles that can break off in a wound or pierce an eyeball. Its juice can also be corrosive. It has many defense mechanisms against those who would harvest its sugars. It is a member of the botanical order asparagales, making it a relative of the Joshua tree and the yucca plant. Its high concentration of starches — easily converted to sugars — is what makes it suitable for distillation. It thrives in altitudes above 5,000 feet and in the so-called Jalisco Highlands.

By law at least 51 percent of the sugars in tequila must come from blue agave, also known as tequilana Weber. The remaining 49 percent may be made of sugars from other sources. The premium brands are usually harvested when the plants are about a decade old. Harvested hearts can weigh between 80 and 200 pounds. The heart is heated to convert its starches to sugars. Then, the roasted core is pressed or crushed to release the sugary clear liquid that is fermented and distilled.

Exports of pure tequila from Mexico to the United States were up 198 percent in the past decade, according to Fortune magazine. Tequila's popularity has been surging in the United States over many years, but consumer palates have grown more sophisticated, and the shift toward 100 percent agave offerings continues.

In 2015 alone, total tequila, by volume, grew 4.5 percent to nearly 14.7 million cases, according to Impact Databank. Luxury brands — those priced over $40 a bottle — grew even more quickly, with the top five brands in the segment climbing 7.6 percent that year. This has placed heavy demand on the blue agave.

Rhizomes grow at the base of agave plants. These "baby" agaves – called "pups," or *hijuelos* in Spanish – are cut and replanted after the "mother" agave is 3 to 4 years old. New fields are planted with these rhizomes. This has led to a loss of genetic diversity in cultivated blue agave. In the wild, the agave is an amazingly rugged organism. It thrives in lackluster soils, dry climates and has strong armor to protect it from animals that may try to make it a water source. But the constant cloning – reproduction without pollination – has led to genetic weakness. The blue agave is no longer allowed to go to seed. The same is happening with other crops worldwide.

The rise and fall of the *Gros Michel* banana, also known as the "Big Mike," is an example of the flame-out of a cloned cultivar that had been taken for granted for nearly a century. Grown in Central America, the Big Mike was, until the 1950s, the dominant export banana to Europe and North America. It was the first banana to be cultivated on a mass scale. If you bought a banana at a corner grocery store in Marion, Indiana, in 1890 or ate a banana split on Coney Island in the 1920s, it would have been the Big Mike, not today's blander Cavendish variety. In the 1950s, a ruinous Fusarium wilt, known as "Panama disease," ravaged immense plantations of the Big Mike in Central America. The blight blackened the banana from the inside out. By 1960, no commercial operations were able to grow the Big Mike in the Americas, the Caribbean, and many other parts of the world. The Big Mike is now virtually gone from the consumer market in the United States. Most people alive today in North America and Europe have never tasted it … with one possible exception.

According to an urban legend, artificial banana flavor tastes "wrong" because it was intended to imitate the flavor of the Big Mike, not the mealy Cavendish banana of today. The main chemical in banana flavoring is isoamyl acetate. It is thought to be closer in taste to the Big Mike because the cultivar had a higher concentration of that chemical. The Big Mike's taste was considerably sweeter, and its consistency, creamier. The Cavendish is more varied in its chemical makeup and tastes less like pure isoamyl acetate.

Discovering the Cavendish cultivar in the hothouse of an estate in Derbyshire in the U.K. was the plant-breeding equivalent of drawing a royal flush in poker. Now, even the Cavendish, which has been cloned like the Big Mike, is also on the brink. A mutation of Panama disease began wiping out the banana crop in Asia in the late 1980s. The wilt has since hit African crops, Filipino crops, and bananas in China, Pakistan, Indonesia and Australia. Like the blue agave, the monoculture — especially those built on asexual reproduction — makes it abjectly vulnerable to attack.

This type of reproduction weakens the immunity of the agave grown in tequila regions, since it thwarts genetic variation. Like the Big Mike, the blue agave has been weakened through cloning. When concentrated in groves, the blue agave is more vulnerable to insects, micro-organisms and nematodes. The latter is a ubiquitous phylum of worm found in every continent and climate. It can inflict enormous damage to crops costing untold billions. Bacterial rot and other diseases have also prospered with the lack of biodiversity. The massive monoculture, reinforced by Mexican tequila purity laws, has required ever-increasing pesticide use. The plant's vulnerability is an uncomfortable truth to any scholar of tequila.

"This is a real threat, one that most people are not aware

of," said Sanschagrin. "The element most often ignored with the clone-versus-seed issue is climate change. The agave is pretty well evolved and has an effective immune system, but now that climate change is making colder winters and hotter summers – which the agaves are not used to – it introduces new stresses, additional random possibilities and increased susceptibility to diseases. So, while it may take up to about 800 years for a new disease to evolve that can get beyond the agave's defenses in a non-changing climate," said Sanschagrin "that time is now shortened. To what extent, nobody knows, but it has people concerned."

The problem with seeds is that it takes longer for the plants originated from them to get through the life cycle, while clones get a two-year head start, said Sanschagrin.

"I am unaware of any brand using agave from seed for their production. It's too early for that," said Sanschagrin, "but there are brands that are starting to experiment in this area. I hear talk of it but haven't actually seen it yet."

After "doing this for so many generations, the agaves are getting weaker, and the only way to protect them is by the increased use of pesticides and herbicides," David Suro of the Tequila Interchange Project told National Public Radio in 2014. Suro's comments painted a picture of an industry sleepwalking into a disaster that could be avoided if it were not for the herd mentality.

As Sanschagrin points out, the summers are getting hotter and the winters colder in the blue agave-growing regions. This is reported to be making the plant grow faster, but they fail to develop the required sugar content and acidity.

Ironically, the often asexually reproduced agave is associated with Mayahuel, an Aztec fertility goddess. Endowed with 400 breasts, she was the deification of the maguey agave, which produced the intoxicating drink pulque, tequila's primordial soup.

Mexican farmers have blown out native species in the past. Unwitting destruction of the blue agave due to genetic weakness would be catastrophic but isn't unthinkable. Plant geneticist Albert Percival with the U.S. Department of Agriculture saw the blowout of an entire body of genetic material while collecting plants in Mexico for breeding cotton. Ancestors of the fine upland cotton that is grown today in California were originally collected in the Acala Valley of Mexico in 1906 and used in a breeding program at an agricultural experiment station in Texas.

But when Percival traveled to the Acala Valley in 1984 to re-collect the original plant material, he couldn't find any cotton at all. "Local farmers told me that in the 1970s, a Mexican consortium had decided they were going to try to grow cotton as a commercial crop. The first year, they had a bumper harvest; the second year was not so good; the third year, boll weevils destroyed the crop," said Percival. Growers in the valley decided to eradicate what they thought was the source of the weevil infestation – the native cotton. By eradicating the native cotton, they not only failed to solve the boll weevil problem but destroyed a genetic legacy that could have been useful to future breeders.

"It would have been nice to have preserved those varieties for the future," said Percival. "There may have been genes for lint quality or some other traits that we would like to breed into today's cotton. Now they may be gone forever."

But back to pulque, an elixir that was sacred to the Aztecs and flowed during many rituals. A version of pulque was likely to have been made by the Olmecs, the earliest known major civilization in Mexico, dating back to 1000 B.C. The lore surrounding the maguey agave, and the intoxicating beverage it yielded, was so powerful, a second Aztec god emerged –

Patecatl, Mayahuel's husband. This deity not only shouldered Mayahuel's fertility and pulque responsibilities, but also took the mantle as Lord of Healing. According to Aztec lore, the deity also discovered peyote. Priests used the spines of the agave to commit ritualistic suicide. The pre-Hispanic Aztecs also used the agave to make nails, pens and needles, along with string to sew and weave with. It was a major part of Aztec life. The Spaniards brought distillation technology to the New World. They sought a source of sugar that could be fermented and distilled. Using pulque as the "mash," they created what would be known today as mezcal.

The Marquis of Altamira, now venerated as the father of tequila, built the first large-scale distillery in what is now the town of Tequila in the state of Jalisco. Not long after, tequila was produced throughout Mexico. Jose Cuervo began commercially distilling it in 1758, followed later by the Sauza family in 1873.

Alongside Juicy Fruit Gum, Cream of Wheat and Pabst Blue Ribbon beer, Tequila Sauza – then called *vino mescal* – was introduced at the World's Columbian Exposition in Chicago in 1893. Notable visitors to the fair were Helen Keller, along with her mentor Anne Sullivan, and Alexander Graham Bell. The expansion of the railroads in the 1880s may have helped spread tequila across the North America, but it would not have been much more than a curiosity at the time.

Don Cenobio Sauza identified the blue agave as the best cultivar for producing tequila, and what we now know as tequila was likely being produced at the early distilleries of the town of Tequila.

The liquor's notoriety outside Mexico emerged from several historical juggernauts of the 20th century. Prohibition in the United States compelled the most dedicated American drinkers to seek intoxicating liquors in border towns; the country's neighbors to the north and south were only too happy to oblige. Like Canadian Club whiskey, distilled across the Detroit River in Windsor, Ontario, tequila became the drink of choice – and necessity – among American drinkers along the southern border during the dry era from 1920 to 1933. Unable to find much beyond rotgut, sacramental wine and bathtub gin, drinkers in the United States began to develop a taste for tequila. The bars and casinos in Tijuana – a warren of cheap thrills – provided much of it.

The Mexican Firing Squad was a prohibition-era drink that incorporated tequila, lime juice, Grenadine and Angostura bitters. It is said to have originated at La Cucaracha Bar in Mexico City. There was also a tequila-based drink called the Lupita, and another called the Sunrise Cocktail.

A newspaperman named James Graham and his wife traveled to Tijuana in 1936, where they ended up drinking at the Turf Bar, one of the surviving bars run by ex-pat Irishman Henry Madden, who was known around the area for his interpretation of the daisy, a cocktail made with brandy, lemon, sugar and Curaçao. Madden's version wasn't made with brandy, though. According to Graham, Madden's recipe came about by mistake – he picked up the wrong bottle one day (cocktail historians assume it was tequila, though there's no actual evidence of that) and went with it. "Margarita" in Spanish means daisy. Madden was a fixture of Tijuana nightlife during Prohibition. His Turf Bar became the birthplace of the margarita.

During World War II, demand for liquor again spiked just as domestic supplies dwindled; distillers had switched to producing industrial alcohol for the war. It was used as a torpedo fuel, among other things. During the war, as during Prohibition, tequila became a prized commodity. A cocktail called a sidecar, made with tequila, became popular. Like the daisy of the 1920s and '30s, it, too, inspired the modern-day margarita.

Meanwhile, the Mexican government declared in 1944 that only spirits distilled in Jalisco could be called tequila. The first set of standards involving purity and processing for tequila were drawn up in 1947.

Although Mexico is the birthplace of tequila, and tequila's development is intertwined with Mexican culture, some distillers *Yanquis* have attempted to craft their own interpretation of the agave juice in the United States. The resultant distillate cannot legally be called "tequila." Tequila must be made from the Agave tequilana that is grown and produced in one of five states in Mexico to claim that appellation of origin.

A source of endless confusion is the more generic term "mezcal." Mezcal can be made from more than 30 different agave species; tequila can only be made from the blue Weber agave. Some mezcals have objects in their bottles such as worms or scorpions. Eating these doesn't make the drinker hallucinate, as the urban legend has it.

Tequila production begins with the fermentation, and later distillation, of the agave sugars from the tequilana Weber – the *agave azul* in Spanish. But distillates are made from many agave varieties elsewhere, outside the regimented blue agave farms of Jalisco. And mezcal is subject to the same vulnerabilities as tequila. Unlike crops like corn, barley, wheat and potatoes, used in other distillates, the agave cannot be harvested annually.

The most common agave variety used to make mezcal is the espadín. Like tequila's *agave azul*, the espadín crop is a clonal monoculture, propagated out of convenience through the replanting of genetic clones of the mother. It brings about the same genetic weakening seen in the blue agave.

The process of allowing agaves to go to seed isn't conducive to the production of tequila or mezcal. Agaves are monocarpic, which means they flower once and then die. The hearts must be harvested before the plant flowers and no one knows what combination of internal or environmental factors combine to induce flowering.

The heavily spined and needle-sharp espadín – It's no coincidence "espadín" is Spanish for "sword" – is used in 90 percent of all mezcal production. It has become the industry go-to. It is the genetic parent of the blue agave. It grows in the Oaxaca desert and is easily cultivated.

But mezcal's growing popularity – a protest, of sorts, to the mechanized and regulated tequila industry of Jalisco – has led to a boom in demand for bottlings made with wild agave varieties. Oaxaca's rare varieties include the arroqueño, tepeztate, tobala, papalome, barril and the madre cuishe.

The squat, broad-leafed tobala grows wild in the rugged coastal mountains and central valley of Oaxaca. This prized agave, which is significantly sweeter than the espadín, is the basis of tobala mezcal. The tobala, which takes more than a decade to mature, is seeing its numbers dwindle and it may soon become the victim of its own popularity.

The tepeztate, like the tobala, is a wild agave. This makes it genetically more robust than espadín or the blue agave. It grows on cliff faces, on rocky outcroppings and amid chaparral in foothills of the Sierra Oaxacan mountains. It can take 25 to 35 years to reach maturity. Before the plant dies, it produces a *quiote* that flowers a rich yellow before turning to seed. A *quiote* is a tree-like stalk – a "peduncle" to a botanist – that emerges from an agave plant in its reproductive death dance. It is edible, or it can be dried and used as fuel or even as a construction material.

Given the massive hurdles facing this agave variety, it,

too, may become the victim of its own popularity. The wild varieties are expected to better adapt to climate change. As of late, the notion of a "wild" agave has been called into question due to the increasing ability of farmers to grow what were previously thought of as wild varieties. The mezcal industry has promoted this. Genetic diversity in the wild occurs over millions of years, but managed populations represent a fraction of such variation and are guided by artificial selection over a short period of time.

Fundación Agaves Silvestres is a non-profit organization dedicated to the reforestation of wild agaves in Mexico. The group's first project aims to "reforest" tobala and madre cuishe agaves in the town of San Dionisio Ocotepec in Oaxaca.

"Some strains are trickier to replant, but there's a misconception that only espadín can be planted," Judah Kuper of Mezcal Vago told the publication Punch in 2016. Kuper, along with other producers, has sought to protect the biodiversity of agaves by planting varieties that are currently being depleted.

He has taken a pledge to uphold a "three-to-one rule," meaning Mezcal Vago will plant three times as much as they use. "There's a boom happening, and Oaxaca is not well-organized enough to deal with it. There are people involved who are trying to keep an eye on it, but there's also greed and money," says Kuper. "There's already agave species disappearing from the hills, and those populations might never come back."

Many an academic paper has been written about the plight of the agave and its significance to ancient cultures – not to mention the current one – in Mexico, but the higher cost is obvious to anyone visiting a neighborhood liquor emporium in the United States.

The global surge in popularity of agave distillates – with a focus on aged tequilas and mezcals from wild agave – could outpace their ability to be reproduced sometime very soon.

Worried about the sustainability of the agave population, some producers are privately throwing up their arms and seeing it as a wretched race to the bottom. The wood required for roasting the hearts and the water required in the process are also increasingly difficult to come by in most of the regions where agave grows.

Some of the world's biggest brands are moving into mezcal, and agave supplies are suffering pressure never seen before.

"There is no question the arrival of [distillers] Diageo, Pernod Ricard [and] Bacardi has put immediate and acute demand on agave availability," David Shepherd, founder and director of Black Sheep Spirits and Corte Vetusto mezcal, told the publication Spirits Business in 2018. "For us as a brand, in two years we've experienced doubling of agave prices. The agreement we have with our producer is we absorb the prices of the agave."

Between the lack of genetic diversity, the long lead times to maturity and the disappearing wild varieties, the agave could be racing headlong toward a Mexican *Götterdämmerung*. The country's federal government, the state of Jalisco and the various grower and distiller organizations and quality councils should not quail from this issue. They would do well to study the lessons of Big Mike.

Chapter Eleven

Hoppy Welfare Queen

STRUGGLING TO REVERSE seven years of declining market share, Anheuser-Busch InBev launched its medieval-themed "Dilly Dilly" ad campaign for Bud Light in 2017. It clearly hoped the meme would be a call to arms, capable of marshalling support, lifting morale and uniting its long-suffering distributors.

The first ad, titled "the Banquet," is a not-so-veiled "Game of Thrones" send-up. It features a king and queen holding court in the presence of a retinue of sycophantic subjects bearing gifts and approaching them one by one. Each offers the sovereign a case of Bud Light, in return for which the king pronounces the subject to be a true friend of the crown. Erupting from the royal court is a universal "Dilly Dilly" of approval. But one supplicant breaks with the others and offers the sovereign a spiced honey-mead wine that he's "really been into." For that, he receives no "Dilly Dilly" from the retinue. Instead, he's introduced to Sir Brad, who escorts him to the Pit of Misery.

So, what exactly does "Dilly Dilly" mean? In the ad, it's

used to voice approval or delight in much the same way one might say, "Bravo!" or "Hear, hear!"

"It can also work as a greeting, a nod of approval [or] expression of gratitude," one of two creators of the "Dilly Dilly" phrase, N.J. Placentra, told Geoff Baker of the Seattle Times.

Placentra, 30, is an art director with the Wieden + Kennedy ad agency in New York. He said he and copywriter Alex Ledford invented "Dilly Dilly" out of thin air while spit-balling ideas for a Bud Light commercial. The ad, called "Banquet," began running in August 2017. Placentra told Baker that he and Ledford needed the king to say something "like 'huzzah' but not actually 'huzzah' when approving the gifts."

Ledford blurted out "Dilly Dilly" and Placentra laughed, so he penciled it in as a placeholder with the idea they could change it later if the client approved the script.

"After we launched 'Banquet,' we began to see sports fans, media, wedding guests and people all over social media using the phrase organically on their own," Andy Goeler, Vice President of Bud Light, told the Thrillist, "with signs on College Gameday, tweets, on-air broadcast mentions, and even Ben Roethlisberger of the Pittsburgh Steelers calling a 'Dilly Dilly' audible" in his snap count.

"'Dilly Dilly' doesn't mean anything," Anheuser-Busch InBev Chief Marketing Officer Miguel Patricio told Business Insider's Graham Flanagan. "That's the beauty of it. I think we all need our moments of nonsense and fun. And I think that 'Dilly Dilly,' in a way, represents that. A lot of people asked me, 'How did you approve that?' To tell you the truth, we never expected this to be so successful," he told Flanagan. "It didn't test that well."

By December, guys in welding shops were saying "Dilly

Dilly"; school kids were shouting it on playgrounds across the land without knowing why; even attorneys and real estate appraisers were playfully signing off emails to colleagues with it. But it wasn't until the Masters golf tournament the following year that things really kicked into high gear for the ad, ensuring the "Dilly Dilly" campaign's place in the pantheon of beer taglines. A directive was handed to security staffers in early April stating that spectators who yelled the phrase "Dilly Dilly" would be ejected from the venerable and hidebound Augusta National at the Masters golf tournament, reported golf editor Bryce Ritchie of the publication Bunkered. That type of publicity can't be bought. Full stop.

The "Dilly Dilly" campaign offered a ray of hope of reversing shrinking sales at the hands of apathetic millennials drinking Mexican lagers, craft brews and other concoctions, if not the "spiced honey-mead wine" that earned the supplicant in "Banquet" a trip to the Pit of Misery.

Sales of domestic light lagers like Coors Light and Miller Lite were also in decline, but no more so than category leader Bud Light.

At the same time, craft beer was fast becoming America's new welfare queen with states and localities lavishing subsidies, one-dollar leases and enormous property tax abatements on enough beer production to paralyze a herd of elephants. America's urban planners now looked to craft breweries as the essential pixie dust to be sprinkled on blighted urban cores to trigger revitalization. The thinking: Encourage a microbrewery or brewpub in the most neglected part of town, and folks will show up. Soon, they'll take their friends there and want additional restaurant options. The suds will make them want to buy things at nearby gift shops. Pretty soon, they'll forget about the fact they're in the worst part of town, and investment dollars will stream in. A big player in all this is the federal government. That a microbrewery, brewpub or taproom can be a catalyst for urban renewal and worthy of tax dollars has now become an ancient wisdom – a tablet descending from on high incised with this *idée fixe*. It cannot be questioned without risking being seen as a crackpot or a civic killjoy.

Vanessa Brown Calder is a policy analyst at the Cato Institute, where she focuses on social welfare, housing and urban policy. Previously, Calder worked as a graduate fellow in welfare studies at the Heritage Foundation, where she analyzed the federal Low-Income Housing Tax Credit and Chicago's housing voucher program. She has sifted through the patois of urban planning-speak; she has pondered obscure corners of how the feds encourage local governments to spend public money on flights of fancy. She believes a lot of this is focused on meeting the needs of a demographic that is different from the one the federal grant money program had envisaged.

"The idea that creating and subsidizing a craft brewery to revitalize a struggling urban core is dreaming," said Calder, who holds a master's degree in public policy from Harvard's John F. Kennedy School of Government.

"The Community Development Block Grant is a federal program," said Calder. "It has funded micro-breweries and minor league baseball stadiums, along with a variety of other unjustifiable economic development projects. Often, subsidies for economic development projects are layered, so it won't just be federal funds. There may also be state grants and local tax abatement.

"The way these grants are typically used is so politicians can point to tangible things like buildings and say, 'I'm responsible for this. I brought you this.' The objectives of those projects are influenced by politics," said Calder. In her view, politicians being able to point to new construction has become the coin of the realm. "Investing in buildings versus investing in people is a problem. Buildings aren't effective in changing people's lives."

In late 2017, craft brewers across the nation reported flattening sales growth, or in some cases, sales declines as new entrants steadily enter the craft beer market. By 2018, there were more than 5,000 breweries in the country. The majors, like Anheuser-Busch InBev, also are piling into the craft market by buying up smaller, regional brewers.

* * *

The federal government's imprimatur has emboldened state and local governments to underwrite microbreweries with tax dollars. The city of Burbank, California, has teamed with a developer to turn a city-owned site on an active rail platform into a beer garden for artisanal brewers. Drinkers will soon be able to throw back pints of their favorite craft brews and then wobble out onto the busy platform as trains whiz by.

In Milford, Ohio, the city council gave the Little Miami Brewing Co. a five-year property-tax rebate. At a time when local governments are falling short in providing even the most basic government services, city managers are patting themselves on the back for landing a favored microbrewery to their city, whatever the cost. Lift Bridge Brewery in Stillwater, Minnesota, is seeking more than $1 million in tax-increment financing to fund an expansion. The city council directed the city's staff to work with the brewery on helping to evaluate various tax incentives.

Crime victims in Bridgeman, Michigan, can forget their troubles over a raspberry ale at Haymarket Brewing Co. Enticed by tax abatements and a good deal on a public building, the Chicago-based brewery purchased a former

Michigan State Police post to build a 100-seat taproom and 30-barrel brewhouse, according to reports.

But what about the start-up that wants to open a new welding shop or janitorial service? Should beer gardens and taprooms be getting tax breaks when other businesses aren't?

"We don't like government picking winners and losers," said Jon Coupal, President of the Los Angeles-based Howard Jarvis Taxpayers Association. "But this isn't nearly as offensive as what local governments do with respect to professional sports teams."

Indeed, in 2015, Missouri and St. Louis tried to keep the Rams in town, dangling $400 million in public money for a new stadium. To justify the public funds, officials argued the team was an economic engine for the region. Looking for public handouts, team owners tout the creation of new jobs near the stadiums, but construction jobs are temporary, and concession workers and ushers tend to work far less than 40 hours a week. And these aren't quality jobs.

Unmoved by the $400 million in proffered public assistance, Rams owner Stan Kroenke promptly ponied up $1.9 billion of his own cash to build a new stadium for the Rams in the Los Angeles area. St. Louis residents and visitors are still saddled with servicing about $144 million in debt and paying upkeep costs for the Edward Jones Dome, the Rams' former home. Hotel and "game day" taxes on concessions and parking were set up to service the debt. "Game day" has now come to define monster truck shows, motocross races, old-timey religious revivals and boy band concerts.

"Grants and tax breaks shouldn't be given to specific businesses. The bad news is that everyone does it," said Coupal. "I think that mindset has been normalized for decades. Another example is counties chasing sales tax dollars by giving car dealerships all kinds of freebies."

A microcosm of the St. Louis stadium is what happened in Buncombe County in North Carolina where the county took $6.8 million of taxpayer money to buy a piece of land to woo Oregon-based Deschutes Brewing to the county. As of this writing, the county was looking to unload the parcel, hoping to get $5 million for it.

In 2015, Richmond, Virginia, put up $33 million in public money and incentives to entice San Diego-based Stone Brewing to build a retail store, tasting room and East Coast distribution center. The city of Richmond continues to rebate a share of the real estate taxes paid by Stone each year in line with the agreement that brought the brewer there. The Richmond Economic Development Authority built the $23 million brewery for Stone, which signed a 25-year lease that gives the brewer the option to buy the property and building for $25,000 at the lease's termination. Stone's estimated real estate tax bill through 2040 is $3.1 million. It would otherwise have been $12.2 million, according to recent estimates.

Shortly after the Stone deal in 2015, the state of Virginia extended $1 million in grants and $1 million in matching tax credits to help Hardywood Park Craft Brewery expand into an office park in Goochland County. The Richmond Times-Dispatch reported at the time that Virginia had specifically "targeted craft beverages as part of the state's economic development strategy."

The city of Beaumont, Texas, plagued by inveterate sewage problems featuring overflowing manholes and toilets across the city during thunderstorms, has been expending city man-hours courting craft breweries. Christopher Boone, the city's director of planning and community development, remarked in 2016 that he was as surprised as anyone that Beaumont didn't have a brewery yet. "We would be able to offer possibly tax incentives such as city tax abatement and fee waivers. We could even offer some lower-cost lease for [a warehouse] building because we own it," Boone told the local ABC affiliate.

In 2017, city fathers in Memphis were on pins and needles as to whether favorite son Wiseacre Brewing would accept delivery of the vacant Mid-South Coliseum as a possible expansion site. The city provided the brewer with an exclusive six-month "look-in" to determine whether leasing the building would be a good fit. Wiseacre ended up taking a pass.

Small towns are getting in on the action, too. At a meeting in November 2016, the city council of Florence, South Carolina, population 38,000, approved an incentive package totaling $180,000 to encourage a craft brewery to set up shop beside town hall. The month before that, the city council of Reidsville, North Carolina, population 14,000, voted to sell a city-owned building for one dollar to a startup brewing co-op. In tiny Perry, New York, population 4,000, a public development corporation matched bank financing to help a microbrewery build in its downtown.

This strategy might work for a while, but it suffers from the same drawback as other attempts at public "investment": Government isn't good at picking assets or knowing when to get in and when to get out. It's not in government's DNA. Don't expect city officials to recognize it — or to turn off the tap of taxpayer money — when the craft beer bubble seems ready to pop.

Between 2008 and 2016, the number of breweries nationwide expanded by a factor of six, and the number of brewery workers grew by 120 percent. Ipso facto, a 200-year-old industry sextupled its locations and more than doubled its workforce within a decade. Even more incredible: This has happened during a time when U.S. beer consumption was declining.

The Brewers Association defines "craft brewery" as an independent beer-producer that makes fewer than six million barrels a year. For sheer saturation, there is no greater laboratory for the concept than San Diego, where a boom has taken place over only a handful of years. Between 1993 and 2009, issuance of brewery licenses was near zero in San Diego County. But since then, the tap handles have proliferated. In 2010, seven licenses were granted. The following year 15 were issued. Then 18 the year after. It is now the most brewery-rich county in the most brewery-rich state.

Beer has a unique regulatory framework, one that creates walls of separation between producers, middlemen and retailers, forming a three-tier system. The structure makes it hard to build vertical monopolies, and that's by design. "In the early 20th century," wrote Bob Alacqua of beernexus.com, "alcohol producers owned or subsidized many bars and saloons. These joints were known as 'tied houses,' since the bars were 'tied' to the brewers and distillers. The tied houses were the mortal enemies of the temperance movement" – a powerful political and social force in America for decades.

Pioneering the business model now used by your corner oil-change-and-lube shop, the tied house enjoyed big economies of scale, pushing down prices, getting patrons drunk on cheap liquor, and then upselling them on prostitution services, gambling and other misconduct. The tied house's villainy was only outdone by its sheer brilliance.

Meanwhile, temperance activists – made up of wives, mothers, grandmothers, preachers and assorted moralists – accused the tied houses of causing poverty and crime, filling the nation's penitentiaries and asylums, robbing women and children, and even wasting the nation's grain supplies. With the motto, "Lips that touch liquor shall not touch ours," angry housewives set about ripping up saloons with hammers and chisels.

One of the main reasons the city of Pasadena, California, was incorporated in 1886 was to abolish saloons and the sale of alcohol. One of the first orders of business for the newly minted city council was an ordinance that banned liquor citywide. The saloon owners in town didn't go down without a fight. A pastor at the city's First United Methodist Church was burned in effigy, and hoodlums were dispatched to disrupt worship services for the next 20 years, according to church records.

When Prohibition ended in 1933, states engineered regulatory barriers to keep one company from owning the production, distribution and retailing of intoxicating liquors. But exclusions for small brewers, along with regulatory tweaks at the state and local levels, have allowed a thousand hoppy flowers to bloom at the local level. States generally allow small brewers and taprooms to sell their beers directly to the public in the style of the tied house. The major brewers can't do this. Thus, it gives Doug's Cherry and Chocolate Infused IPA or Big Ed's Hoptopia Citrus Stout a natural advantage – to a point.

It has allowed little beers to develop a local following and then grow somewhat. But when they reach a certain size, they can no longer legally avoid the three-tier system.

For the big brewers, it spells death by a thousand flea bites. Throwing the guy who's really into the spiced honey-mead wine into the Pit of Misery would be wildly satisfying for a big brand like Bud Light.

By 2014, more than half of all brewing facilities in the United States were microbreweries, as the chief economist for the Brewers Association, Bart Watson, has written. This changes, slowly but surely, what beer-drinkers throw back.

Since many craft brands have limited, often casual, distribution, it implies a lopsided dependence on local customers, often those physically present at the brewery.

But here's the rub: Demand for beer overall has been sliding in the U.S. for years. Twenty years ago, nearly three-quarters of young people said it was their favorite alcoholic drink, according to surveys by Gallup and Goldman Sachs Investor Research. Fewer than half feel that way now. The market is shrinking, and craft beer has grown at the expense of national brands like Budweiser, Miller and Coors.

How long can that trend continue? Particularly given that upstart brewers are also cannibalizing market share from pioneer craft houses like Sam Adams, Sierra Nevada and New Belgium?

These are open questions. There are signs that craft brewing is being driven by what a late-night drinker might call irrational exuberance. If private investors alone were sidling up to the bar to throw down the cash, this might not be any public concern. But in many cases, they're dragging taxpayers along for the bender — and, when it comes, the hangover. Besides picking winners among craft brewers to fight urban blight, city halls and statehouses have begun making common cause with on-the-go drinkers by creating open-container zones. The hope is that the revelers will drink a sufficient amount of liquor to think they're in the French Quarter of New Orleans or on Beale Street in Memphis. They'll then begin spending wads of cash at spaghetti parlors, public houses and gift stores, but without getting so sozzled that they stumble into verboten areas outside the zones and make a scene with the neighbors.

These new go-cup zones are popping up in unlikely places in the Bible Belt, the Rust Belt, the Plains and the Mountain States. Not everybody is thrilled with the idea of legalizing the go-cup, especially in places where public intoxication has been a problem.

Besides the underwriting by taxpayers of winners and losers in the craft-brew crapshoot, and the civic pride now welling up over new open-container zones, even the U.S. State Department is getting into the act, awarding EB-5 visas to moneyed foreign nationals with alcohol-fueled business plans and a hankering to sink roots in the U.S.A.

The Immigrant Investor Program, also known as the "EB-5 Visa Program," was created by Congress in 1990 to stimulate the U.S. economy through job creation and capital investment by immigrant investors. It's a program that allows foreign nationals to apply to become legal U.S. residents in return for as little as a $500,000 investment in a business that creates or preserves at least 10 jobs. There are 10,000 EB-5 immigrant visas available annually.

One such EB-5 Visa project is Europa Village – a winery, residence, hotel and event space partly bankrolled by $60 million from over 100 investors from China brandishing EB-5 visas, reported Los Angeles Times business writer David Pierson in mid-2017. It will be developed to a "village of wineries" on around 30 acres of vineyards in Temecula, California. It contains an inn with ten recently redecorated rooms, according to its website. Europa Village offers 88 EB-5 investment units in an attempt to raise $44 million. A total of 1,329 qualifying jobs will need to be created to satisfy the terms of the EB-5 visas, according to the Invest LA Regional Center in 2018. As a frame of reference, a resort hotel typically has a staff-to-room ratio of 2 to 2.5 full-time employees per room, according to industry benchmarks, and the average vineyard in California requires the equivalent of 1.8 employees per acre, according to the Wine Institute, so a 30-acre vineyard and 10-room resort hotel would only require about 80 direct full-time jobs at the high end.

In Eastern Washington, a 368-acre, $24 million "vineyard-oriented" enclave called E'ritage received approval from U.S. Citizenship and Immigration Services in May 2015, reported the publication Wines & Vines. Documentation associated with the project indicates that E'ritage would create 288 jobs in Walla Walla, backed by at least $14.5 million in EB-5 funds with 90 percent of participants from China. Several Chinese-language websites addressed the project, according to Wines & Vines, indicating that developers were seeking 29 investors willing to contribute at least $500,000 each. The Seattle Times reported in 2015 that Seattle-based Pacific Viniculture was seeking $10 million in EB-5 capital for a new 500-acre vineyard and winery.

Even the Von Trapp Family – yes, the ones from the "Sound of Music" – have gotten into the EB-5 Visa act. After the war, members of the singing family settled in the mountains of Vermont and opened a resort. Now, they're singing the praises of a new $20 million project: the Trapp Lager brewery and restaurant. EB-5 dollars from Chinese investors were being solicited for the new brewery, reported Aljazeera America in 2015. Construction was reported to be underway and the resort has already employed dozens of workers. The Wall Street Journal reported the offering materials indicated the project would preserve 200 jobs at the lodge, but also create 904 new jobs within three years – 66 jobs at the Trapp Lager brewery and restaurant, and the rest "indirect" jobs as the capital spending ripples through the Vermont economy.

Difficulties in accessing traditional financing brought on by the Great Recession, along with a rise in the number of wealthy investors in developing countries, have led to a recent spike in interest in the EB-5 program, according to a 2014 report from the Brookings Institution and the Rockefeller Foundation. In 2017, Senators Dianne Feinstein and Chuck Grassley introduced legislation to eliminate the program, claiming it was replete with fraud and abuse as it lacked a verifiable way to measure job creation. "The EB-5 program is inherently flawed," said Feinstein. "It says that U.S. citizenship is for sale. The Securities and Exchange Commission has filed charges in case after case of fraud connected to this troubled program."

* * *

In 2015, Ohio Governor John Kasich signed a bill allowing the creation of open-container zones across the Buckeye State, where they've been given the somewhat misleading designation "outdoor refreshment areas." Middletown, population 49,000, set up the state's first such district. It relies on potentially crapulous pub-crawlers reading maps and signposts lest they wobble into hostile climes and get ticketed. Gripped by civic boosterism, no state has become a bigger fermentation vessel for the go-cup than Ohio.

The Canton City Council voted unanimously to create one. Developers of Cleveland's Flats East Bank residential-retail project applied for that city's first open-container zone under the new law. Cincinnati, not to be outdone, was weighing the creation of its own open-container district at The Banks, a mixed-use development.

In Lincoln, Nebraska, advocates for the Railyard district hope that its open-container zone will keep millennials from moving away after graduating from the University of Nebraska. That thinking doesn't consider the possibility that some Cornhuskers may commit to moving away precisely as a *result* of walking the zone. As they leave Nebraska, they may, like Lot's wife, take one final look back on a once-historic district now filled with perambulating drinkers. The Omaha City Council, not to be outdone by Lincoln, unanimously passed an ordinance allowing developers to create open-container zones in that city.

But while many city officials, civic boosters and local developers believe parts of their localities are perfect for alcohol-fueled walkabouts, there are many unanswered questions from a public policy standpoint. For one, are taxpayers absorbing more liability when cities encourage drinkers to imbibe outside the stern gaze of a bartender? Are the zones putting city police into the role of determining which open-air carousers are consuming verboten bring-your-own intoxicating liquors and which are buying from approved watering holes. There are also the practical issues of increased littering, public urination and public drunkenness. Historical ironies abound, too, since some of these cities were founded to control the proliferation of alcohol in unincorporated county areas.

Perhaps the greatest irony involves New Orleans, the nation's sidewalk-daiquiri capital. As of this writing, the city was weighing measures to keep drinkers behind closed doors on Bourbon Street as it deals with a series of deadly shootings in the French Quarter and the threat of vehicle-borne terrorist attacks. In 2017, Mayor Mitch Landrieu unveiled a $40 million plan to cut crime in the city. The very un-*laissez les bons temps rouler* plan includes closing the doors of bars after 3 a.m. and police sweeps of Bourbon Street to move people inside bars and discourage patrons from taking road sodas on vision-quests. A recent incident in which a suspected drunk driver injured dozens of revelers has only intensified the effort. And after high-profile shootings in its open-container zone in 2016, Mobile, Alabama, re-evaluated its public-drinking zone.

But clearly most of the momentum is toward legalizing

the go-cup. Roswell, Georgia, City Councilman Mike Palermo wanted to expand an existing open-container zone into the city's historic downtown square. He hoped drinkers would gain a greater appreciation for civic history (if through beer goggles). But the expanded zone would contain two parks, which may become stumbling points – literally and politically. Another Atlanta suburb, Sandy Springs, is preparing to welcome restaurants into its new open-container district. Meanwhile, in Virginia, a state that has provided public matching grants to craft brewers as part of its economic-development strategy, a pair of bills is being debated in the legislature that could allow open-container districts in the Old Dominion.

And in Colorado, bar owners in Fort Collins are hoping to generate interest for an open-container zone at the city's East Lawn at Foothills Mall. That may be fitting, because as any city gardener will tell you, lawns are a big hit with migratory drinkers seeking temporary relief.

Chapter Twelve

Wheys and Means

ATTENTIVE VIEWERS TUNING in to NBC's coverage of the closing ceremonies of the Pyeongchang Winter Olympics probably noticed a commercial directed by the documentary film director Louie Psihoyos. In it, a group of Olympians make common cause in their dislike of dairy products, encouraging viewers to drink plant-based products (but not specifying any particular product). It aired in six U.S. markets.

"I did it and I got stronger," says U.S. Olympic weightlifter Kendrick Farris in the spot's opening seconds. The commercial, created by an ad agency called Effect Partners and another named Pollution was as simple as it was evangelistic: ditch dairy.

The spot hit the airwaves as Psihoyos's film, "The Game Changers," was screened at Sundance and the Berlin Film Festival. The film follows James Wilks, a retired MMA fighter who now trains elite special forces members in hand-to-hand combat. It promotes a plant-based diet and is a quest to understand the relationship between athletic performance and animal products. Psihoyos gives Wilks a producer credit in the film. But the commercial seemed like just another blow to long-suffering dairymen, who have witnessed a trade embargo against Russia, a plateau in demand from China, the removal of European production quotas and the strengthening of the U.S. dollar, resulting in a protracted period of low dairy prices globally. And it's not just American dairymen who are suffering.

In watering holes and froufrou hotel suites around Brussels' Place du Luxembourg and along the Avenue Louise, between bites of triple-crème dessert cheeses and crab croquettes in citrus aioli and steamed mussels – a Belgian favorite – urbane Eurocrats tut over the ultimate sacrifice to be made by the heroic Dutch dairy cows. With a hand cupped under the chin so the juices don't drip onto a Turnbull and Asser pocket square here or a Charles Tyrwhitt slim-fit wool blazer there, sallow-faced members of the supra-national class lament the hardship that could result from the slaughter of a half-million cows, "but it's not as if the dairy farmers hadn't had ample lead time…" they rationalize between delicate swigs of Veuve Clicquot. European Union edicts regulate how much dung dairies may produce. Dutch cows are making too much of it. Dutch dairymen must also contend with the massive market consolidation that has been allowed to congeal in one company, mega-processor FrieslandCampina, which handles a reported 80 percent of Dutch milk.

With Holland's dairy herd of 1.8 million cows (about the size of California's), the reduction to Dutch manure doesn't amount to a hill of dung on a global scale. Consider India, which has the world's largest dairy herd at about 300 million animals owned by 70 million small-scale dairy farms. The Indian herd is almost 170 times the size of Holland's. In India, slaughtering a cow is considered a hate crime. The government has expanded cow sanctuaries, such as one outside Delhi.

* * *

"We started making cheese in November 2000," said fourth-generation CEO Brian Fiscalini, and scion to the Fiscalini farmstead, which has been raising dairy herds at the site in the Central Valley near Modesto, California, since 1914. His great-grandfather started the operation with 12 milk cows.

"Mariano came on shortly after that in 2001, and we like to joke that before Mariano came, we thought we were making cheese [but] once he finally got here, he showed us *really* how to make cheese," said Fiscalini, who, along with his sister, Laura Genasci, oversees the day-to-day operations of the dairy, along with their semi-retired father, John. Both siblings graduated from Cal Poly San Luis Obispo as their great-grandfather had a century earlier.

As for Mariano Gonzalez, Fiscalini's master cheesemaker, he's been making cheese for 30 years, starting in his native Paraguay. Fiscalini's dairy and Gonzalez's experience perfectly complement one another. Fiscalini Farms Bandage Wrapped Cheddar won Best Farmhouse Cheese in America just a year after Gonzalez joined the dairy.

"The milk we work with," said Gonzalez, "we never heat above the temperature of the animal. All our products are basically raw. We like to maintain that part of the traditional process of the cheese, maintaining high quality."

A couple of curious Holsteins look in, waiting their turn, from the milking barn's entrance gate. The "brisket bar" opens, and the exalted creatures stream in anew. Trusted workers spray teats with an iodine mixture and wipe udders with towels. Natural light floods the barn. The cows seem happy. With a total of 54 milking stalls, the milking barn on the Fiscalini property was built in 1993. The barn operates for about 23 hours a day and shuts down for an hour to be cleaned. "We maintain control the entire time – the cleanliness, the sanitation, the training of our employees, the care of our animals – all of that leads to a great, high-quality, healthy milk," said Fiscalini.

But making cheese with raw, unpasteurized milk requires strict adherence to food safety standards and frequent inspections. The dairy presses its curds in interconnecting square "hoops" under tremendous pressure for at least 18 hours, says Gonzalez.

A short walk from the milking barn, two methane digesters built in 2009 serve as artificial stomachs, capturing methane gas from the manure and converting it into electricity. The dairy was among the first in the region to build them. Besides consuming manure, they also consume the whey left over from the cheese production process. This produces enough renewable energy to power the dairy, cheese plant and 300 nearby homes.

The milk cows are outfitted with devices some farmers began calling "Fitbits for cows." The devices sense motion and track the cows' activity and core temperature. They relay data back to the dairy farmers, so they can catch problems early on and be on top of estrous cycles on a cow-by-cow basis.

Fiscalini makes every shovel and rake on the farm by hand, which is an unusual thing and a tradition passed down to him by his forebears. In 2015, he had about 1,500 cows in production and a total of about 3,000 animals. His dairy, which employs 26 people, sends 12 percent of the milk to the cheese plant, which produces about 350,000 pounds a year, mostly cheddar. The cheese plant employs another 15 people. The rest of the milk in a recent year went to the Carnation evaporated milk plant in Modesto, where it was made into sweetened condensed milk. Fiscalini said he hopes to eventually use all of his dairy's milk for cheese and other dairy products made on site. Elsewhere, 500 acres of crop land is fertilized entirely with manure from the Fiscalini dairy. Nothing goes to waste.

* * *

The average cow has more than 40,000 jaw movements daily. It eats nearly its weight in vegetation each month, almost five tons of forage a year. Cows are red-green colorblind, have almost total 360-degree panoramic vision and can hear lower and higher frequencies better than people. They're social animals and generally like humans. They make friends, bonding to some herd members and avoiding others. They get used to their surroundings and like routines.

"It's important to understand the complexity of a modern dairy," said a cost estimator and colleague of mine. "The milking barn is the whole operation. When they build a milking barn, they build the whole dairy complex around it. The companies that build these barns use the same tried-and-true designs for every build. They've been perfected over many decades," he said.

"The milk from the tank is loaded onto tanker trucks at regular intervals, sometimes several times a day. They drive the trucks in and load them right in front along the building. Everything is laid out very strategically for production – from the front of the building, where the milk is stored, cooled and pumped onto tanker trucks, to the area [where] cows are milked with wash areas behind that," he said.

"The cows are shunted from a barn in the back. They rotate around in a certain fashion. They must be milked twice or three times a day, rain or shine, no matter what. A dairy is a food processing plant like any other. If a dairy doesn't have maximum efficiency, given its thin margins, it will run at a loss."

Between 1969 and 2008, an inverse relationship existed between the number of dairy facilities in California and the number of cows and total milk production in the state, reported the California Department of Food and Agriculture. During the period, the number of dairy farms steadily decreased, while the number of cows and milk production steadily increased in the Golden State. Milk production per cow has been on the rise over the past 65 years. Annual milk production per cow between 1951 and 2015 rose by 204 percent. Meanwhile, the number of dairy farms – following the trend for all farms in the state – has declined, from 18,479 in 1951 to a mere 1,438 in 2015. Average herd size per dairy farm during this period soared from 42 milk cows to 1,215.

Since 2008, the trend toward fewer dairies has continued, while the number of milk cows has declined, leaving milk production relatively flat overall. Based on state estimates, the number of the beasts peaked at 1.88 million in 2008 and has since trended downward to 1.74 million in 2016. While the overall herd in California has declined, the number of dairies milking the smaller Jersey cow has increased over the last two decades, especially in the San Joaquin Valley.

Still, the Holstein is the most prominent of the seven dairy breeds. Cows of Holstein (pronounced HOHL-steen) extraction make up over 90 percent of the cows on U.S. dairy farms. They are recognizable by their distinctive black-and-white markings and are the largest of the U.S. dairy breeds. The cows in Chick-fil-A's "Eat Mor Chikin" campaign are Holsteins, though the ad gets it wrong, since dairy varieties aren't raised for beef.

A mature Holstein typically weighs in at about 1,500

pounds and stands about 58 inches tall at the shoulder. They eat about 100 pounds of feed and drink a bathtub full of water every day. Miss one milking and the cow can begin to go dry. Miss consecutive days of milking and mastitis can develop. The milk comes out of the cow at about 102 degrees Fahrenheit. It's then chilled to 35 degrees. Farmers have a choice of whether to milk their cows twice or three times a day. It changes production and costs. It's common for a Holstein to produce 9 gallons of milk daily. They produce about 25 percent to 30 percent more milk per cow than the smaller Jerseys but require larger equipment and more space than the Jersey. Most crossbred herds are the result of breeding a Holstein and its offspring to the Montbeliarde, Swedish Red or Red Dane breeds – "ProCross" is the term used to describe the hybrids.

Between 2011 and 2015, organic dairies in California increased milk production year over year. Annual milk production per cow for organic herds increased by 8.8 percent. Several factors contributed to this increase including availability of quality organic feed, better herd management, and stable organic milk prices. In 2015, organic herds represented about 1.6 percent of the total milk production in the state.

* * *

Postwar Europe, more than America, has created a self-perpetuating governing class. Like their urban counterparts across the Pond, they, too, tend to be generally ignorant of agriculture. They play to their cosmopolitan constituents and exploit the urban-rural divide in Europe. A rigid, one-size-fits-all nitrates directive in the European Union has been in place since 1991, but Holland has been exempted from it – until now. The directive's goal is to protect water quality from pollution by agricultural sources and to promote the use of good farming practices. "Good farming practice" might be defined as a practice devised by a disconnected working group in a no-risk, no-cost environment in Brussels with the power to compel farmers in far-flung corners of the European Union to adopt the practices, with the farmer assuming all the risk and all the cost. In 2006, the Dutch government secured an 11-year exemption from such practices for its dairy farmers. The exemption expired at the end of 2017. Since then, another chemical directive, this one for phosphate, has complicated matters.

About 80 percent of dairy farms in Holland produce more manure than they can dispose of on their properties. To skirt the restrictions, farmers pay to have the manure removed, but some have resorted to fraud. A recently uncovered scheme showed many had been avoiding the expense by falsifying documents in something called "calf fraud." According to the Dutch Minister for Agriculture, a significant number of farmers registered calves as multiple births in a pencil-whipping exercise to make their herds appear smaller. About 2,100 farmers have been implicated. The E.U. edicts have not only led to the normalization of white-collar crime among dairy farmers but may now require a "dairy police" to enforce the fiats – something Brussels didn't consider. Also, this type of fraud has lasting effects on farm data, the lifeblood of ag research and policymaking. The fraudulent data now shows more than 10 percent of Dutch cows give birth to twins or multiples (up from 3 percent to 5 percent normally). One hallmark of the two major famines of the 20th century was the proliferation of fraudulent agricultural data.

"We don't want to be seen as part of the intensive livestock sector," Richard Scheper, a dairy analyst at

Rabobank, told the Guardian. "The Netherlands is like a big city. Everyone has a house, good life and enough to eat so they think about nature. The pressure is higher than in poorer or more rural countries." Translation: Most people in the Netherlands are too busy enjoying a high standard of living to worry about such trifling matters as where their food comes from or how they came to have such a high standard of living in the first place. Food abundance has allowed the Dutch – and the European Union – to focus on more esoteric concerns, like climate change and the need for draconian mandates from a central government to kick everyone in line. Complying with the mandates should be no problem provided farmers are willing to euthanize about a third of the nation's dairy cows.

* * *

In June 2018, creditors seized the Triple V Dairy, owned by U.S. Congressman David Valadao and his family. Located in the San Joaquin Valley, Valadao's 21st Congressional District includes Kings County, western Fresno County, southwestern Tulare County and northwestern Kern County. Rabobank, which held the note, began selling off the congressman's milk cows and equipment piecemeal to pay back more than $8 million in unpaid loans, according to media reports. Inventory sheets in court filings showed that the dairy had almost 17,000 cows, heifers, breeding bulls and calves, as well as more than 4,000 tons of feed.

As if the gods of agriculture, commerce and bureaucracy had conspired to play a cruel joke on Valadao, the day his dairy farm was foreclosed was also the day the U.S. Agriculture Department threw a lifeline to California dairy farmers. That day, it made them subject to something called the "Federal Milk Marketing Order System." Valadao had proposed the change through legislation in 2013, saying it would help California dairy producers compete in the national market. No doubt, it will. But the relief came too late for him personally. Instead, Congressman Valadao became the standard bearer for what is happening to dairy farmers in California.

California accounted for about 18 percent of all U.S. milk production in 2018. With the policy change, over 80 percent of the U.S. milk supply will now fall under the federal regulatory framework. California dairy producer prices were typically some of the lowest in the country; joining the federal order system, milk prices paid to the state's dairymen and the method for setting milk prices will be brought in line with prices paid in the federal system.

While the federal system is far from perfect – itself having the feel of something concocted by a people's commissariat – farmers in California prefer the federal system. The change, according to dairymen, eliminates an even worse system in California in which rumpled lifers in the state civil service, under the direction of an appointed political myrmidon, monitor the prices of butter, cheese, powdered milk and whey on open exchanges and weigh them against the costs of feed, labor, utilities, veterinary care, packaging and administration. After considering the forces of supply and demand in dairy markets, they arrive at the ideal market-based number to compensate dairymen for their risk, provide investors an acceptable rate of return, allow bank loans to be serviced and supply consumers with high-quality and affordable dairy products. What could go wrong?

California had thusly been regulating dairy prices since 1935. At that time, California was isolated on the West Coast, far from the nation's major population centers. Dairy markets of the era were local in nature; products were not transported long distances. That geographic separation brought significant differences in market conditions that supported California staying out of the federal system and having its own program, or so the reasoning went.

California processors paid for milk according to its class. Class 1 was fluid milk; Class 2 was cultured products like yogurt, sour cream, cottage cheese, buttermilk and egg nog. Class 3 was ice cream and frozen dairy desserts. Class 4a was butter and dried milk powders and Class 4b was cheese and whey protein powders. Under California's system, all money was pooled – you can't make this up – and then paid out equitably to dairy farmers. "I never thought I'd see this day," Kevin Abernathy, general manager of the Ontario, California-based Milk Producers Council, told Western Farm Press. "This is our opportunity to end the insanity of the state order," he said. Congressman Valadao, despite being the state's most recent victim, was more measured in his comments.

"As a dairy farmer myself, I experienced firsthand the serious disadvantages dealt to California dairy producers and I came to Congress to ensure Central Valley farmers and ranchers had a voice in Washington," Valadao said in a news release. "Many family dairy farms in the Central Valley are struggling. Over the last five years, at least 50 dairies in Fresno, Kern, Kings, and Tulare [counties] have been forced to close their doors."

Perhaps inspired by the heavy-handed treatment of the Dutch dairy farmers, California Governor Jerry Brown signed a bill in 2016 intended to reduce methane gas from cows in the Golden State. The law recognizes that California leads the nation with a dairy herd of 1.7 million and about 4 million beef cattle. Part of the law calls for cutting methane from livestock 40 percent by 2030 from 2013 levels. It's intended to reduce "short-lived climate pollutants." Methane accounts for only about 10 percent of U.S. greenhouse-gas emissions. But methane's greenhouse effect is greater than that of carbon dioxide. Nonetheless, methane is a fleeting gas. It stays in the atmosphere for only about a decade; carbon dioxide's potential is 200 years or more. Cows are the main culprit of livestock methane through belching, flatulence and manure.

At the venerable World Ag Expo in Tulare, California, states like Nebraska, Iowa, Kansas, North Dakota, South Dakota, Texas and Nevada routinely set up booths with the aim of selling their states' superior business climate to the long-suffering California dairymen. "Increasingly every year, there are more states showing up at the expo to entice California dairies to relocate to their states, and they're finding a receptive audience," Western Milling market analyst and commodity manager Joel Karlin told NBC. "California has been losing cows to other states such as Idaho, Texas and New Mexico – and now a lot of operators are looking at the Midwest more favorably since feed is cheaper, labor is cheaper and water is more plentiful."

* * *

Mexico is the largest importer of U.S. milk. The Asian markets, especially China and South Korea, are also major importers of American dairy products. According to the U.S. Dairy Export Council, U.S. exports set a new high in March 2018 on a total volume basis, surpassing the previous high set in March 2014. Exports of milk powder, whey protein concentrate, and lactose were each at record highs.

Dairies can hold onto their fresh milk for only so long. Then, they must make storage decisions. At that point, three things can be done with the milk. It can be made into butter and skimmed milk powder; cheese; or whole milk powder.

In March 2018, U.S. suppliers exported 204,453 tons of

milk powder, cheese, butterfat, whey and lactose, up 26 percent from March 2017. U.S. exports were valued at $510 million, 8 percent greater than in March 2017 and the highest total value since April 2015. Ingredient sales drove much of the gains. Shipments of skim milk powder to Southeast Asia were nearly double the prior-year level and sales to Mexico were the second-most ever. Shipments of lactose to China were at a record high.

When milk prices fall, it puts downward pressure on the price of other dairy commodities like milk powder, cheese, butterfat, whey and lactose. Milk is sold per so-called hundredweight; butter, by the ton.

In 2017, Michigan and the U.S. Northeast saw milk being dumped as production surpassed processing capacity. Global milk supplies increased in the third quarter of 2017, rising year over year by 2.2 percent. This weighed down commodity prices. Some large dairies turned to cheese plants. Over the past half-century, milk use in the United States has shifted gradually from fluid forms, like milk and cream, to manufactured products like cheese and butter. In 1950, fluid milk and cream took about half of the milk supply. By 2000, it was less than one-third.

More traders than ever purchased cheese and butter contracts, which are traded in Chicago. In 2017, the measure for settled butter options and futures rose to an all-time high. By July 2017, Bloomberg reported that Europeans were consuming so much butter that the EU's stockpiles were nearly empty, adding to a spike in demand that sent global prices soaring. France's Federation of Bakeries has called the price spike a "major crisis." Spot prices for butterfat in Western Europe doubled from midyear 2016 to midyear 2017.

But minimum prices paid to producers are dictated by a complicated system of reference prices and formulas. The milk producers often don't fully understand these complexities themselves. Like many other types of farmers and ranchers, dairy farmers are increasingly involved in futures-based risk management.

Meanwhile, the market for dairy alternatives is booming. In 2017, the market was valued at $7.37 billion. The plant-based milk market is predicted to be worth $35 billion by 2024. According to data analytics firm Nielsen, lactose has emerged as one of the leading ingredients consumers actively avoid. Total per capita consumption of fluid milk has been steadily falling as the U.S. population ages, while plant-based "milks" are gaining popularity. In California's fertile Central Valley, even dairy farmers are being drawn by the great collective transgression, entering the plant-based milk industry by diversifying into almond orchards instead of growing silage for their herds on lands once used for that purpose. Some are now buying feed from out of state.

In early 2018, the publication Dairy Herd Management reported a former dairy processor had doubled-down on nut milks after unveiling another alternative to dairy with "peanut milk." Elmhurst Milked, LLC, already produced nut- and grain-based drinks including milked cashews, milked almonds, milked hazelnuts, milked walnuts, milked oats and milked brown rice. The latest addition to the lineup is the milked peanut.

Elmhurst began as a dairy with a small herd outside New York in the early 1900s, a time when much of Manhattan remained covered in farmland. The cows were purchased on Manhattan and driven across the Williamsburg Bridge to the Elmhurst neighborhood in Queens, where the buyer's sons, Max and Arthur Schwartz, began hand-bottling the milk in their father's milk house in the 1920s. Calling the operation Elmhurst Dairy, they delivered milk throughout Brooklyn and

Queens in a truck filled with ice blocks.

In November 2016, Elmhurst CEO and scion Henry Schwartz decided to radically change the family business. He changed its name from Elmhurst Dairy to Elmhurst Milked and went vegan on the good people of Gotham.

"They were innovators," Schwartz says of the founders. "They went from bottling small batches of cream on a hand filler to selling dairy products to millions of New Yorkers ... I think they would respect my decision to continue to innovate in a new direction," he told the publication Dairy Herd Management. Elmhurst was billed by the publication as the only entrant into peanut milk at the time.

NAFTA uncertainties in the Trump era are causing enormous hand-wringing and teeth-gnashing for American dairy producers over Mexico, their largest export market. A report released in 2017 by CoBank showed American dairy farmers each year were producing about 3 billion more pounds of milk than the year before. Then, the U.S. Dairy Export Council released its numbers for March 2018, laying out record highs in total volume for exports of milk powder, whey protein concentrates and lactose.

A 2017 report published by Variant Market Research estimates that the global plant-based cheese market is predicted to grow rapidly in the coming years. This could push more milk out of cheese. By 2024, the vegan cheese market is expected to reach $3.9 billion from $2.1 billion in 2016.

Others believe raw milk is the salvation of the dairy industry. Raw milk is milk from cows, sheep or goats that has not been pasteurized to kill harmful bacteria. This raw, unpasteurized milk can carry dangerous bacteria like Salmonella, E. coli and Listeria, which are responsible for causing numerous foodborne illnesses, reports the FDA. The Raw Milk Institute, a non-profit international organization promoting the safe and hygienic production of raw milk, points out that raw milk is the first food for all mammals. It's a living whole food that contains enzymes, a biodiversity of beneficial bacteria, sugars, proteins, fats, minerals, antibodies and other essential elements needed to nourish a growing baby. One survey of raw milk drinkers in Michigan found they drank raw milk to support local farms, for the taste, for "holistic health benefits" and because they didn't feel processed milk was safe. Raw milk contains more fat than pasteurized milk, according to Real Milk, a campaign promoting the raw alternative.

The FDA doesn't allow raw milk for human consumption to be transported across state lines. In 2012, the Centers for Disease Control and Prevention released a study showing that the rate of disease outbreaks linked to raw milk was 150 times greater than outbreaks linked to pasteurized milk.

Raw milk sales are illegal in Virginia, but residents of the Old Dominion can own a "share" of a cow, or of a herd, since it isn't illegal for a person to drink raw milk from his own cow. Proposed legislation could close this loophole. It would compel farms whose cows are owned by shareholders to provide the names and addresses of those shareholders to officials in Richmond.

* * *

The new Tillamook Creamery Visitor's Center is months from completion. The 38,500 square-foot facility will allow visitors to watch Tillamook Cheese being made and packaged. The number of visitors, the cheesemaker reports, has soared over the years – to more than 1.3 million each year, with as many as 10,000 on many days.

This day the pasturelands and thickets on each side of

U.S. 101 are so brilliantly emerald and sylvan the area could be mistaken for the back nine of some iconic golf course. Leaves on the hemlocks, maples and alders dance in the wind. In the sky, amid fast-moving mottled clouds, distant jet engines whir. That evening, the heavens erupt into a spectacular thunder-and-lightning show with reports of a waterspout off the coast. Coastal Tillamook County in north Oregon is named for an American Indian tribe living in the area in the early 19th century when settlers arrived. The Lewis and Clark expedition traded with them for blubber the tribe had harvested from a whale that had washed ashore. The tribe's staple food was salmon. It knew no cheese and had no knowledge of dairy farming.

Dairy farming is today the biggest agricultural activity in Tillamook County, which touts itself as the Land of Cheese, Trees and Ocean Breeze. There were 45,063 head of cattle in the county but just 27,000 humans. The top field crops in the county are hay, silage and green chop — all used to feed hooved animals.

The 100-year-old Tillamook County Creamery Association is a dairy cooperative. It makes and sells products under the Tillamook name. Its best-known product is Tillamook cheese, including Tillamook Cheddar. Its cheese factory is the county's largest business and the largest private employer. It employs one in 10 people who live there. By Tillamook's own account, almost half of its employees are women.

* * *

On 7,288 acres along the Columbia River in north-central Oregon, the Lost Valley Farm mega-dairy opened in April 2017 as the state's second-largest dairy. It would supply the Tillamook County Creamery Association. Dairyman Greg te

Velde bought the massive farm along Interstate 84 in early 2016 for about $8,900 an acre and then developed it to a dairy, it was reported. It was formerly a poplar tree farm.

By early 2018, the state alleged the dairy had put at risk nearby drinking water sources by violating environmental laws. Officials wanted it shut down. The Oregon Department of Agriculture asked a Multnomah County judge for an injunction that would stop the dairy's ability to create or discharge wastewater after eight months of alleged permit violations.

Te Velde, a 60-year-old Californian, had run a dairy with 8,000 animals on land leased from the state's largest dairy, the 93,000-acre Threemile Canyon Farms in Boardman in northeastern Oregon. That farm produces 170,000 gallons of milk daily, according to its website. It has 24,000 Jerseys and Holsteins. The mix between Jerseys and Holsteins provides milk that is richer in butterfat and valued by cheese makers. It raises its own replacement dairy cows in its 4,500-calf nursery. It has 25,000 replacement heifers on the farm. Cows are tagged and tracked in its computerized database, which contains detailed health history records on each. Te Velde leased Threemile Canyon Farms from his family, the Oregonian reported. It's partially owned by fellow California dairyman A.J. Bos, who is related to te Velde through marriage.

With this new dairy, he had permission for 30,000 mature cows, heifers and calves. At the time of this writing, he was battling lawsuits that could result in foreclosure of the besieged dairy. Lost Valley Farm's wastewater permit allows it to generate 187 million gallons of manure per year, reported the Statesman Journal. Regulators approved the dairy despite objections from about 4,000 people and a dozen state and national health and environment organizations. They raised concerns about air and water pollution, water use and health effects on nearby communities.

Now, the state alleged the mega-dairy was endangering nearby drinking water by violating environmental laws and should be shut down immediately, according to a state's lawsuit. The dairy failed numerous inspections and has been cited four times and fined $10,640.

Te Velde responded that he had only had about half the 30,000 cows allowed, and those would need to be sold for slaughter if he could not milk them. The cows would need to be sold at a discount, and te Velde said he doubted his ability to buy them back quickly, resulting in a loss of revenue of an estimated $30 million.

"Oregon sues to shut down new mega-dairy, citing repeated manure spills," blared the headline of an article by staff writer Tracy Loew in the online edition of the Salem Statesman Journal in February 2018. Just under the lede in the 800-word story, readers are told of the dairy's proximity to the Columbia River, its association with Tillamook County Creamery Association and the 4,000 objections regulators had logged prior to issuing permits for the mega-dairy. Readers are also reminded, high up in the story, that te Velde is a Californian. He was in the Beaver State but not *of* the Beaver State. A good chunk of the article also seemed to tell readers: See? This is what can happen when state officials don't listen.

The reader must keep reading to the 14th paragraph before Loew gets around to mentioning that the dairy is situated in an already contaminated special groundwater management area. The reader must then make it to the 16th paragraph to learn that state officials don't know how much wastewater (if any) was improperly released by the dairy. Te Velde contends the dairy was meeting all permit requirements.

The aforementioned lawsuit seeks an immediate and

permanent injunction prohibiting the dairy from creating any more wastewater. But as any naval procurement officer will attest, a newly built capital ship requires an extensive shakedown cruise before it's commissioned into the fleet. "In my experience and discussion with other dairy farms, the approach to inspections and the Oregon Department of Agriculture's approach to notices and penalties against Lost Valley Farm is much more stringent than at other dairies in Oregon," dairy manager Travis Love wrote. "The dairy is a new facility. [The state] is aware of this but is approaching compliance with the permit as if it is an established dairy that has been in operation for some time."

As the story's buried lede indicates, the new mega-dairy is in the Lower Umatilla Basin Groundwater Management Area, one of three districts already designated for special oversight due to higher levels of groundwater contamination. The Oregon Department of Environmental Quality declared the area contaminated as early as 1990, nearly 30 years before te Velde's mega-dairy. Was this the source of the existing contamination? High nitrate concentrations in the Lower Umatilla Basin already exceeded the federal safe drinking water standard. Nitrate, or, as one academic eloquently calls it, "animal excreta," is associated with dairy waste.

In the summer of 2017, te Velde was among 10 people arrested in a tri-county prostitution sting. Meanwhile, it was reported that Tillamook County Creamery Association had stopped buying Lost Valley's milk. Thus, a tale that seemed like a figurative morality play in the first act took on the character of a morality *lesson* in its final act.

"Te Velde was going to beat the environmental stuff," one dairy broker in California told me, asking that his name not be used. "The state was going to work with him. He had the support of the governor. But the hooker incident…he lost his bank over it. He lost all his political support."

In 2018, Rabobank, the Dutch agricultural lender, filed a separate lawsuit in Morrow County seeking to foreclose the dairy in connection with the foreclosure of two dairies te Velde owns in California. According to the suit, two of three commercial loans the bank made to te Velde are more than a year past due. He was reported to owe $37.4 million on those two loans. The month Rabobank filed, feed and equipment companies sued him for over $1 million plus interest for what they alleged were unpaid invoices.

"The problem is with lagoon overflows," said Terry Silbernagel, a Salem-based agricultural broker. "The governor supported him but then the governor himself left in disgrace. The Oregon Department of Environmental Quality has landed on him now. I think maybe they landed on him pretty hard. You don't just shut down a new dairy. There will always be problems. But Oregon has a reputation, like California, of being unfriendly toward business. They ought to have given him a chance. There are two other mega-dairies in that area." According to reports, former Governor John Kitzhaber had supported the mega-dairy until his resignation under the cloud of a federal criminal investigation for allegedly steering official favors to his fiancée's consulting firm.

"There aren't that many mega-dairies in Oregon. This is a heavy-handed state [environmentally]," said a western Oregon-based ag broker who asked not to be identified. "Dairymen are moving to red states like Idaho and Texas. Traditionally, the sweet spot for dairies here are those with herds between 500 to 2,000 head. We sold a farm with 600 cows with a Tillamook [contract]. Everyone was very happy. Buying a dairy here hinges on the cooperative that will buy your milk. Tillamook is a good one, but you don't just join them. You have to buy your way in. You just don't open up a dairy farm in Oregon," he said. "If you don't have a good market for your milk, you're done."

Hannah Connor, an attorney for the Center for Biological Diversity, one of the groups that opposed the mega-dairy, said the violations detailed in the lawsuit were a preventable disaster. The Center for Biological Diversity recently made headlines for suing the Trump administration for failing to protect humpback whales from such things as ship strikes and oil spills.

In June 2018, Oregon took the first step toward shutting down the Lost Valley mega-dairy by revoking the water pollution discharge permit it needed to operate. In the modern regulatory state, the wastewater discharge permit is the lifeblood of any dairy and dictates how many milk cows, heifers and calves a dairy is permitted to have. It's a way in which state officials can control herds in their states politically under a veil of well-meaning environmental stewardship. The announcement of the revocation was an opportunity for a phalanx of critics to pile on and broach the familiar "factory farm" discourse.

"The very model of factory farms like Lost Valley Farm and other mega-dairies operating in Oregon is flawed," Tarah Heinzen, an attorney at Food & Water Watch's Portland office, penned in an op-ed in the Statesman Journal: "It's time for the state to take a hard look at this model and take appropriate action to protect Oregon's natural resources," she wrote.

"Appropriate action" – yes! Oregon could simply contact all its formerly bankrupted small dairy farmers who were forced to hand over their dairies to creditors in the face of mounting regulations, fees, mandates, quotas, wage floors, wastewater caps, taxes and permitting costs. It could then compel them to buy back their dairies. Unfortunately, that's not the way it works. Those dairies are gone and probably for good.

For Lost Valley, like so many dairy farms in the Western ag states, the end came slowly, then quickly, and, in te Velde's case, ignominiously. A bankruptcy judge cleared the way for the U.S. Department of Justice to take over management of Lost Valley Farm. Te Velde would also lose control of his two California dairies – GJ te Velde Dairy in Tipton and Pacific Rim Dairy in Corcoran, the Statesman Journal reported. Judge Fredrick Clement, United States Bankruptcy Court for the Eastern District of California, in his written decision, seemed to delight a bit too much in the dairyman's personal demons, which we learn from the judge are gambling and drug use. If estate money was spent or loans taken without the court's authorization, then fine, remove te Velde as fiduciary. This is the judge's prerogative. But unless you're willing to run the dairy yourself, your honor, spare us the churchy obiter dicta from on high about the man's moral failings. We get it. He has problems.

The predicament is revelatory of what residents of the Beaver State have come to expect: well-paying jobs; a high standard of living; pristine nature; clean water; a Disneyland-like creamery to visit; and the pride of producing wholesome products like cheese, ice cream, yogurt and butter. Oregonians would just rather not be confronted with the smells and unsightliness of the concentrated herds required to produce the necessary milkfat on razor-thin margins in the modern regulatory state. What Oregonians should be learning is that when the smaller dairies are driven out of business, there is no getting them back.

Chapter Thirteen

Fifty Shades of Nuts

IN EARLY 2018, riots erupted in France when a supermarket chain, Intermarché, put Nutella – the hazelnut-and-cocoa spread – on sale at a 70 percent discount. A jar was advertised at 1.41 euros ($1.75) rather than 4.70 euros, the chain's usual price. The discounted Nutella managed to erode the thin veneer of civility among French consumers. Viral videos showed French consumers pushing and punching each other. One elderly woman was hit over the head with a box. "People just rushed in, shoving everyone, breaking things. It was like an orgy," one Intermarché employee in northeast France told a French news outlet. Similar scenes played out across the Cinquième République.

The popularity of Nutella has never been at issue. It has longevity on its side. The founder of the Ferrero candy company first combined hazelnuts and cocoa during the darkest days of World War II when chocolate was rationed and difficult to come by.

At this writing, Nutella alone takes down 25 percent of the world's hazelnut crop. Other makers of confections, from pralines to truffles, take down much of the remaining global yield.

Europe represents the largest bloc of hazelnut eaters. Hazelnuts – less commonly known as filberts – have become a global commodity, consumed mostly as a luxury food. Besides their place in Nutella and confections, they're consumed as in-shell nuts for the Christmas market, mixed nuts, hazel butter and high-end salad oil, which resembles olive oil in its chemical profile. In the United States, 98 percent of commercial production is in or near Oregon's Willamette Valley. This is thought to be the only region in the United States where the standard European varieties do well. The United States sates only about 20 percent of worldwide demand. As a nut, it processes well. Demand for nuts that process well is always high. In 2014, each jar of Nutella was reported to contain about 50 hazelnuts.

A few months before the Nutella riots in France, a German consumer protection group announced it suspected Nutella had been reformulated. The Hamburg Consumer Protection Center reported it had observed an increase in the spread's skimmed milk powder and sugar content, which already amounted to half of the chocolate-hazelnut spread's make-up. The group found Ferrero had increased the content of powdered skimmed milk from 7.5 percent to 8.7 percent, and sugar from 55.9 percent to 56.3 percent.

Nutella's Italian manufacturer copped to "fine-tuning" the spread. It insisted the nutritional value of the new version resembled that of its predecessor.

The spread seemed to have more sugar and fat – but it also seemed to have fewer of one key ingredient: hazelnuts. "As the color of the new Nutella is lighter, we are working on the assumption that skimmed milk powder was added at the expense of cacao," a spokesperson for the center went on record saying. Ferrero, along with other companies, doesn't have to list the quantity of ingredients in its products.

Of the million metric tons of hazelnuts grown globally, Turkey produces some 70 percent. In Europe, the hazelnut tree is mainly grown as a bush or multi-trunked shrub for ease of harvest. A heavy frost in late March 2013 cut Turkey's output from 660,000 metric tons to 549,000. In 2014, after another unusually cold spring battered trees, the Turkish yield fell to 381,000 tons, according to one source, although other sources put the total Turkish yield at just 65,000 tons. Farmers burned straw and tires in their orchards to combat the frost.

The surge in hazelnut prices brought on by the short supply proved a bitter pill for confectioners like Ferrero, already grappling with high cocoa prices in 2014 due to fears the Ebola outbreak could spread to the top-cocoa growing countries in Africa and throttle the flow of cocoa beans to ports.

All of this led to a spike in prices, causing companies to reduce hazelnut content in their products or increase prices or both. Ritter Sport increased the price of its whole hazelnuts bars by 8 percent in 2015. The company's hazelnut offerings are reported to account for 40 percent of Ritter Sport's U.S. sales. Nutella is reported to have taken the opposite tack, reducing its hazelnut content from 17 percent to 13 percent the same year. Dependence on Turkey has left Ferrero, Kraft Heinz, Mondelez International and Nestle vulnerable. During the pinnacle of the hazelnut crisis in 2014, Turkish suppliers held back from selling, which kept supplies even tighter, trader Adam Johnston of Edinburgh, Scotland-based commodities firm Freeworld Trading told the Wall Street Journal in late 2014.

It's not uncommon for growers to hold back supply when prices are rising in anticipation of achieving even better prices down the line. To control its own hazelnut supply, Ferrero acquired Oltan, Turkey's largest hazelnut producer.

The trouble in Turkey has increased the demand for U.S. hazelnuts. Oregon farmers grow 99 percent of the U.S. crop, but the United States is still a relatively small player. In Oregon, growers primarily raise hazelnuts as a single-trunked tree that grows 50 to 60 feet tall. In 2014, Oregon contributed just 36,000 tons. But by 2016, that number had climbed to 44,000 tons. As with any tree nut, supply can't be adjusted quickly to meet demand. Necessary lead time must be built into the equation to develop new acreage and nurture immature trees to the point they begin yielding. This comes with substantial holding and opportunity costs. The average nut production in the state is 2,100 pounds per acre.

In 2015, Oregon had about 34,000 acres of producing hazelnut trees. By 2016, that number had increased to about 37,000 acres, up nearly 9 percent, according to the state's agriculture department. Some believe the shortage of Christmas trees in the United States in 2017 was at least partially due to an increase in acres being planted to hazelnuts in Oregon, which is also the nation's largest producer of Christmas trees. Oregon does not consider Christmas trees in the same category as agricultural crops and does not track acreage under production to the same extent as nut orchards.

Besides the time and cost involved to bring a hazelnut orchard into full production, there is uncertainty. Turkey has had a veritable lock on hazelnut production over many years and there is considerably less institutional knowledge and confidence elsewhere.

In 2017, the Canadian government provided a grant to farmers to test tree varieties in the province of Ontario. Ferrero, hoping to crack Turkey's grip on the hazel, is partially funding the project in Canada and hopes to see farmers plant

25,000 acres of hazelnuts by 2027, from about 400 acres in 2017. According to one model, a farmer in Canada's corn belt can earn 10 times more per acre from hazelnuts than corn. Similar projects have sprung up in Serbia, Chile, Australia, South Africa and New Jersey in the United States. "Everyone is looking for new places to plant hazelnuts," Jaime Armengolli, owner of Chilean grower and processor Agricola La Campana, told CNBC. "Yields are good. Costs are low. Growers are very optimistic." Chile's shelled hazelnut exports exceeded 6,500 metric tons in 2016, almost five times the previous year's exports, according to government statistics.

Hazelnuts have generally not been grown in the Eastern United States because the standard varieties are not cold-hardy and are highly susceptible to a disease known as Eastern Filbert Blight, a fungal pathogen carried by wild hazels. That pathogen, which is spread by the wind, has slowly made its way to Oregon over the years.

Hazelnuts are generally cross-pollinated. This means two or more varieties of trees are used to produce nuts. About 6 percent to 10 percent of the trees in a typical orchard are so-called "pollinizer trees." Also, hazelnut trees are one of the few tree varieties that bloom before the leaves emerge. With separate male and female flowers on the same tree, both species of hazelnut require the wind for cross-pollination.

Hazelnuts, which are green during development, turn brown when ripe, about seven to eight months after pollination. This is around the end of August or early September and harvest takes place in late September and October. The nut falls out of the husk when ripe. The trees begin to bear about five years after planting. On average, trees produce for more than 50 years. Hazelnut orchards in the United States are harvested by machine. Harvesting in Turkey and elsewhere in Europe is done by hand. Like almond farmers in California, hazelnut growers in Oregon sweep the fallen nuts into rows and then vacuum them up using a machine called a harvester. Unlike the almond tree, the hazel tree isn't shaken first. The nuts are deposited into wooden totes and then taken to processers who clean, dry and sort them. About half of all nuts are shelled for the market.

* * *

In early 2018, Oregon State University was set to release a new hazelnut cultivar dubbed the "PollyO" to honor Polly Owen, a hazelnut luminary, an Oregon State alumna and the director of Oregon's hazelnut office from 1995 to 2017. In Oregon's hazelnut region, Owen is something of a rock star. The PollyO is the latest hazelnut tree developed by OSU breeder Shawn Mehlenbacher, and it is resistant to the Eastern Filbert Blight. The OSU hazelnut breeding program began releasing immune varieties in 2005. "We've had a lot of disease pressure in our field with no cankers on these trees," Mehlenbacher, known for an iconic mustache – Wilford Brimley meets Ron Swanson – told an audience during the Nut Growers Society's annual meeting. These varieties and Mehlenbacher's work have been a ray of sunshine to Oregon's hazel farmers. Farmers with older plantings make do. The blight was first detected in southwest Washington in the 1960s. It slowly spread south. The industry has been battling to manage the effects of the disease since. Techniques to manage it include surveillance, pruning out infected tissue, the use of fungicide sprays and the introduction of blight-resistant varieties.

"A tree can be infected for 18 months before you see signs of it," said grower Garry Rodakowski. "Cankers are small football-shaped pustules. You can get three or four on the head of a pencil eraser. They pop out through the bark. Each one has a million fungal spores in it. They act like volcanos shooting the spores out to infect other trees." Rodakowski, besides being a grower himself, is chairman of the Oregon Hazelnut Commission.

Researcher Nik Wiman, Oregon State University's orchard specialist in Western Oregon, is looking at the post-blight world. Wiman, who holds a Ph.D. from Washington State in entomology, believes that while the focus has been on combating Eastern Filbert Blight, the study of production fundamentals has gotten short shrift.

"Everybody's been chasing the Eastern Filbert Blight. We knew very little about the disease when it first came in," Wiman told the Capital Press in 2018. But now that an arsenal of countermeasures has been developed, including the introduction of several hazelnut cultivars resistant to the pathogen, Wiman is focusing on the basics – using science to work out nutrient demands for the newly developed cultivars, some of which contain genetic material from across the globe. He studies the timing of fertilizer applications to maximize tree and nut development. It's something of a moving target, since a tree's response to nutrients depends on the accumulation of heat over a given season. "There is so much change, even in a [short] time frame like a month," Wiman told the Capital Press.

He has also focused on irrigation techniques and combating the Pacific flatheaded borer, a beetle whose larvae attack many trees and shrubs in the Northwest; it is especially attracted to young hazelnut trees. The females lay their eggs on the trunks, and the larvae enter the wood. It's a big issue, since more than half of Oregon's hazelnut acreage contains young trees.

The flatheaded borer has an enemy in the wild – a parasitic wasp that lays its eggs into the larvae and kills them. Carpenter ants also eat both the larvae and pupae from the wood. Using broad-spectrum chemicals will kill the larvae but will also kill the helpful insects. For that reason, says Wiman, pesticides must be used judiciously to avoid killing off these "biological controls."

Meanwhile, a relatively new agricultural pest from Asia, the brown marmorated stink bug, has become a serious threat to crops in the East and to hazels in Oregon. It was accidentally introduced into North America in the late 1990s from China or Japan. It's believed the pest hitched a ride in packing crates or on machinery. "They can actually feed right through the shell and damage the kernel inside," Wiman said.

But as fate would have it, a parasitic wasp that targets the stink bug followed it to American shores. The insects are now being bred at OSU's research center in Aurora and released at infested sites. "It showed up on its own. It followed its host," Wiman said. "We think it's going to have a huge effect long term."

Meanwhile, after decades of work, members of a research team at Rutgers' New Jersey Agricultural Experiment Station claim they've developed a cultivar that can be safely grown in New Jersey and elsewhere in the Northeast. "We are getting so close to being able to get a new agricultural industry off the ground in New Jersey," Tom Molnar, head of Rutgers' hazelnut tree breeding program, told the Star-Ledger. After gathering seeds in Eastern Europe, Central Asia and Crimea and growing thousands of trees and cross-breeding them, Molnar says his team has successfully bred a blight-resistant tree they believe will grow in New Jersey and nearby states. They are preparing to distribute the trees to Garden State farmers in 2018 for trials.

The Rutgers team also used pollen provided by fellow researchers at OSU. Commercial plantings are reportedly now being made in the Upper Plains States and elsewhere in the

Midwest, along with several Canadian provinces.

It's a feel-good story for Oregon and New Jersey. It helps diversify the worldwide sourcing of hazels. But, like almonds in California's Central Valley, it could one day become a monocrop, crowding out the grass seed, peppermint, corn and bean fields of the Willamette Valley.

The Turkish lira is in freefall as of this writing due to political turmoil and U.S.-imposed sanctions. This means a good Turkish growing season could flood world markets with dirt-cheap hazelnuts. China has become the top consumer of Oregon hazelnuts, but that could now change with the devalued Turkish lira. Meanwhile, big players are showing up in Oregon prospecting for hazelnut land. A pistachio powerhouse from California recently bought 1,000 acres, said Rodakowski. A group from Turkey now has about 1,000 acres. Rodakowski is hearing about hedge funds making inquiries. Although the Oregon hazelnut story is still in its first act, count on no government czar to sound a claxon when crop diversity has been lost in the fertile Willamette Valley. Man cannot live by Nutella alone.

Chapter Fourteen

One World under Hummus

DEMAND FOR HUMMUS, made from chickpeas, is on a sustained upswing in the United States, squeezing out the once-ubiquitous sour-cream onion, salsa and warm artichoke dips of an earlier generation. Hummus has been a big disruptor. It has moved the shared-consumption needle.

Hummus consumption has risen to a point that a few daring Virginia tobacco growers, whose families have farmed the leaf in the Old Dominion for generations, began test-planting precious acres of their enriched soils to chickpeas. Its rise as a U.S. crop has been meteoric. In 2003, U.S. plantings were about 50,000 acres. By 2017, it had risen to more than 600,000 acres, according to the Agriculture Department. From 2016 to 2017 alone, the number of acres grew by nearly 86 percent.

In Great Britain – from the anonymous, grimy burbs of North London to the manicured estates of Surrey – the groundswell in hummus consumption is even more pronounced. A 2013 survey crowned Britain as Europe's hummus consumption capital. It found that 41 percent of Britons, double the number of any other country, had hummus in their refrigerator. In 2017, hummus shortages were reported across the United Kingdom with shelves being cleared out at Tesco, Sainsbury's and Marks and Spencer.

* * *

To follow the hummus, one must follow the chickpea, once humbly known as the "garbanzo bean" in the United States. Despite the surge in acreage planted to chickpeas in the United States as I write this in early 2018, poor global crop yields are sparking a shortage of them. Britain's Independent reported in early 2018 that the price of hummus had escalated by around a third over the previous year in Britain. Australians – in another hummus-loving corner of the Commonwealth – have been resorting to a faux-hummus of mashed beetroot and roasted capsicum. But there was scant sign of a hummus shortage in the United States in the run-up to the 2018 Super Bowl.

Americans are seeking out more gluten-free products and more healthful and varied snacking, the Agriculture Department wrote in a recent report. In 2006, hummus was reported to be in 12 percent of U.S. households. By 2016, it was 25 percent. Data provided by the consultancy Technomic shows that mentions of chickpeas on menus were up 3.8 percent in the fourth quarter of 2016 from a year earlier, while hummus gained 3.7 percent. But drought conditions in the Northern Plains States can affect the yield and put pressure on supplies.

Millennials tend to be more daring in trying new flavors than their boomer parents. They're more apt to try things like Sumbal Matah Indonesian salsa or order beef weaned on fermented cottonseed or throw back a mixed drink containing lychee boba balls. Millennials' attraction to shiny objects is partly responsible for the positive momentum of the quinoa chip and warm fennel dip.

* * *

Chickpeas belong to a crop group known as "pulses." These are high-protein, low-fat seeds in the legume family. India is the world's largest producer and consumer of the chickpea. The United States comes nowhere close. In 2016, U.S. farmers produced about 250,000 metric tons of chickpeas on about 320,000 acres. By contrast, Indian farmers produced about 9 million metric tons of chickpeas on over 20 million acres. In the United States, chickpeas are grown mostly in the Palouse region of Washington and Idaho; the latter is the leading producer of small desi chickpeas; the former leads the nation in the production of the larger kabuli variety. The Palouse accounts for about 70 percent of U.S. chickpea production, with Montana producing around 20 percent and California around 4 percent. Most of the U.S. chickpea crop goes to hummus.

U.S. Senator Maria Cantwell is a pro-business Democrat and junior senator from Washington State. She helped defeat attempts to strip the Asparagus Market Loss Program from the 2008 farm bill. It provided $15 million in assistance to help offset losses to Washington asparagus farmers due to the Andean Trade Preferences Act – part of the War on Drugs. By incentivizing farmers in Latin America to grow legal crops, the act allowed U.S. growers to be undercut, gutting many established U.S. crops, including a highly developed cut-flower industry in California's coastal counties. (In rich irony, some of the very flower greenhouses shuttered by the act are being repurposed by the state's now-legal marijuana industry.) Left unsaid in the farm bill is that federal assistance to asparagus farmers is now also offsetting other things like increased record-keeping requirements, worker's compensation, state unemployment insurance premiums, compliance with Washington's agricultural employment standards and its minimum wage act. In the Evergreen State, farmers are increasingly caught in a hall of mirrors caused by the forces of globalization and a stream of taxes, fees, surcharges and labor fiats from the statehouse in Olympia. The federal farm bill has become a shambolic conduit not only to promote enormous monocrops in the Midwest and South, but to inadvertently backstop redistribution schemes in California, Washington, Oregon and New York. The farm bill has been pushing its shelf life going on nine decades.

These days, Cantwell, a 60-ish Midwesterner who came west to work on the failed 1984 presidential bid of the late Senator Alan Cranston, has been spreading the gospel on the state's booming chickpea crop. Retail sales of hummus is expected to exceed $1 billion by 2022, increasing from $250 million in 2013, up from $192 million in 2007 and up from just $5 million in 1997. She helped push a provision in the 2014 farm bill for a pilot program she authored to include more peas, lentils and chickpeas in school lunches.

In 2016, the leading American hummus maker was the Sabra Dipping Company, which has been owned jointly by PepsiCo and the Israeli food manufacturer Strauss Group since PepsiCo purchased a 50 percent stake in Sabra in 2008. Kraft Foods owns Athenos, another pervasive hummus brand. A few industry watchers are beginning to use the term "Big Hummus." With a reported 62 percent market share for hummus sales in the United States, Sabra is the powerhouse of hummus, with a vision of dominating guacamole, salsa, baba ganoush and Greek yogurt dips. Its sales were forecast to exceed $1 billion in 2017.

The national dry pea, lentil and chickpea industry office is in Moscow, Idaho, separated from the Washington state line only by a Walmart Supercenter. Officially called the USA Dry Pea & Lentil Council, it engages in marketing, research and government relations. It works with breeders and researchers at Washington State University, which is about 10 miles to the west. Its representatives in Mexico, China, New Delhi, Barcelona, Paris and Bangkok promote U.S. pulses in their respective regions. These are heady days for U.S. pulse crops. Pulses are generally harvested by hand in the Mideast, North Africa and West Asia. In the gently rolling slopes and flatlands of the Palouse, they can be harvested mechanically.

While the snacking trend may be unfortunate for the traditional sit-down meal, it's working for PepsiCo and Sabra. One source tracked a 7 percent increase in chip-and-dip sales in the United States between just 2013 and 2015 with sales reaching $16.4 billion. CNBC reported in 2016 that dips alone — excluding salsa — saw growth of 26 percent in the preceding five years. The category is expected to grow an additional 20 percent by 2020.

In 2017, snack food maker Hippeas confirmed that Strand Equity Partners, a private equity fund co-founded by Seth Rodsky and actor Leonardo DiCaprio, had invested in the company. Hippeas, a new brand of organic chickpea puffs, is sold in over 20,000 stores in the United States and the United Kingdom, with customers including Starbucks, Whole Foods, Wegmans, Albertsons, Safeway, Boots, Waitrose, Amazon and others.

Chickpea production can't keep up with U.S. consumption. Domestic production has soared, but imports have been needed to sate domestic demand. In 2017, over 58,000 metric tons of chickpeas were imported into the United States, a 27 percent increase from the previous year. In past years, Mexico has been the top supplier to the United States, but Canada topped the list in 2016 with 41 percent of chickpea imports.

There was much media buzz in 2013 about the surge in U.S. hummus consumption – to the point that the aforementioned Virginia tobacco farmers were beginning to replant portions of their soils to chickpeas. Hummus giant Sabra partly funded research at Virginia State University – not far from its largest hummus plant near Richmond – aimed at determining which chickpea varieties would grow best in the Old Dominion. It is feared, however, that the state's high summer humidity will prove insurmountable and make chickpeas more vulnerable to a fungus known as Ascochyta blight, which has threatened chickpea crops across the United States. The university's college of agriculture is researching canola, white lupin, tepary bean and summer grain legumes with names like lablab, pigeonpea and guar, and winter grain legumes like chickpea, lentil and winter pea. It's become a hotbed of pulse research.

* * *

Hummus has become just one more friction point in the Mideast. Recently, Lebanon accused Israel of appropriating its national dish. In 2009, Lebanon fired the first salvo as that country's Minister of Tourism, Fadi Abboud, threw the government's backing behind an effort to create the world's largest hummus bowl. It weighed in at 4,500 pounds. The undertaking was a reaction to a perceived slight at a French trade show in which a claim had been made that hummus was an Israeli invention. Both hummus and falafel are the objects of a gastronomic donnybrook between Israel and Lebanon. In January 2010, Israel took the record back with a 5,000-pound bowl of hummus. Later in 2010, Lebanese chefs in a village near Beirut wrested back the title with a dish of hummus that weighed in at over 25,000 pounds.

The government of Lebanon attempted to register the name "hummus" with the European Union to receive a protected appellation. It would require foods labeled "hummus" to be prepared in a certain fashion and have originated in Lebanon, in the same way Roquefort cheese must be made from milk from a certain breed of sheep and aged in caves outside the town of Roquefort-sur-Soulzon in southern France.

The Association of Lebanese Industrialists went to the European Commission to seek protected status for hummus, fried chickpea balls and other traditional dishes. The move was designed to counter a growing number of Israeli brands that have found their way into U.K. supermarkets. "What we are trying to do is simply what the Greeks have done with feta cheese," Abboud told Britain's Telegraph in 2008. He was referring to a European Commission decision in the early aughts that gave Greece exclusive rights to the name feta cheese. "The word Lebanon is not mentioned on one hummus tub in all the U.K.," he told the publication. "It makes me so mad."

The word "hummus" comes from the Arabic word for "chickpea." Ultimately the European Union didn't grant Lebanon protected status as it found the food belonged to an entire region. As it turns out, every country in the Mideast claims hummus as its own, including Israel, where hummus has become a unifying food for a country less than a century old with most of its inhabitants from outside the region.

Like the Lebanese, Palestinians have long been making and eating hummus, too, and Israel's adaptation of hummus has become a gastronomic lightning rod for wider friction between Israelis and Palestinians. If the trend continues, hummus could come to represent any generic admixture of a pulse, seed or grain. Toom, a dip made from garlic, lemon juice, oil and salt, is a riff on a traditional Lebanese sauce called "toum." While toum is known for its dominant garlic flavor, Toom has a more mainstream flavor, Matt Joyce, Toom's creator, told CNBC. In the United States, the grocery chain Trader Joe's sells an edamame hummus. One U.K. company has launched a fava bean hummus using domestic rapeseed rather than olive oil. "What Sabra does for hummus, they basically have their original hummus and they just kind of sprinkle different stuff on top to make different [flavors]," said Joyce. "I wanted to create flavors that are distinctly different tastes," he said.

"While millennials gravitate toward authentic tastes, they're not necessarily staunch purists about form and function," Marc Halperin wrote in the fast-food trade publication QSR. "They have a soft spot for ethnic mash-ups, which combine authentic elements of two or more ethnic cuisines in familiar, accessible formats. Sushirritos, naanwiches, Korean barbecue tacos, Mexican dumplings — this is a generation that has no trouble with hybrids of any sort." Pulse farmers have no problem with it.

Chapter Fifteen

An Inconvenient Fruit

AMERICAN LIME CONSUMPTION has exploded, from a half-pound of per person each year in 1980 to three pounds in 2013. Since the middle of the last century, Mexico has been the largest global producer and exporter of limes, and it remains the main supplier to the United States. By one estimate, the United States gets some 97 percent of its limes from Mexico. The second-largest importer of limes to the United States is Guatemala, at just 1.5 percent. Mexican growers focus on two varieties: the key lime and the Persian lime (also called the Tahiti lime); the latter was introduced into Mexico by Americans. John Bearss developed a seedless variety in 1895 in his nursery in Porterville, California.

Persian lime production in Mexico, in turn, is heavily dependent on the U.S. market, where Mexican cuisine ranks in the top three menu categories. In 2014, the United States had more than 54,000 Mexican restaurants in operation, and Mexican restaurants constituted about 8 percent of the total U.S. restaurant-scape, according to the food-service and hospitality consultancy CHD Expert. Mexican food had just unseated the hamburger for the third-most-common U.S. menu type, with the burger and fries falling into fourth-place territory. In lockstep with the rise in Mexican food's popularity in the United States was the rise in lime production, and exports were made more profitable by the North American Free Trade Agreement. Lime production in Mexico has also grown due to the rise in per-capita lime consumption in the European Union. In the United Kingdom, Mexican food has been growing in popularity. The results of a study by Future Thinking, as reported in the publication Food Manufacture in 2015, found 30 percent of U.K. families had bought or eaten Mexican food in the previous year. The publication attributed this to the rise in television programs in the United Kingdom that featured Mexican cuisine – both in cooking shows and in comedies and dramas in which actors were seen eating Mexican food. This has driven up the prices of Mexican limes. Limes are typically sold by the 40-pound box.

Lime prices pick up in the United States from about December through February. In some years, this period can include March and stretch to just before Easter. In April, volume from Brazil declines, provided weather patterns are normal. At that time, Mexican supplies slowly begin to rise. The Mexican volume hits its apex in the United States from June through August. Lime prices typically fall in April after a period of higher prices.

A rise in operating costs in Mexico in 2017 and early 2018 – marked by higher fuel prices and other operating expenses – forced growers to invest less in their orchards, skimping on fungicides, herbicides and fertilizers. This resulted in lower-quality fruit. Exports to the United States increased because it was the only market that would accept this low-quality product, an unnamed source told the publication Fresh Plaza. The Veracruz lime-growing region in Mexico has been pummeled by atypical weather in recent years. The state of Veracruz, an elongated swath of land that hugs the Mexican coastline along the Gulf of Mexico, varies dramatically in climate and topography, from snow-capped mountain peaks to humid tropical zones along its coast. Half of Mexico's citrus is grown in the state. Most is produced in the north, and much of the lime crop is exported. The exports support a frenetic Mexican packing and shipping industry. Limes are also grown in the states of Michoacán, Colima and Jalisco, but they aren't considered as conducive for lime production as Veracruz.

When the Veracruz lime-growing region is hit with cold conditions, it results in excessive fruit drop. In January 2018, moisture and cold temperatures resulted in frozen buds, with small fruit forming and blossoms falling off trees. Mario Cisneros of Santis Produce told the publication Fresh Plaza that this weather was just another chapter in the climate anomalies that have occurred in Mexican lime-growing regions. "The climate has not been predictable in recent years," he said. "The seasons have been sporadic with rainfall at times we don't expect it and dry conditions when we expect rain. This recent cold weather is another example of the challenges growers are facing with the local climate."

Whatever the case, it won't likely match the abominable market conditions of the Great Lime Shortage of 2014, when both heavy rainfall and drought conditions knocked blossoms and forming fruit off trees, and members of drug cartels began looting groves and hijacking delivery trucks. In 2014, limes shot up from $20 to $120 a case.

* * *

A procession of vehicles, mostly small pick-ups, packed with flowers and many small children makes its way down a dirt road somewhere in the rural state of Michoacán. Today, the Cortez, Marin and Rivera families are burying 15 family members ranging in age from three months to 60 years old, thirteen from one family. All were lime pickers or the family members of pickers. The families' story is featured in the 2015 documentary "Cartel Land."

We learn the grower had been extorted by the Knights Templar cartel. When he didn't pay the ransom, the syndicate killed some of his workers and their families, smashing the children's heads against rocks and throwing their bodies into a well. "I would like the government to bring the men who did this to justice, but it hasn't been the case. That's the situation in Michoacán. All we want is justice," one of the survivors told the documentarians.

"Most people in the U.S. don't realize how highly dependent we are on Mexico for certain products," David Shirk, a security specialist at the Mexico Institute of the Woodrow Wilson International Center for Scholars, told CNN Money in 2014. "They don't understand how much our economies are intertwined. The bad things happening in Mexico do have an impact on U.S. consumers and U.S. exporters." Stepped-up efforts to keep drugs out of the United States have had the unintended consequence of encouraging drug cartels to diversify their operations. They've branched into limes and avocados.

If weather and violent gangs weren't enough, lime suppliers are now also facing truck shortages that are pushing up costs. Much produce from Mexico is affected, especially as suppliers try to ship produce to markets across the United States.

A new and contentious rule by the U.S. Federal Motor Carrier Safety Administration requires freight carriers to install electronic monitors – so-called E-logs – to replace the written duty logs truckers have had to maintain since the 1930s. The device connects directly to a rig's engine and automatically records driving hours. But the devices, like all technology, aren't capable of reasoning. That's a big problem. The devices don't consider, for example, if a trucker has had to sit in line for hours waiting to load or offload. Time spent in line butts up against the government's nonnegotiable hours-of-service rule that requires all work be completed within a 14-hour window. This means that once a driver starts his truck, he's on duty and the 14 hours begins ticking down toward a mandatory rest period. The technical wizardry and the newly unearthed duty hours are driving up freight prices. This is both being passed along to the consumer and forcing failures and industry consolidation.

"Freight has become a huge issue for suppliers," Cisneros of Santis Produce told Fresh Plaza. "Prices are astronomical," he said. "I have a client in Chicago who was quoted $10,500 to bring one truckload of fruit from Texas to Chicago. Another in Fresno was quoted $12,000 from Texas to Fresno. There is a lot of demand for trucks in Mexico and it's adding to the issues we are having with the supply of limes."

Meanwhile, Colombia has been paying attention to the lime issues in Mexico and the inelastic demand in the United States, Europe and the Caribbean. Also in the wings has been Peru, which is anticipating export growth in Persian limes witnessed by an increasing number of plantings in the northwest of the country; they are beginning to bear fruit. Exports grew 75 percent year over year in 2017 to about 1,600 metric tons, according to the publication Fresh Fruit Portal. "I think that during the campaign this year, exports of Persian limes will rise by a similar percentage to that of 2017, because many plantings have gone in the ground over recent years," said Peruvian Citrus Growers Association General Manager Sergio del Castillo Valderrama. The growth in new plantings of Persian limes is the result of a hike in prices caused by the lower production in Mexico.

Also setting the stage for a future global lime glut is Brazil, where the Portuguese word for both the lemon and lime is *limão* – causing no end of statistical confusion. Brazil competes with the Mexican lime in Europe. In 2014, Brazil was Europe's largest supplier of limes. Joey Deen of the produce import-export firm Denimpex told the publication The Packer that acreage planted to limes in Brazil was continuing to increase. More limes, though, are staying inside the country because of the growing domestic market.

Even tiny Guatemala is ramping up its lime plantings. Before 2012, reported Fresh Plaza, Guatemala's lime crop had little market potential, since 100 percent of the demand of its main market, the United States, could be filled by Mexico. But things have changed. With some 27,000 acres planted to Persian limes, Guatemala has managed to gain access to Europe, and its lime crop continues to grow.

The United States has not always been dependent on foreign limes. It once had a thriving lime industry in Florida. In the years after World War II, growers around Homestead, Florida – about equidistant from Miami and Key Largo – developed a booming lime industry. South Miami-Dade's tropical monsoon climate was considered ideal for the growing of unique tropical and subtropical fruits like mangos, avocados, carambola, lychees, bananas, sugar apples and passion fruit. The area was ideal for growing limes, which could be harvested year-round. It brought steady work for farmworkers and uninterrupted cash flows for growers. At the same time, a period of heavy immigration from Latin America and a fascination with Tiki and tropical cultures fueled a domestic demand for drinks and cuisine garnished with lime.

The first blow to the U.S. lime industry came in 1992 in the form of a Category 5 hurricane. Andrew was the most destructive to hit Florida up to that time. It made landfall in Dade County and leveled about half the commercial lime groves in the region. According to the University of Florida Institute of Food and Agricultural Sciences, the lime industry generated about $25 million annually in revenues ($44 million in 2018 dollars) just before Andrew ravaged the state.

The season just after Andrew, the Miami-Dade County commercial lime industry packed a paltry quarter-million bushels of limes, an 87 percent reduction from the nearly 1.7 million bushels that were packed the season before Andrew. A 2014 feature article on America's vanished lime industry in Time magazine by writer Katy Steinmetz sheds more light.

"The impact on lime trees was devastating," Craig Wheeling, a former fruit-company executive, told Steinmetz. "The hurricane picked up the trees and blew out the fences and the irrigation risers, virtually destroying all the plantings of the industry."

The larger growers with more resources replanted their trees, Wheeling told Time, and by 1999, "we had a fabulous year." Things were looking up for the U.S. lime. Florida growers printed labels with a little American flag on each piece of fruit, so consumers would know they were grown in the United States. As Florida rebuilt after Andrew, savvy Mexican citrus growers spotted the disruption and increased lime production in the area around Veracruz with its cheap labor and land.

Signed in 1994, two years after Andrew, NAFTA opened up the U.S. market for Mexican citrus growers. After the agreement was signed, additional Mexican lime plantings began, followed several years later by a rise in imports into the United States of limes from Mexico. Consumers in the United States prefer the larger and relatively seedless Persian limes, so Mexican growers boosted planted areas of Persians over Mexican limes.

Then came Florida's 1995 citrus canker panic. Citrus canker, believed to have originated in Southeast Asia, is a disease caused by the bacterium Xanthomonas axonopodis. Trees infected with it exhibit lesions on the leaves, stems and fruit. The disease has a long history in Florida, according to the American Phytopathological Society, a group of scientists dedicated to plant pathology research. The disease, which was first identified around 1912, spread throughout the southeastern United States on imported seedlings from Japan, but was declared eradicated from Florida and adjacent states by 1933. It was again discovered in Manatee County, south of Tampa Bay, in 1986 and again declared eradicated in 1994. But three years later, the disease re-emerged in the same general area on the west coast of Florida where the 1980s outbreak had occurred. Then a new infestation of citrus canker was discovered in urban Miami in 1995, with an estimated introduction some time in 1992 or 1993, about the time Andrew hit the Homestead area.

The canker affects limes, oranges and grapefruit most profoundly; other citrus varieties are less susceptible or, in some cases, resistant. The canker affects the vitality of infected trees, causing leaves and fruit to drop prematurely. Fruit infected with canker is safe for human consumption but considered unmarketable. The disease is extremely persistent when it gets established in an area. Wind-driven rain plays a big role in its dispersal. Cases are more acute in areas with high average rainfall and a high mean temperature, such as south Florida, where state and county quarantine officials have ordered the destruction of whole groves.

A new eradication program was established in 1996 to destroy all citrus trees planted anywhere near an infected one. "The state of Florida agriculture department would order them destroyed, send in bulldozers, pile up the trees and burn them," Wheeling told Time. It was literally a scorched-earth policy. The state did everything but salt the soil. By 1999, the U.S. Agriculture Department was proposing an enhanced program in cooperation with the Florida Department of Agriculture and Consumer Services to eradicate newly discovered citrus canker infestations.

At that time, other citrus insect pests to Florida defied eradication efforts; physical damage to citrus caused by these pests contributed to a greater number of entry points for bacterial citrus canker infection. In particular, damage from the insidious citrus leafminer has been linked to the increased spread of citrus canker. The larvae of the ignoble creature, a native of Asia, tunnel into citrus leaves, deforming them, leaving behind excrement. Research shows a leafminer infestation can hasten the spread of citrus canker up to 300-fold.

At the height of the panic in 2000, the state of Florida, as if calling in the Marines, ordered in hand crews with chainsaws to hew thousands of citrus trees down to stumps, even if they showed no symptoms of infection. At that time, reported the Miami Herald, the state Department of Agriculture and Consumer Services removed any residential citrus tree within 1,900 feet of a canker-infected tree.

Fearing for the welfare of Florida's larger citrus growing regions to the north, officials imposed a prohibition on replanting citrus in those areas for years, fearing that new trees would also contract the canker. Farmers planted avocados and vegetables instead. For the U.S. lime growers, the area near

Homestead had become Dante's Third Circle of Hell. By that time, the low cost of lime production in Mexico was impossible to resist. It seemed easier to just outsource lime production to Mexico than to find solutions in the United States.

Limes are the most "cold-tender" of citrus trees, pomologist and self-described fruit detective David Karp told Steinmetz. Karp has worked as a plant specialist at the University of California, Riverside. "Ninety percent of the time you'd be fine, but if there's one cold day, you lose your trees and crops die."

* * *

In 2005, Huanglongbing, or citrus greening disease, was first reported in Florida. It would have been the knock-out blow to domestic lime had not the citrus canker and NAFTA already TKO'd the U.S. crop. Within three years, greening disease – more commonly known by its acronym "HLB" – had spread to the majority of citrus farms there. Spread by an aphid-size flying insect, HLB was first described in 1929. The rapid increase in the disease, one of the most destructive ever, threatens the citrus industry worldwide. Leaves of newly infected trees develop a blotchy, mottled appearance. Fruit from infected trees is small, misshapen and poorly colored. The juice is high in acids, making it abnormally bitter. It has already cost Florida growers more than $4.5 billion. Since its discovery in the Sunshine State, citrus acreage has declined significantly. Greening is now in Mexico. It was first detected there in 2009 and has since spread to 23 of Mexico's 31 states, according to Gro-intelligence. com. This includes crucial lime-growing states like Veracruz and Michoacán. It is thought the worst of the citrus greening disease in Mexico is in the state of Colima, on the Pacific coast. In 2011, Colima produced

493,686 metric tons of limes (23 percent of total Mexican output). By 2014, production in Colima was down to 174,616 metric tons, according to Gro-intelligence. Veracruz, the state that produces the most U.S.-bound Persian limes, has already experienced production shortfalls due to citrus greening. This has led to abandoned orchards.

A rare bright spot in the greening mess: Western FarmPress reported in 2015 that the National Clonal Germplasm Repository for Citrus and Dates in Riverside, California, had discovered uninfected pomelo budwood imported with a shipment of otherwise HLB-infected citrus from India. As the pomelo tested negative for HLB after significant exposure, it might prove highly-valuable to researchers and breeders. Pomelo is a grapefruit-like citrus variety with flesh that is sweeter and milder than a grapefruit.

The word "lime" no longer appears anywhere in the 2017 annual report for fruits and vegetables published by the Florida Department of Agriculture and Consumer Services. (The absent lime crop aside, the report makes for dismal reading. This is a bleak period for Florida citrus.) Slightly more upbeat is California's annual statistical review for crop year 2017. While that state's Department of Food and Agriculture doesn't bother to break out any numbers for limes (it does for nearly all other citrus varieties), it wastes no opportunity to inform readers that California leads the nation in lime production, whatever that may mean.

Research by Steinmetz of Time magazine put California's lime-growing activity at a paltry 400 acres, enough to support some local farmers markets; And importing limes from Hawaii isn't worth the cost, especially when Mexico is so close.

In 2016, Wonderful Citrus, the U.S. integrated grower, shipper and packer of fresh citrus, announced the purchase of

I. Kunik Company, a major distributor of Persian limes grown in Mexico, and the purchase of the operations of B&S Grupo Exportador, a major supplier of Persian limes to the global market. As part of the transaction, Wonderful Citrus also acquired nearly 2,000 acres of Persian lime orchards in Mexico, making it the largest lime grower in the country when combined with its existing lime holdings.

Headquartered in the city of Martínez de la Torre on the River Filobobos in lush, tropical central Veracruz, B&S has longstanding relationships with leading growers and suppliers, as well as a 264,000-square-foot packing house. With the addition of these orchards, Wonderful Citrus has a total of 7,100 acres of lime orchards in Mexico.

The acquisition appears to have dodged, for now, the teeth-gnashing by critics over the influence and the concentration of the ownership *Yanqui* in Mexican limes. The Resnick-haters have been slow to the party. If the pair can do for limes what they've done for a handful of other fruits and nuts north of the border, it will get interesting.

Meanwhile, a company founded by a league of self-described "produce legends" based in dazzlingly tranquil Carmel, California, began marketing Persian limes in 2018 under the billion-dollar Margaritaville brand controlled by singer-songwriter and tropic lifestyle-spirit guide Jimmy Buffett. The limes – mostly Mexican – will be sold in heavily stylized grab-and-go bags and shipped in display-ready boxes. The company, Fresh Alliance, says it's packing for quality and uniformity and looking to spark impulse buys. The company reports it is looking for additional partnerships with Colombian growers. Buffett was also in the news in 2018 for licensing the "Coral Reefer" name to a medical marijuana startup. (It was inevitable.) He also licensed the Margaritaville name, music and knowhow to a Broadway production,

"Escape to Margaritaville," a happy yarn about a beach bum who lives on an island in the tropics – where else? – and looks something like a young version of Buffett. Fresh Alliance is hoping hordes of Parrotheads will flock to the limes.

Gutting it out, innovating and nurturing the Florida lime industry in the face of adversity was inconvenient considering it could so easily be offshored to Mexico once NAFTA was in place. It's emblematic of the capitulation and loss of control that comes with offshoring. If the Resnicks can be as successful marketing limes as they've been with pomegranate juice, pistachios, mandarin oranges, almonds and artesian bottled water, it will be deliciously ironic. American lime growers will once again be competitive, but only by owning lime groves in Mexico.

Chapter Sixteen

Peanut Republic

FORREST PARKER WAS chef at the Old Village Post House in Mount Pleasant, South Carolina. The restaurant, in an immaculately preserved front-gabled wood-frame building with clapboard siding, wood corbels, dormers, three dining rooms and a tucked-away courtyard, is in Mount Pleasant's historic Old Village. It is on the mainland across the Cooper River from Charleston Harbor. It's widely praised for its shrimp and grits, crab cakes and ribeye steaks.

In 2016, Parker was among four chefs named by then Governor Nikki Haley as South Carolina's Chef Ambassadors to represent the state's culinary heritage. Ex officio, he was the first chef to receive a sample of the ancestral peanuts that he later described as "the most peanutty peanut of peanuts."

The ancestral peanut was once America's defining peanut. The Carolina African runner peanut faded after the Civil War but made a resurgence during a boll weevil infestation in the late-1910s and '20s. When "Mr. Peanut" — the dapper gent in spats, white gloves, top hat and monocle — was unveiled in 1916 by the Planters Nut and Chocolate

Company, the illustrator would likely have had the Carolina African runner in his mind. When peanuts were hawked to crowds at the newly merged Ringling Bros. and Barnum & Bailey Circus in Rockford, Illinois, in 1919, this would have been the variety sold. When the Tin Pan Alley song "Take Me Out to the Ball Game" was first played at a ballpark in 1934, at hearing the line, "Buy me some peanuts and Cracker Jack!" many would have made the connection to the African runner, not the larger, blander Virginia and Spanish varieties.

But by the late 1930s, the Spanish and Virginia varieties had again replaced the Carolina African runner. The latter fell out of favor by growers so completely that just 40 seeds remained in a cold-storage vault at North Carolina State University. They were placed there in the late 1930s in an act of extreme prescience by a largely forgotten plant breeder. Those 40 seeds, as it turned out, were the last on Earth.

The Carolina African runner was the first peanut in the colonies. The cultivar was brought to the port of Charleston in 1690 on a slave ship from Africa; it is denser, sweeter, smaller, and has a higher oil content than the peanut varieties grown today. But by the 1800s, the tables had turned in favor of the aforementioned Virginia snack peanut and the Spanish peanut in the northern cities. But in the late teens and early 1920s, the African runner re-emerged. The boll weevil had infested all cotton-growing regions of the United States, devastating the South during that decade. The infestation had the dual effect of causing a national shortage in cottonseed oil; cotton farmers rotated into the Carolina runner peanut due to its high oil content. But the peanut's diminutive size caused problems at harvest time. And it was susceptible to certain diseases, which made it an issue for growers who needed to produce larger crops as World War I heated up in Europe.

Historians believe the last commercial crop of Carolina

African peanuts was harvested in the late 1920s. It was thought that by the late 1950s, the Virginia and Spanish varieties had driven it to extinction.

David Shields, a food historian at the University of South Carolina, tracked down seed samples that had been labeled simply "Peanut No. 4." He believed these were the only known Carolina African runner seeds in existence. In 2013, horticulturist Brian Ward at Clemson University's Coastal Research and Education Lab planted the seeds Shields had given him at his field lab. "I didn't know at the time I'd been given half the seeds in existence," he told the publication Modern Farmer. Twelve sprouted.

When the plants blossomed that summer, Ward and Shields were certain they'd recovered the lost Carolina runner peanut. It looked exactly like a photo Shields had seen of the plant in the Sloane collection, then in the British Library.

Ward and a South Carolina farmer by the name of Nat Bradford painstakingly multiplied the seeds to 1,200 plants the following season. "The Carolina African peanut is so tiny that when it runs through a modern shelling machine, only about 70 percent will make it into a pile of good seed, then the sheller has to throw the rest out," Ward told the National Peanut Board. Ward has nurtured the seeds and helped bring about a revival of the variety. In the early years, he hand-shelled the 30 percent the shelling machine didn't pick up. "It takes about six of us cleaning and separating to get about 20 extra pounds of seed in a day," he said at the time.

Other farmers helped in the effort. The 1,200 plants became 60,000 in 2014, a million in 2015 and 15 million in 2016. About 30 small growers produced crops in 2016. The project has been funded by the Carolina Gold Rice Foundation, grain purveyor Anson Mills and its founder, Glenn Roberts, and the South Carolina Peanut Board.

"The peanut when roasted," chef Parker told National Public Radio, "has the most intense peanut flavor I've ever experienced and continues to be a revelation every time I taste it."

* * *

Delta Air Lines announced in 2017 it would no longer serve peanuts, the official state crop of the airline's home state of Georgia. Peanut allergies have been on the rise in most industrialized countries. The allergy is lifelong in most affected children, although 15 to 22 percent will outgrow their peanut allergy, usually before their teenage years.

In just a decade, from 1997 to 2007, the prevalence of reported food allergy increased 18 percent among children under 18, according to the U.S. Centers for Disease Control and Prevention. It hasn't reduced peanut demand. "Domestic consumption is at an all-time high," Adam Rabinowitz, a University of Georgia professor and peanut economist, told the Atlanta Journal-Constitution in 2017. "Even exports are at an all-time high." U.S. per-capita consumption of peanuts was about 7.4 pounds a year in 2016, according to the Agriculture Department. That's the highest since at least 1980 (when it was 4.8 pounds). It eclipses almonds (less than 2 pounds per capita). In fact, it eclipses all tree nuts combined. And peanuts are technically not even nuts, but legumes.

A 2015 article in the New England Journal of Medicine detailed the Learning Early about Peanut Allergy (LEAP) trial. Its findings gobstruck the pediatrics and food-allergy world, and cheered growers in the peanut-sphere. It demonstrated that among infants at high risk for allergy, the sustained consumption of peanuts, beginning in the first 11 months of life, resulted in an 81 percent lower rate of peanut allergy at 60 months of age than the rate among children who avoided peanuts. A follow-up study a year later took it a step further. It indicated a 12-month peanut avoidance period was not associated with an increase in the prevalence of peanut allergy among the same children to whom peanuts had been introduced in the first year of life and continued until 5 years of age.

"Parents of high-risk children should feel more confident, and perhaps even elated, that they can reduce their child's potential risk of allergy to peanut through early introduction," pediatrician J.J. Levenstein, M.D., told the National Peanut Board. The National Peanut Board provides an instructional video for parents on making their own peanut-containing infant and toddler foods.

Kavin Senapathy, a science writer and mom of two living in Madison, Wisconsin, wrote a piece for the publication Slate titled "Your Kids Don't Need Training Wheels for Peanuts." In it, she points out that the recommendations on when and how to introduce these allergenic foods have been in a state of flux. Previous recommendations called for delaying some of the most common allergenic foods—cow's milk was delayed until 1 year of age, eggs until age 2, and peanuts and shellfish until age 3.

But in 2008, the American Academy of Pediatrics reversed its guidelines, stating there was no evidence that delaying solid foods beyond 4 months to 6 months of age, including foods considered to be highly allergenic, like fish, eggs and peanuts, had a significant protective effect on the development of food allergies. The National Institute of Allergy and Infectious Diseases guidelines suggest recipes that thin peanut butter (so a baby can swallow it) and how peanut flour can be added to an infant's food.

Senapathy contends this has led to confusion among parents and to a cottage industry of smartly packaged infant food supplements in convenient pouches and stir-in packets that, in some cases, ratchet up the dose of common allergens, including peanut proteins. The products, according to Senapathy, tend to rest on the findings in the LEAP study, the LEAP-ON study (the aforementioned study that looked at LEAP trial children after a peanut hiatus of one full year between 60 and 72 months) and the 2016 EAT (Enquiring About Tolerance) study, which found that introduction of six allergenic proteins before 6 months of age is not associated with increased risk of food allergies.

The findings of these studies, as Senapathy points out, don't offer direct support for the kind of dose-specific products being marketed in the packets and pouches. To assess efficacy, you'd need to collect clear and specific data on the products themselves, she points out.

* * *

Howard Valentine is the Executive Director of the Peanut Foundation. He is square-jawed and trim, and today, in the field, wears jeans and a ball cap. He could come right out of Central Casting. He fits the part as *éminence grise* of American peanut farming. "Every crop has a germplasm collection, not just peanuts," he said. "The germplasm collection holds the secret to our future. Without the germplasm, we would probably end up with a disease that we couldn't handle, one that would wipe out the crop."

The National Clonal Germplasm Repository is a branch of the Agricultural Research Service of the U.S. Department of Agriculture. It's a gene bank that preserves genetic material for every significant crop – and many an exotic variety – used to feed humans on Planet Earth. There are nine clonal repositories spread across the United States. They manage a total of 19 gene bank facilities, collectively storing 570,000 unique samples of 15,000 plant species that make up the National Plant Germplasm System. Collecting and sharing plants and seeds that grow around the world is one of the U.S. Agriculture Department's longest-running programs. Just behind national defense, it is one of the most valuable uses of U.S. tax dollars, and it is wholly unknown to most Americans.

The mission of the gene bank system is to conserve the germplasm – the tissues or seeds containing crop genetics – and provide them for research, breeding and education. It serves as the core of U.S. food security and helps ensure the nation's agricultural economy. Plant exploration and collecting are vital for agriculture, since crops must be continually enhanced to defeat the many cankers, wilts and blights that attack them and the pests that serve as disease vectors or that attack seedlings, plants and roots directly. Breeding also expands tolerance to drought and temperature, helps crops adapt to new growing conditions, and makes them heartier, more productive, more nutritious or better tasting. The plants that collectors bring back often provide the genetic material for breeding improved varieties.

The locations of the repositories and their satellite stations largely mirror the crops in the areas in which they're based. For example, the germplasm of citrus plants and dates are preserved in Riverside, California; a distribution center for grapes, temperate fruit, walnuts, almonds and pistachios is in Davis, California. The National Clonal Germplasm Repository in Corvallis, Oregon, stores the germplasm for pears, quince, hazelnuts, berries, butternut, mint, hops and other specialty crops. In Hawaii, the system maintains one of the world's largest and most genetically diverse pineapple collections on 33 acres in Hilo. It is part of the National Clonal Germplasm Repository for Tropical Fruit and Nut Crops. Both familiar and obscure pineapple cultivars are kept there.

Some, like the Smooth Cayenne, are industry leaders. Others, like the miniature Saigon Red, brought to the repository from Vietnam in 1938, are more obscure. Saigon Red is too tart to eat.

The base gene bank for the National Germplasm System is the National Center for Germplasm Preservation at Ft. Collins, Colorado. This center holds seeds of agronomic crops, cryo-preserved clonal plant materials, and animal and bacterial germplasm.

In 1898, experts predicted food shortages and famine in the United States by 1931, as population growth was on track to outpace America's ability to grow enough wheat. That year, U.S. Department of Agriculture special agent Mark A. Carleton was sent on his first plant exploratory trip to Russia. He returned with durum and hard red wheat varieties to grow in the United States. He became the Meriwether Lewis of U.S. agriculture. His boss would later write, "We have forgotten how poor our bread was at the time of Carleton's trip to Russia. In truth, we were eating an almost tasteless product, ignorant of the fact that most of Europe had a better flavored bread with far higher nutritive qualities than ours."

In 2012, the U.S. peanut industry tasked the Peanut Foundation with mapping the genetic code of the peanut plant. With a price tag of $6 million, the Peanut Genome Initiative became the largest research project ever funded by the peanut industry. Noelle Barkley is a geneticist and peanut curator with the Agriculture Department. She maintains the peanut germplasm collection. "The goal of this project is to look at as many traits as we can in the field and use a laboratory-based approach to look at genetic markers, trying to link those genetic markers to the traits we [observe]." Of the collection of 10,000 peanut lines in the germplasm, researchers associated with the project are assessing 800 elite lines of peanuts in a physical grow-out. Researchers can go back and select for various traits. It will provide a comprehensive catalog of the peanut germplasm.

The cost has been shared equally among growers, shellers and manufacturers. But for the data to be useful to peanut breeders, the voluminous quantity of genomic data must be searchable in advanced on-line databases. The peanut genome ended up being a tough nut to crack, since the total genetic information in the peanut is very large compared with other legumes. In fact, it's about as large as the human genome.

Also, like many domesticated plants, the peanut's genetic information contains about twice the number of chromosomes compared with its relatives in the wild. The industry now knows the modern-day peanut originated in a rare, natural crossing of genomes from two wild peanut species about 10,000 years ago in the foothills of the Andes.

The U.S. Peanut Belt comprises the major peanut producing states. They grow nearly all the U. S. peanut crop. If their goal was to rule the free world, peanut farmers made significant progress in 1977 when Georgia favorite son and peanut farmer Jimmy Carter ascended to the U.S. presidency. If you don't count cattle herds owned by Theodore Roosevelt and Lyndon Johnson, Carter was one of few presidents since the close of the 18th century to have been born into farming. Harry Truman and Abraham Lincoln were the two others.

* * *

Peanut butter accounts for about half of the U.S. edible use of peanuts. The other half is divided equally between snack nuts and confectionery. Cotton is the peanut's rotation partner of choice in the heavy production areas of the belt.

In 2014, Georgia grew 46 percent of all U.S. peanuts,

followed by Florida (13 percent), Alabama (11 percent), Texas (9 percent), South Carolina (8 percent) and North Carolina (7 percent). Unlike other countries where peanuts are turned into oil, cake and meal, the primary market for U.S. peanuts is in edible consumption, according to the American Peanut Council. Only about 15 percent of U.S. production is typically crushed for oil. The peanut crop is the 12th most valuable cash crop grown in the United States with a farm value of well over $1 billion.

"If a grower plants the same crop in the same field over and over, the pathogens – often molds, fungi and nematodes – become problematic," said Bob Kemerait (pronounced with Southern vowel breaks as KIM-reyt – the first "e" turns to short "i" and the second "e" disappears altogether). He is a professor of plant pathology at the University of Georgia, Tifton, campus. Nematodes are a type of ubiquitous worm that can't normally be seen with the naked eye. They exist in every continent and climate and can inflict heavy damage to crops costing untold billions of dollars. When it comes to identifying the many vile afflictions to which the peanut plant is subject, Kemerait, a bull-necked man with vise-grip hands attached to a football lineman's wrists and muscular forearms, repeats the medical doctor's dictum to his students, that when they hear hoofbeats, they should think horses, not zebras. He does caution, though, that if they don't consider zebras, they'll miss some very interesting diagnoses.

A constant threat to peanuts is white mold and leaf spot. Both are caused by fungi. There's also target spot, areolate mildew, boll rot, peanut rust and northern corn leaf spot. Growers spend millions combating these diseases. It's often an interaction of the wet years and the amount of disease that was already present from previous years, said Kemerait, a graduate of the University of Florida who's worked with indigenous peanut farmers in Guyana, and small-scale farmers in Haiti and the Philippines.

Peanuts are generally rotated with cotton, since peanuts, unlike cotton, aren't affected by the Southern root-knot nematode and will reduce future damage to the cotton crop. "One of the main reasons we rotate peanuts and cotton is they both attract a nematode, but it's a different nematode. One doesn't affect the other," said Glen Harris, a soil and fertility specialist with UGA Tifton. "If you plant cotton after cotton after cotton, you build up a nematode problem. You throw peanuts in there, it knocks them back for at least a year."

Crop rotation benefits the soil, too. If a crop is re-planted, the same nutrients and minerals in the soil are consumed. "If you continually grow peanuts, which have a high calcium requirement, you're going to continuously be pulling a lot of calcium out of the soil. If you put in corn, which doesn't have as high a calcium requirement, it's not going to be removing calcium as quickly from the soil and you have a chance to replenish and recycle some calcium into the system when you leave the residues there," said Scott Tubbs, a UGA peanut systems agronomist. Peanuts, like soybean, alfalfa and clover, are so-called nitrogen-fixing, which means they improve the soil by taking nitrogen from the air and adding it to the soil when the plant dies.

World peanut production – peanuts are classified as "groundnuts" in U.N.-speak – totaled about 36 million metric tons in 2016 with China producing 46 percent of the global supply, India at 19 percent, and Nigeria at 8 percent. The United States is the world's fourth-largest producer at 7 percent with about 3 percent of the world's peanut acreage. Argentina, Brazil, Malawi, Senegal, South Africa and Sudan account for the remainder of the world's peanut production.

Worldwide peanut exports are about 1.25 million metric

tons, according to the National Peanut Board, an organization sponsored by the Agriculture Department to help market U.S. peanuts. The United States is a leading peanut exporter, with average annual exports of between 200,000 and 250,000 metric tons. Canada, Mexico, Europe and Japan account for more than 80 percent of U.S. peanut exports. The largest export market for U.S. peanuts in 2010, the most recent year for which data was available, was Canada, which purchased peanuts valued at more than $80 million, followed by Mexico, which purchased peanuts valued at more than $54 million.

The U.S. peanut program, as laid out in the 2014 farm bill, was nothing short of inspired if you were a peanut farmer. It led to substantial increases in direct subsidy payments to about 6,500 farm businesses that have averaged over $800 million a year since 2015, expanding domestic peanut production and increasing U.S. exports, creating the potential of otherwise unnecessary trade disputes, reports the American Enterprise Institute, a nonpartisan public policy group.

The peanut lobby's acumen for obtaining government aid is evidenced by the average annual payment of over $340 an acre being extricated from the pocket of the U.S. taxpayer between 2014 and 2016. That number is legendary. The payments almost matched revenues from the sale of peanuts in the market, reported the conservative think tank. No other grower category, says the group, not producers of rice, corn, wheat or any other commodity, came close to receiving such levels of government subsidies for a single crop. Although the farmers of the Peanut Belt may have a reputation for being thick as thieves, at least in the eyes of the American Enterprise Institute, they're breaking no laws. They're doing what the system incentivizes them to do.

According to data released by the National Agricultural Statistics Service, total U.S. peanut consumption has risen from more than 720 million pounds in 1994 to about 1.3 billion pounds in 2016. The Southeast FarmPress reported that U.S. peanut farmers had produced a total of 3.52 million tons of farmer stock peanuts in 2017, the highest ever in single a season based on data going back as far as 1909. Individually, farmers are yielding an average of 4,176 pounds per acre, the second-highest yield and only slightly less than the record set in 2012. Peanut production jumped 30 percent to 7.2 billion pounds, reported the Agriculture Department. "The U.S. peanut market will carry out from the 2017 crop and into the 2018 season an oversupply of about 1.28 million farmer stock tons, one of the largest carry-out supplies ever," U.S.D.A. National Peanut Research Laboratory Technologist Marshall Lamb said in a 2018 interview with the Southeast Farm Press.

Like the "more cowbell" pop culture touch point, if more peanuts is the desired goal, the subsidies appear to be working.

Chapter Seventeen

Jacked Crustaceans

A BIG ATTRACTION of shrimp in the United States is its aspirational quality. People aspire to eat more of it. Shrimp references are reported to be way up in rap songs, a sign of those aspirational qualities. Consider the following lyric from rapper Drake's conceptual track "305 to my City":

"Tonight was your night, go get you some lobsters and shrimp … You smart and you know it, I get it, I get it you outdo these pimps."

It is unlikely any "pimps" were ever "outdone" by such humdrum protein sources as pork chops or Salsbury steak. And Americans have clearly stepped up their game. Of the 15.5 pounds of seafood each man, woman and child in the United States ate in 2015, about 4 pounds of it was shrimp, which is now more popular in the United States than tuna, according to the National Marine Fisheries Service. In the 1970s, shrimp was mostly reserved for fine valet-parked restaurants with table captains in mess jackets, crimson trousers, sleeve braids and lapels with gold piping. Today, shrimp has become so plentiful that we expect to find it as a protein option at Popeye's or in a fast-food burrito or in a honey-garlic sriracha shrimp bowl in the frozen-dinner aisle of a supermarket. Americans are eating twice the amount of shrimp they ate in 1985. (A corollary to this is that Americans are now eating less than half the fish sticks they ate that year – just three-quarters of a pound per capita per year – according to the Marine Fisheries Service.)

Marine shrimp farming began to take shape in the 1970s. Prior to that, less than one percent of the world's shrimp was farm-raised. One reason: Prior to the 1980s, shrimp farmers hadn't been able to coax shrimp to reproduce in captivity. Aquaculture at the time relied solely on eggs recovered from wild-caught shrimp – it still does in parts of the world – and the tank-raised crustaceans of the day were highly susceptible to viruses. Also, little was known at the time about how salinity affected growth.

Most shrimp imported into the United States are now farmed in large tanks or in man-made ponds covering terrific expanses of land. The crustaceans are fed commercially produced feed pellets that are sometimes laced with antibiotics. But global shrimp farming has emerged as a source of concern that goes beyond food safety. A thick residue of chemicals, waste and uneaten feed pellets can build up in tanks. This sludge is sometimes released into nearby streams and rivers, causing environmental damage.

"Bacteria and algae can begin to grow and disease can set in, prompting farmers to use drugs and other chemicals that can remain on the shrimp and seep into the surrounding environment," Urvashi Rangan, Ph.D., executive director of the Consumer Reports Food Safety and Sustainability Center, wrote in a 2015 report.

There is now extensive commercialization and an increased consumption rate of aquacultured seafood. By 2014, more than 90 percent of the seafood consumed in the United States was imported from about 140 countries, according to the U.S. National Marine Fisheries Service. To sate our boundless appetite for the arthropod, the United States has become an enormous importer: About 94 percent of shrimp consumed by Americans comes from countries like Indonesia, India, Malaysia and Thailand.

"Import pricing (dumping) collapsed the U.S. fishery. Shrimp fishing in the Gulf of Mexico is now approximately 70 percent less than the 2001 to 2003 baseline level," reported the Tarpon Springs, Florida-based Southern Shrimp Alliance. Yet, shrimp remains the most valuable fishery in the Gulf, according to the group, and it's in the top three nationally in any given year. The industry represents a significant component of the coastal economies of eight U.S. states. The United States imposed anti-dumping duties on six nations in 2005.

With the growth in world shrimp aquaculture in recent decades, disease has caused substantial economic losses. The first big virus to hit the commercial shrimp industry was IHHNV, also named Penaeus stylirostris densovirus. It was first reported in blue shrimp from Hawaii in 1980. To date, more than twenty viral diseases have been reported that affect shrimp and prawns. This has given rise to aquaculture's growing dependence on antibiotics, which, to say the least, is controversial. In 2017, the industry used considerable antibiotics and antimicrobials. Antibiotics are considered an easy fix for promoting growth and well-being in shrimp aquaculture; barring government bans, farmers will continue to use – and overuse – antibiotics. "The penetration of antibiotics through the food chain is a big problem," Dr. Martin Blaser, a professor of microbiology and an infectious diseases physician at New York University Langone Medical

Center, told Bloomberg in a piece of devastating journalism by Jason Gale, Lydia Mulvany and Monte Reel.

Research has found that as much as 90 percent of the antibiotics given to pigs pass undegraded through their urine and feces. This has a direct effect on fish farmed in China, reported Bloomberg. Antibiotic-laced fish ponds drain into canals that empty into the Pearl River estuary. The estuary receives 193 metric tons of antibiotics a year, Chinese scientists estimated in 2013.

The dependence on antibiotics in aquaculture – especially in Asia – has led to the emergence of superbugs, bacteria that are highly resistant to antibiotics. It is thought about 90 percent of bacteria from seawater are resistant to at least one antibiotic type and up to 20 percent are resistant to at least five antibiotics. The U.K. government estimates that about 700,000 people die annually from antibiotic-resistant infections worldwide. It projects that number will explode to 10 million a year by 2050.

Knowing where shrimp is coming from and what's being done to it before it reaches U.S. tables is problematic. Seafood in general has been permeated by fraud and deception. Of seafood bought and laboratory-tested in 12 parts of the United States, the findings of a 2013 study were dismal. In the 120 samples of fish labeled "red snapper," 28 different species of fish were found, including 17 that were not even in the snapper family, according to the study by the nonprofit ocean protection group Oceana. It also contained surprises about where consumers were most likely to be defrauded. Sushi restaurants topped the list in every city studied. Grocery stores were most likely to be selling fish honestly. Restaurants overall ranked in the middle.

Almost two-thirds of the wild salmon samples, according to Oceana's finding, were discovered to be farmed salmon.

Some consumers seek out wild salmon because it tends to be higher in minerals like potassium, zinc and iron. The interaction between aquaculture and the world's oceans is illustrated in a 2017 salmon spill in which a pen near Washington's Cypress Island collapsed, releasing tens of thousands of non-native Atlantic salmon into the Pacific Ocean in Puget Sound, reported the High Country News in early 2018. The coastal Swinomish, Samish and Lummi tribes asked tribal fishermen to capture the non-native species, which they feared could imperil the native salmon. A state of emergency was declared and more than 43,500 of an estimated 160,000 escapees were caught. The Lummi Nation protects the native salmon runs, as they play a critical role in the tribe's economy. Now, it's dealing with the ecological and political fallout of one of the region's largest salmon spills. As of this writing in March 2018, it was unclear what damage – if any – the spill had had on native species.

Cooke Aquaculture told the press the recaptured Atlantic salmon had empty stomachs, implying they hadn't competed with the native fish for food. Also, the spilled Atlantic salmon weren't sexually mature, so they hadn't bred with native stocks. But biologists and members of the Lummi Nation worried about one more troubling possibility: Canadian studies show that farmed salmon have harmed wild and hatchery salmon by spreading sea lice and viruses. Sea lice have been plaguing salmon fisheries and the aquaculture of salmon with increasing intensity, as the small marine parasite flourishes in salmon farms. Some salmon farmers have reported large numbers of salmon dying due to the infestation. The planktonic sea louse is a parasitic creature and just a few can kill a healthy fish. Some farmers are experimenting with lasers to kill the parasite.

The Washington Commissioner of Public Lands Hilary

Franz has since terminated Cooke Aquaculture's lease to operate Atlantic salmon farms at the site, where a second fish farm was recently at risk of collapse.

The $90 billion aquaculture trade accounts for almost half of all seafood harvested or caught, according to the United Nations. China supplies nearly 60 percent of the global total and is the world's biggest exporter. U.S. food regulators have known about the country's antibiotic problem for more than a decade. The European Union threatened to ban imports of Indian shrimp, saying Indian aquaculture's compliance with limits on antibiotic use was also insufficient.

In 2015, the retailer Costco elected to focus on its sale of antibiotic-free Norwegian salmon over Chilean salmon. Marine Harvest became the first company in Chile's forested Los Lagos region to obtain an antibiotic-free certification for one of its Atlantic salmon farms. A Chilean official characterized this as a milestone in aquaculture.

Seafoodnews.com reported the FDA had rejected about twice the amount of imported shrimp during the first three quarters of 2015 compared with rejections during the same period the year before. The top violator was Malaysia. The following year, Bloomberg reported Chinese pass-throughs – called "transshipments" – via Malaysia were resulting in antibiotic-tainted seafood winding up on U.S. tables under the guise of being a product of Malaysia instead of China.

Chinese companies, the article claimed, had managed to import tens of millions of dollars of shrimp into the United States using forged records and exploiting lax oversight in China. In April 2016, the U.S. Food and Drug Administration issued Import Alert 16-136, directing district offices to detain and test shrimp and prawns from peninsular Malaysia for residues of unapproved animal drugs and unsafe chemicals that may have an adverse effect on human health.

The drugs being tested for were nitrofurans and chloramphenicol, both antibiotics and both carcinogens. Also, according to the FDA, both can contribute to the emergence of antimicrobial resistance in bacteria, reducing the effectiveness of these antimicrobial drugs vital for treatment of human disease. From October 2014 to September 2015, the FDA sampled and tested 138 shrimp shipments from Peninsular Malaysia. Of those, 32 percent tested positive for the presence of antibiotic residues.

Besides nitrofurans and chloramphenicol, residues from other antibiotics were found, including those from tetracycline, sulfonamides and streptomycin. Tainted shrimp is likely to be slipping through due to inadequate enforcement.

"The FDA simply isn't testing enough on the imported market to really find all of the violating residues, Rangan of Consumer Reports told Al Jazeera. Of the 205 imported farmed samples we found, 11 of those had illegal residues of antibiotics on them. The fact that the FDA only tests 0.7 percent of all the shrimp in this country for those antibiotic residues suggests that the agency is not actually testing enough shrimp to catch the amount of illegal residue products that are coming into the market," she told Al Jazeera.

"When you feed low levels of antibiotics every day, you're not feeding them enough to necessarily kill bacteria. Those bacteria become resistant to those antibiotics and that can make those antibiotics less effective in people if we are infected by those bacteria. We found about a third of the shrimp [tested] had vibrio contamination – vibrio is one of the few food-borne illnesses on the rise. Seven percent of the samples had MRSA," said Rangan. MRSA is a Methicillin-resistant Staphylococcus aureus infection caused by a type of staph bacteria that's become resistant to many of the antibiotics used to treat ordinary staph infections, according to the Mayo Clinic.

"Shrimp farm unit production costs were dramatically reduced through use of veterinary drugs – antibiotics and perhaps fungicides – banned for human consumption by the FDA," reads a statement by the Southern Shrimp Alliance. "Their use allows for very high stocking densities and disease prevention. Direct human health threats include aplastic anemia and cancer. Indirect threats include antibiotic resistance – evolution of superbugs."

The Malaysia Ministry of Health made assurances it would confront the transshipment issue head-on with better regulation of the country's processers. It vowed to take over the authority of issuing certificates of origin. In the past, chambers of commerce have been accused of rubber-stamping certificates.

China tends to ramp up its stocked inventory for Chinese lunar new year. Leading up to the holiday each year, the global market is thrust into a frenzy as wholesalers stock up on the farmed shrimp but worry about overpaying. The site Alibaba reports a 300 percent surge in consumption of fresh food, especially imported seafood, during this holiday. Chinese consumers seek out Chilean king crab, Boston lobster, fish from New Zealand, Canadian prawns and Vietnamese black tiger shrimps, as statistics from Alibaba's T-mall show.

China's domestic seafood supply is set to stagnate while demand for seafood continues to rise. Senior Analyst Gorjan Nikolik of the Dutch bank Rabobank specializes in the global seafood sector. "China will strongly influence the global seafood industry for at least the next decade," he said. "China is the leading seafood nation, with the highest consumption, production and export rates."

As more Chinese consumers penetrate the ranks of the middle class, they tend to switch seafood species from freshwater varieties like carp to ocean species, like saltwater crustaceans, many of which are imported. Sundry crackdowns on the so-called gray trade add to market volatility. At the close of 2017, a crackdown by the Chinese government roiled markets as seafood was found to have been shipped to Haiphong in Vietnam, then smuggled into China to avoid duties.

Based on an analysis of global trade data and industry sources by the publication Undercurrent News, smuggling is the main driver of Vietnam's increase in seafood imports from $25 million in 2001 to over $5 billion in 2016; an average growth rate of 42 percent a year each year for 15 straight years is unmatched by any other nation. The growth totals 9,000 percent for the decade-and-a-half period.

Japan once dictated the shrimp market; then it was the United States. Now Chinese consumption is dictating market terms. The Chinese market is considered something of a free-for-all, since there are no certification requirements and the product standards are loose. Production in China is driven mainly by the country's live market; it's expected to increase.

A microcosm in the global frenzy for shrimp is tiny Ecuador. It is the world's third-largest producer of white-leg shrimp. It focuses on the export of head-on shell-on shrimp instead of peeled shrimp, and its producers have become highly dependent on China. In 2017, China accounted for 55 percent of Ecuador's exports. Ecuadoran shrimp is viewed as a premium product by the Chinese restaurant sector. According to the Seafood Trade Intelligence Portal, Ecuador increased it shrimp production from 260,000 metric tons to about 420,000 tons in 2017. It is believed much of the shrimp from Ecuador goes into Vietnam, then is smuggled into China through the gray market.

* * *

Under the best of circumstances, life has never been easy for small farmers in the coastal district of Khulna in Bangladesh. It is now the heartland of the shrimp-farming monocrop. Farmers once grew fruit and vegetables or raised livestock and poultry here. Many now raise prawns.

A gold-rush mentality caused many to strike a Faustian bargain to convert their farm fields to shrimp ponds. The shrimp ponds literally sow the earth with salt. It ruins it for agriculture. There was a reason the Romans salted the soils of Carthage. Salt not only penetrates the soil, but it leaches into groundwater and adjacent lands. Once the ponds are dug, the land can't accommodate vegetables or livestock for at least five years after all aquaculture ceases. In the shrimp-farming regions of Bangladesh, salinity creeps ever-further inland as more farmland is poured into the gullet of the beast. An upriver dam throttles the fresh water supply to the area, adding to the saltwater leaching problem.

Although there are 81 prawn hatcheries in Bangladesh, a lack of technical knowledge, inadequate skilled manpower and an insufficient supply of wild broods have limited hatchery production, according to a 2010 paper by Nesar Ahmed, Department of Fisheries Management, Bangladesh Agricultural University; and Max Troell of the Beijer Institute of Ecological Economics, Royal Swedish Academy of Sciences. Many thousands of landless poor and unemployed are engaged in "fishing" for wild prawn larvae along the coastline during a few months each year. When peasants are mobilized and paid piecemeal to target a specific species, bad things tend to happen (see the Chinese campaign to eradicate the Eurasian sparrow).

To get at the larvae, peasants crawl around in muddy river inlets and drag fine mesh screens attached to box frames.

To get one shrimp larva, an average of 50 juvenile fish and crustaceans of other species are killed, according to the Swedish Society for Nature Conservation. The Bangladeshi government has imposed restrictions on larvae collection, but the ban, according to researchers Ahmed and Troell, hasn't been adequately enforced. The practice has decimated biodiversity in Khulna. Instead of simply tending to their farm fields as they once had, local peasants are invading riverine environments and destroying ecosystems far from their farms.

These days, the children of Khulna now eat mostly starches like potatoes, rice and lentils. They no longer get nutrients from green vegetables, milk or eggs. They're growing up with permanent vitamin deficiencies. According to a national rickets survey, the condition is way up in children from the highly saline areas compared with other areas. No farmer can afford to reclaim his farm fields by fallowing his land for five years, so the beast grows.

By late 2017, rejections of antibiotic-contaminated imported shrimp made up nearly one-quarter of the FDA's seafood entry line refusals, according to the Southern Shrimp Alliance. The group has been vocal on the use of banned substances by companies selling shrimp into U.S. markets. Over three weeks in September 2017, a Venezuelan company had one entry line refused, a company from Vietnam had two entry lines refused and a single Chinese company had fourteen entry lines refused, all for shrimp contaminated with veterinary drug residues, according to the group. The FDA also issued a public notice of additional seafood entry line refusals in the month of August, including the identification of two more entry lines of Vietnamese shrimp refused for reasons related to banned antibiotics. Shrimp lines contaminated with banned antibiotics that were rejected in August came from China, Hong Kong and Vietnam.

Through the first three quarters of 2017, the FDA had reported refusing 67 entry lines of shrimp for reasons related to banned antibiotics. As bleak as it sounds, this was substantially below the refusal levels reported in 2014, 2015, and 2016. All the while, anti-dumping duties remained in place for five nations; Brazil, China, India, Thailand and Vietnam, according the Southern Shrimp Alliance.

* * *

About 75 miles northwest of Indianapolis lies Fowler, Indiana, population 2,265. Before RDM Aquaculture came along, Fowler was best known as the birthplace of slugologist Otis "Ote" Johnson of baseball's 1911 New York Highlanders of the American league. Off East State Road 18, a two-lane road that runs through town, is RDM, otherwise known as Karlanea and Darryl Brown's farm. For almost eight years, the Browns have raised Pacific white shrimp in tanks connected to a tangle of PVC pipes and tubing. Their pioneering spirit won them the 2015 Indiana Innovation Award. The farm uses no antibiotics or hormones. It started in 2010 when it received its first batch of post larval shrimp. At the time, it was one of just three privately owned shrimp farms in the United States. It grew to six production and two nursery tanks and began with a 40 percent survival rate. It now has 36 tanks total and has consistently maintained 70 percent to 90 percent survival rates.

The couple had experimented with farming tilapia but dreamt of shrimp aquaculture. With $500,000 from an inheritance, they purchased a six-tank system. It was tough at first. They purchased post-larval shrimp from a Florida hatchery. They lost the entirety of their first two batches and three-quarters of their third batch when pump and filtration systems failed and a storm caused a power outage.

They don't see themselves as shrimp farmers but meticulous guardians of water. They believe that if they mind the water characteristics, the shrimp farming will take care of itself. RDM does nine tests on its water every day. It tests the water for temperature, dissolved oxygen, nitrites, CO_2, salinity, alkalinity, pH, ammonia and floc. The farm is a closed-loop system, and there is essentially no discharge, which means lower costs of replenishing water and salts. The couple has designed their own system using regenerative blowers to pump air from outside. They add only fish food, salt and baking soda to their water. The closed-loop system works like this: The shrimp eat the feed and excrete ammonia. Bacteria turns that into toxic nitrites. Other bacteria turn the nitrites into benign nitrates. Aeration dissipates the nitrates as a harmless gas. The Browns share what they've learned.

"I get asked all the time: Why are you helping set other farmers up?" Karlanea Brown told the Chicago Tribune in 2018. "I'm not naive enough to think that I can produce all the shrimp in the U.S. I need help. With all the shrimp farmers coming up, a lot of people are worried about another shrimp farmer close by. They don't understand, you can't supply the whole market. I don't care how large you are." The company is diversifying into saltwater aquaponics and raising Australian Red Claw Crayfish. It also has oysters and a fresh water aquaponics system on the horizon. It has helped set up farms from Peru to the Ukraine.

David Love, a microbiologist at Johns Hopkins University is the *éminence grise* of shrimp aquaculture research. He lavished rare praise on RDM's practices but questioned whether they would be able to make it work in the long term due to costs. It's hard not to pull for them.

Epilogue

The many forces buffeting salty snacks, the guacamole bowl, the suds, the voodoo-blackened buffalo wings, the tequila, the limes, the shrimp platter – the entire party spread – are so whipsawed, so conflicted, so contradictory, so incongruent and sometimes so subtly awful that it feels like not much can be done to comprehend, let alone secure, these markets. But reform is possible; there are many roads that lead to Damascus.

Free-traders envisage a utopia of pristine markets in which nations grow the commodities they are best-suited to grow and then trade with other nations who, in turn, grow crops *they* are best-suited to grow. But globalization wrongly assumes a Western-style rules-based system. In practice, the prevailing country is the one that can cut costs most ruthlessly; manipulate its currency most effectively; use whatever pesticides, herbicides and antibiotics that might be most effective whatever the long-term cost; and even leverage conscripted labor. The playing field is never level, and the differences can be skillfully gamed by growers in individual countries.

In globalized ag markets, countries with overlapping

government power structures – those with federal, state, county and municipal governments – will compete at a disadvantage to countries with strong centralized governments, tilting the playing field.

Another enormous problem is the government handout – farmers receiving wads of cash from their governments to grow favored crops, produce favored dairy products or raise favored hooved animals. In the United States, successive farm bills over decades have been a boon to grain, wheat, cotton, rice, oilseed and peanut farmers. A menu of expected subsidies has evolved and shaped markets. Trimming or eliminating one subsidy has often resulted in funding for other programs swelling in a costly game of Whac-a-Mole.

In America, the federal government is picking winners and losers as never before. Sops to farmers lead to monocrops, stifle innovation and erode Americans' diets. However well-meaning or effective farm subsidies are when they're first established, they tend to long outlive the problems they were created to remedy. It's an inherent problem with government.

And then there is the government's acceptance – even promotion – of consolidation in agriculture. A tremendous concentration of ownership has formed under the noses of the U.S. Departments of Justice and Agriculture. It is shocking and un-American.

Finally, state governments are sticking a separate pitchfork into ag. The negative-multiplier effects hard-wired into the regulatory state are doing to ag what they've done for housing in these same states. They are adding directly and indirectly to what farmers pay for fertilizer, fuel, seeds and land; labor cost and benefit edicts demonstrate that no effort has been made to understand life on the farm patch, let alone the effects of state-level taxes and regulations on the national diet. For one, it has farmers pushing into crops that can be mechanically harvested. Freed of inconvenient workers, the surviving growers get bigger and widen their embrace of the demon spawn – the monocrop. The insidious cost spiral often knocks small farmers out of farming completely. Western ag states, after having replaced much messy manufacturing with service industries, may one day look to gorge themselves on the juicy white meat of farming, too, with its unpopular smells, clutter and pesky need for water. The result? More bedroom communities, more premium ag land paved over, more irrigation water used to flush toilets in Los Angeles and San Francisco, and less food security for the nation.

But there is one ray of hope for those humans who seek a varied diet and don't believe production of the nation's fruits and vegetables should be offshored or reserved for only those who can afford to shop at the most fashionable grocery parlors. The regulatory state has been like crack cocaine to roboticists. Engineering companies like Abundant Robotics in Hayward, California, and Israel-based FFRobotics are poised to take off. We can hope their products are soon within financial reach of the nation's long-suffering carrot, broccoli, parsnip, squash, cherry, apricot, onion, peach, apple and berry farmers. If not, farmers won't grow hand-harvested produce in America, and our diets will contain even more carbs and more cheap proteins. Here are a few strategies that will help:

1. Break up, uncouple, diversify

Government is failing at one of its most basic responsibilities in a free-market economy. The Agriculture and Justice departments have sat idly by while an enormous consolidation of economic power has formed across all food and ag segments in the United States. It's ghastly. It has suppressed experimentation and entrepreneurship and lobotomized the marketplace of ideas. It's not America's duty to martyr its free-market system to keep the world's growing middle class in cheap protein. The United States isn't a planet. It's a country.

The concentration of power is affecting what crops are planted and what foods are available to American consumers. The resulting corporate giants are now throwing their weight around. Some threaten small farms with lawsuits when they choose not to use patented GMO seeds and the GMO seeds from nearby farms contaminate their fields. Companies that provide seed separation services are getting hounded out of business. Oftentimes the big seed-chemical companies know they can't win in court but can force a small farmer to submit with the mere threat of a costly lawsuit.

In his 2016 book "Concentration and Power in the Food System: Who Controls What We Eat?" Michigan State University professor Phil H. Howard dissects the consolidation and what it's doing on all levels of the food supply chain. "At almost every key stage of the food system," said Howard, "[consolidation has meant that] companies have the power to drive up prices for consumers and reduce their rate of innovation. These trends are often hidden from most of us – and even from people who work in these industries." It's gotten worse since Howard's book was published. In May 2017, ChemChina merged with the Swiss chemical and seed company Syngenta. Four months later, Dow Chemical completed its merger with DuPont; In June 2018, Bayer completed its $66 billion purchase of Monsanto, creating the largest seed and agrochemical company in the world. The new companies will promote agriculture based on the beneficial interaction of their patented chemicals and seeds.

In the grain market, the so-called "ABCDs"— ADM, Bunge, Cargill and Dreyfus control, by some estimates, 90 percent of the global grain market. Now, according to analysts, ADM may be making a play for Bunge. This consolidation is dangerous and needs to be reversed.

2. Recognize Ag as a net victim of climate change

Over time, climate change will throttle crop yields – some models show grain and corn yields decreasing by half over the next 35 years. Meanwhile, the global population steadily rises. Today it is 7.5 billion. It's expected to reach 8.5 billion in 2030, 9.7 billion in 2050 and 11.2 billion in 2100, according to the United Nations Department of Economic and Social Affairs. The science may not be settled, but farmers, who aren't strangers to preparing for adversity, should take note.

The American small farmer is the quintessential conservationist. The farmer fears drought. He has a special interest in recharging aquifers. Any farmer in the game for more than one generation is vested in the sustainability of the land. They worry about the 1.7 billion tons of topsoil being blown or washed off U.S. croplands each year. Government should not vilify agriculture or take its bounties for granted.

U.S. cattle, sheep and goats represent a corner of the ag world that creates methane gas. The beasts also create nitrates that can seep into groundwater. Hog farming generates lagoons filled with bacterial nasties. Each year, tens of millions of people worldwide are joining the ranks of the middle class and can fill their diets with more and better animal proteins. But it's not America's duty to pollute its groundwater with nitrates to produce cheap protein for the planet. It's our country and we should have a say in how its resources are used and maintained. The electorate has been asleep at the switch. But penalizing small farmers for climate change will cause more farm failures and further consolidation. Agriculture isn't a net cause of climate change but a net victim.

3. Reform the farm bill as we know it

The farm bill's exploitation of the American taxpayer has
become so ghastly, so absurd, so breathtakingly awful, so
surreal, so unctuous that a ray of hope consists only in Senator
Grassley telling the think tank Heritage Foundation in the
lead-up to the 2018 farm bill that he didn't believe subsidies
for farmers should be unlimited. (Grassley's mere mention
that subsidies *could* be unlimited was a surreal indication of a
New Deal program gone mad.)

But the farm-patch politician took his comments a step
further. "Why can't we require farmers who collect huge sums
of money from the government to actually *work* on the farm?"
pondered Grassley, who was promoting a hard cap of
$125,000 per person in annual payments and limiting
payments to farmers, their spouses, and one manager per
farm, regardless of size. One can imagine Grassley explaining
these handouts to nonfarmers in his state – welders,
accountants, first officers aboard merchant ships, mail
carriers. How can they and their spouses qualify for even the
paltry $125,000-per-person benefit?

There are also many arrows in the ag welfare quiver.
Seventy-five years after the end of the Great Depression,
Congress finally got around to closing the book on the direct-
payments program with the 2014 farm bill. It's a testament to
the stickiness of big entitlement programs once they build a
head of steam. Federal programs seldom go quietly into that
good night simply because they are no longer useful or the
problem they were created to solve no longer exists. Farms
reaped hundreds of billions of dollars since the end of the
Great Depression, even if they didn't plant a single seed.

If the direct-payments program stays dead, there are still
counter-cyclical payments to grain, wheat, cotton, rice, oilseed
and peanut farmers – a program based on targets that can get

growers to chase subsidies rather than market prices. There is the Average Crop Revenue Election program with a $65,000 per person limit, crop insurance covering 100 different commodities (with taxpayers footing much of the premium cost), direct loans and loan guarantees, along with special disaster assistance. The subsidies aren't only cherished by the big-ticket commodity farmers but seen as a birthright. Farm Belt politicians love to point to them to curry favor with – and donations from – their constituents. Conservatives, Libertarians and free-marketeers loathe these payments. Average Americans would, too, if they were aware of the scope. Data show the payments go overwhelmingly to the largest operations, and they feed monocrops. Overlapping programs often results in farmers being paid twice.

During the 1970s, Farm Belt lawmakers formed an unholy alliance with their counterparts from America's inner-cities. The urban politicians promoted big payments to farmers while the Farm Belt politicians pushed for more food stamps and subsidized school lunches for the inner-city districts. The two groups – with plenty of special-interest backing – have pushed back against every effort to reform the farm bill and separate the two programs. The food stamp program – rebranded the "Supplemental Nutrition Assistance Program," or "SNAP" – and nutrition programs account for around 80 percent of the modern farm bill. The goal of SNAP, which requires a permanent underclass to receive the aid, isn't to wean people off public assistance or make people more self-sufficient over time – indeed, the percentage of recipients has increased since 1976 – but to provide cover for sumptuous welfare payments to agriculture. The big players then pump money back into lobbying efforts to keep the thing going until the next farm bill.

Typifying non-Farm Belt politicians who help normalize

SNAP dependency, dangling the program as catnip to cash-poor but vote-rich constituents, is 24-year-old Andy X. Vargas, a Democratic member of the Massachusetts House of Representatives. He's young but he's learning the playbook quickly. The seat of his 3rd District in Essex County is the city of Haverhill, population 63,000. Clustered mostly in the city's "numbered" streets – a low-rent grid peppered with junk cars, burglar bars and broken glass – about 15 percent of the city's residents are on SNAP. While Congress goes through the bidecenial Gilbert and Sullivan comic opera of debating cuts to the 2018 farm bill, progressive officeholders in the Bay State like Vargas prepare to brandish the artfully contrived results. Innocent of the long-term conceptual thinking required to get people *off* SNAP, they participate in a feel-good event called the "SNAP Challenge." (While Vargas is a state legislator and the farm bill is a federal affair, he still epitomizes the type of urban politician who derives a benefit from SNAP.) The challenge was to buy healthy food while spending just $4.56 per person a day — that's the average amount received per person from SNAP. "It was exhausting," nutritionist Adriene Worthington, who just barely succeeded in meeting the challenge's requirements, told the Boston Herald. "I can't imagine trying to do that, at that level, with children or with an older parent," she said.

"As a legislator, I always try to best understand the lives that my constituents live," said Vargas. "In this scenario, I get to walk a week in the shoes of those 9,685 constituents of mine." If Vargas had truly walked in their shoes, he'd have quickly learned that the roughly 15 percent of Haverhill residents who receive SNAP assistance are statistically most likely to spend 20 percent of their month's allotment on sweetened beverages, desserts, salty snacks, candy and sugar. Of those snacks, desserts and elixirs, the top subcategory, according to a study commissioned by the Agriculture Department, was "sweetened beverages," which includes soft drinks, fruit juices, energy drinks and sweetened teas. "In this sense, SNAP is a multibillion-dollar taxpayer subsidy of the soda industry," Marion Nestle, a professor of nutrition, food studies and public health at New York University told the New York Times in 2017. "It's pretty shocking."

Worse, because SNAP benefits are distributed in a lump sum each month, and because many recipients spend those funds within a week of receiving them, stores have figured out that sales and foot traffic change in predictable ways during those periods. Food companies have learned to time advertisements for sugary drinks to the days states distribute the SNAP benefits. The study relied on 2011 data from the New York State Department of Health. This study, according to the Washington Post, was the first to link food advertising to the timing of the disbursements.

Worse, the SNAP program, which appears to be directly or indirectly underwriting increased junk-food and soda consumption, may be contributing to obesity among America's poor, particularly its minorities. The prevalence of obesity among low-income Hispanic 2- to 4-year-olds was about 17 percent. It was 18 percent among American Indian/Alaska Native children. This was considerably higher than the rate for low-income non-Hispanic whites, who were obese at a rate of 12.2 percent. Whether the SNAP program is making low-income minority kids more obese than their peers is an open question, but it warrants further study. One thing that can be said is kids in all income brackets are heavier in America today than they were in 1960. According to a study by the Centers for Disease Control children aged 6 to 11, with an average weight of almost 74 pounds in 2002, were almost 9 pounds heavier than the same age group in 1960. That held true for teen boys aged 12 to 17. They were heavier by more than 15 pounds. Teen girls in the same age bracket were up about 12 pounds.

Enormous government subsidies for one likely suspect, high-fructose corn syrup, have underwritten many calorie-dense processed foods and drinkable sugar bombs. SNAP money is then used to purchase the foods to complete the loop. In 2017, 43 million people in the United States received SNAP benefits. It was the lowest number since 2010, when 40.3 million people were on food stamps. It peaked in 2013, at 47.6 million. The number dips during economic booms and rises during recessions, but the program, as part of farm bill, depends on the permanent dependence of a large number of Americans. Much is then spent on unhealthy foods.

4. Nurture automation and harness 'big data'

As the bicoastal ag states legislate labor rates that are pricing out domestic vegetable and fruit production, automation may hold the key. Israel-based FFRobotics has developed a robotic fruit harvester – the FFRobot. It is a harvesting platform that emulates the hand-harvesting process. The company says the FFRobot can provide bruise-free automated fruit picking. It is reported to be able to pick 10 times more usable fruit than the average picker in the same time period, all the while collecting and analyzing the fruit picked per tree and per acre.

In 2017, Abundant Robotics received a $10 million investment. The company builds apple-picking robots that could eventually be adapted to harvest other fruits. Its chief executive and co-founder, Dan Steere, told techcrunch.com that his company began working with the apple industry four years earlier to figure out how to automate the cumbersome task of picking apples. "It's very difficult to locate fruit that's ready to be picked within a canopy and then retrieve it without turning it into apple sauce," he said.

Every fall in the United States and Australia, the company's engineers can be seen in orchards conducting field trials and working alongside farmers. The company's robots are designed to work around-the-clock, identifying and picking apples even at night.

A machine being perfected by a Spanish entrepreneur, reports the Wall Street Journal, automates the process of picking small produce like strawberries.

Robotics and automation have also made strides in irrigation. In 2014, the California Department of Food and Agriculture launched the State Water Efficiency and Enhancement Program with the acronym "SWEEP." The state provides grants for irrigation systems that save water.

Seth Rossow is a vegetable farmer in his thirties — significantly below the average age of a farmer in America these days. At his farm outside Merced, he's growing 57 acres of cannery bell peppers and 94 acres of cannery tomatoes. He's also growing 30 acres of organic grain corn. He exhibits a young man's ambition and optimism. His wife, Michelle, walks the fields with him once a week. She, like her husband, is from a farming family.

"You never know the challenges you're going to face in agriculture," he said in the dazzling stillness of his pepper field. "You think we've got a consistent climate here in the San Joaquin Valley, California. In 2015, we planted our bell peppers, the first bell pepper crop we ever had, and a couple of weeks later — it was in May — we got hailed on and almost lost the entire field. A half-mile away, I had tomatoes that didn't even get rained on. Even in the San Joaquin Valley, there are significant differences in weather."

Rossow felt he didn't have the wherewithal for capital improvements like an automated drip irrigation system. With the SWEEP program, he was able to install an automated soil-moisture monitoring system.

"The bell peppers don't like [the heat], especially when they're flowering and trying to set fruit, said Rossow."

SWEEP funded a computer near Rossow's well that will control pressure regulators in his fields. When it's hot, he still has to drag his sprinkler system out. The farm saw three days in a row with highs of 109 degrees.

"One thing we noticed after installing the soil moisture sensors," said Rossow, "was that after 45 minutes to an hour of running our drip tape, water was not going up any more, it was only going down as gravitational forces overwhelmed the capillary reaction of moving water up. So, with installing a computer system, I'm able to pulse-irrigate, pulsing little sets. I'm able to control the moisture and move it up to where I want, to feed the top roots."

Still echoing in Rossow's head is a certain axiom he heard at Cal Poly San Luis Obispo, one of the state's preeminent ag schools: "The best thing the farmer can observe in the field is his own shadow." He's the embodiment of a young man's thirst for experimentation, to harness technological innovations.

If it is encouraged, big data combined with massive new computational power and cloud computing, will create new opportunities for farmers, improve food security and contribute to human health. It will help to analyze climate change, outbreaks of disease and pests, and land degradation. It will usher in an era of smart farming. New sensor technology and the data this provides will lead to unprecedented new decision-making capacity. We're at the cusp of a revolution. In dairy farming, wearables for cows are already telling dairy farmers when animals are in estrus, when they're running a fever and what their activity level is.

On a 1,000-cow dairy farm just south of Sacramento, a generator is masked by a shed. A thick, black plastic barrier is slightly inflated as it is stretched across two acres of manure lagoon, trapping the methane gasses the manure emits. Microbes break down the manure into methane, which is piped to the generator and burned to create electricity. The system is known as a biogas digester. Methane is a more potent greenhouse gas than carbon dioxide and livestock release a lot of it. The Fiscalini Cheese Company near Modesto has a similar digester. "[It's] where we take all the manure and waste from the farm and turn it into electricity," said fourth-generation CEO Brian Fiscalini. "We can fuel our entire farm here. We have enough electricity for our dairy barn, our cheese operation, and enough electricity for an additional 300 homes in the area."

State lawmakers in California, Washington, Oregon and New York are rapidly making production of stone fruit, row crops and dairy unfeasible at any scale. Barring a dramatic rollback of layer upon layer of state regulation and taxation, a tech revolution will need to occur.

5. Redefine globalization

Globalization in its current form has created a world in which America's farmers and merchants must roll in the dirt with the regimes of all manner of murderous plutocrat, blood-caked potentate, capo di tutti capi, maximum leader, caudillo and president for life. Absolute leaders, not surprisingly, can control ag costs absolutely, allowing them to deliver goods into the United States at lower prices. Globalization has brought out the worst in Americans, too. Look no further than Mountain View, California-based Google's confidential plan to develop a censorship engine for China called Dragonfly or its Silicon Valley neighbor Facebook allowing its platform to be co-opted for foreign influence campaigns.

But here's where globalization has helped farmers: "No one country or even one continent has all of the genetic resources necessary to sustain crops at the level that is needed today," said Allan K. Stoner, leader of the ARS Germplasm Laboratory. "Conditions and needs continue to change, and collecting genetic diversity is how you have the resources to deal with them." Only one of 20 major crops worldwide originated in North America: the sunflower. Cultivated sunflowers are today one of the five largest oilseed crops in the world. Strawberries, blueberries, cranberries, forage grasses, pecans, grapes and tepary beans are also indigenous to North America. Those are collected by U.S. and foreign plant breeders. Russian researchers used the U.S. sunflower germplasm to breed the varieties that started the sunflower oil industry. "Our major crops came here from elsewhere," said Stoner. "And when you are looking for genetic diversity, the most important places to look are the centers of origin for crops – that is, the places where they evolved and where people have been cultivating them the longest."

* * *

Some critics propose doing away with the U.S. Department of Agriculture as a cabinet-level entity, since so few Americans today are involved in farming. They say that no American is entitled to a guaranteed income or to have his business guaranteed from failure by the U.S. taxpayer. They contend farming is simply not a great business model.

Small farmers believe they themselves are subsidizing the untenably low produce prices paid by consumers. That's why they must have off-farm jobs to survive. Farmers are good at understanding their own small part of the picture but are too distracted – or too sleep-deprived – to think much about the big picture. They're easily divided and easily conquered. Increasingly, they're no match for the urbanized masses, who expect an abundance of food but are clueless about where it comes from or the sacrifices that must be made to produce it.

Asparagus is labor intensive, because harvesters must work each row repeatedly over a season. A proficient cutter can cover up to 2 acres a day. On each pass, cutters harvest only those spears that are 8 inches to 9 inches long. They must be careful not to damage the plants while they do this. Harvesting asparagus requires skill. Growers typically pay cutters at least a dollar more than Washington State's minimum wage of $11.50, reported the Yakima Herald in 2018. At $12.50, this hourly wage is $2.50 below the $15 benchmark selected by big city labor as the ideal for everyone. This $12.50 is the current "sweet spot" when federal assistance from the current farm bill is factored in. It's the maximum the harvester can achieve based on the market; it's the minimum the grower can get away with paying based on the market. Remove the federal assistance and the wage would need to be lower. Farmers are price takers, not price makers. If they try to raise the price to the grocer, foreign growers – unaffected by high domestic wages – are ready to step in at the lower price. The only option for the farmer is to plant a different crop, fallow his fields or lease or sell his land.

The "fiscal cliff" deal passed by Congress in 2014 included a menu of obscure provisions. One of them extended assistance to asparagus growers. It was part of the farm bill extension included in the package. The farm bill is morphing. Instead of being *merely* an incoherent confusion of make-up payments, patronage, 11th-hour sneak-ins, sops to Farm Belt favorites, nods to the K Street slagheap and pork to excite voters in heavy food-stamp districts and the Heartland, it is becoming a pass-through fund in which residents of fiscally responsible states underwrite losses to farmers under siege by their free-spending progressive state governments on the coasts.

Taxes and edicts mean more carbs for the poor. Two big ag states – California and New York – have passed laws that double the federal minimum wage. Oregon and Washington are well on their way. They now have a tiger by the tail, and it affects the nation's food supply. Obviously, if enhancing economic opportunities or bringing prosperity to the masses were as simple as raising the minimum wage to a specific number, it would have been done long ago. The same holds true for other failed market controls on the historical scrapheap of bad policy decisions.

The federal government sets a national minimum wage of $7.25 per hour as of this writing. Seattle was one of the first cities to more than double it to $15 with a multi-year phase-in period. A 2017 study by researchers at the University of Washington found that the costs to Seattle workers of the increase outweighed the benefits by 3 to 1. The fixation with the jingoistic, one-size-fits-all $15 benchmark hurts the ag world, too, but it's less studied. A working paper released in 2018 by the National Bureau of Economic Research examined employee pay data from 2011 to 2016. It concluded that employers who were forced to raise minimum wages for lower-paid workers also raised the hourly wages of higher-paid workers to maintain parity. It also found evidence that employers who had raised minimum hourly wages also reduced the amount they paid for their employees' health-care benefits to offset the costs.

The co-founder of seven Marmalade Café restaurants told the Los Angeles Business Journal in 2018 that he has reduced hours for his staff, laid off some of his 500 workers and outsourced most of his back-office operations. Two of his restaurants are in Los Angeles, where the minimum wage is rising incrementally each year toward a legislated $15 an hour in 2020. He's now trying to negotiate lower prices with his vendors and suppliers, who've likely also been cost-cutting and de-staffing. A study by Michael Luca at Harvard Business School and Dara Lee Luca at Mathematica Policy Research found that every $1 hike in the minimum wage brings a 14 percent increase in the likelihood of a 3.5-star restaurant on Yelp! closing.

An early adopter of an elevated minimum wage has been San Diego. There voters approved upping the city's minimum wage to $11.50 per hour in 2017 after it had been increased from $8.00 an hour in 2015 – meaning the city imposed a rise in hourly costs of 43 percent in two years. A die-off of mom-and-pop restaurants is now rippling through the city. Stephen Zolezzi, president of the Food and Beverage Association of San Diego County, warned of it in the San Diego Business Journal in 2017. A year later, his divination appeared to be coming true. To name just a few, after 28 years in business, Cafe Japengo in La Jolla went dark in 2018, as did the iconic Nati's Mexican Restaurant in Ocean Beach after nearly 60 years in business. Diners hoisted their last dim sum at one of San Diego's longest-running Chinese restaurants, Emerald Chinese Cuisine, after 26 years in business, while the locally famous Mexican Fiesta in Little Italy closed after 35 years in business. But the apex came when the celebrated Café Chloe in the East Village announced it would be closing down after 14 years in business.

"Stop Killing Chloe's: How California is very knowingly killing the mom and pop restaurant," a headline in the online version of San Diego Magazine howled shortly after the announcement. Economist Lynn Reaser, Ph.D., at Point Loma Nazarene University, found nearly 4,000 San Diego food-service jobs may have been eliminated or failed to be created over a two-year period beginning in 2016. University of Michigan professor Mark J. Perry concluded in 2017 that San Diego was hemorrhaging 200 food-service jobs a week. Restaurants are a canary in the mineshaft for ag.

The big flaw in the push to double the federal minimum wage at the state level is that it rests on the assumption that the typical business owner has an additional $7 or $8 an hour to spend on operating costs for each employee. As simplistic as it sounds, the thinking promoted by labor unions and lawmakers has been that the restaurateur – in fact, every business owner – cruises up to his business from time to time in his Maserati, walks through the place, glad-hands everyone and then drives away to spend his surplus cash. It lacks the humility to recognize that accomplished restaurateurs are successful only *because* they grasp the importance of paying their employees as much they can afford to. If they fail to pay the best people adequately, a rival will snap them up. As it turned out, most restaurateurs in San Diego had no such cushion and couldn't pass on the cost to their price-conscious patrons. The fast-food chains could afford order-taking kiosks, kitchen robotics and creative outsourcing at scale. Four-star restaurants were positioned to pass the costs onto their affluent customers. It's the mom-and-pop restaurants – those that cater to the middle class – that are dying out.

The foodie website Eater recently reported on a trend in high-minimum-wage states like Oregon and California in which the local greasy spoon reopens as a worker-owned restaurant cooperative. Co-op members then share the rewards and risks directly and duck the requirement to pay the bloated minimum wage, since everyone's an owner and no one is an employee. A teenager looking for her first summer job seating tables may be out of luck without a $10,000 partner buy-in. Look for more such job-killing workarounds if models to skirt mandated wages become *de rigueur*. The regulatory state created by the European Union has made wine-growing unfeasible in some of the most fertile grape-producing lands in Baden and the Middle Rhine Valley in Germany. It's become so expensive to hire workers that some growers have abandoned their vines altogether or formed coops.

In Venice, Italy, some restaurants have eliminated their kitchens and serve patrons food produced on an industrial scale elsewhere. In Venice, California, "ghost restaurants," battling high labor and rent costs, have sprung up without dining rooms and only deliver food. Some are transitioning to a counter-service model that eliminates servers. A unique job-killing aspect of the aggressive minimum-wage hikes in California is that the state counts tips as employee income and requires employers to remit an additional payroll tax based on the tips *and* the higher minimum wage.

The degree to which restaurant die-offs are a harbinger for ag is an open question. Small farmers have more options than restaurateurs when officeholders capriciously tinker with market mechanisms.

The site Lendedu surveyed the owners of 500 small businesses in California, New York and the District of Columbia, all early adopters of the $15 wage. About 43 percent of small-business owners responded they were planning on, or considering, relocating their businesses due to the wage floor. About 43 percent of respondents were unsure whether their businesses would survive the new labor costs. Transfer this poll to small agriculture. The Beaver State, to its credit, has at least adopted a bifurcated minimum-wage scheme that recognizes the economic frailties and the lower cost of living in the rural counties of eastern and southern Oregon.

When the Oregon legislature is in session, Jenny Dresler, state public policy director for the Oregon Farm Bureau, said she practically lives at the statehouse. One imagines this energetic and affable young woman driving the streets of Salem after dark, ready to slam on her brakes, pop out in a whir of blond hair and enlighten any hipster or aloof techie about how he'd better thank his flippin' stars for the Oregon farmer. She told the Capital Press that even with Oregon's more farm-friendly minimum wage, it's become a make-or-break issue for some operations. Farmers and ranchers are price takers, not price setters, she said. That, in a nutshell, is why wage floors cause farm failures, force farmers to sell or get them to re-crop. If they're unable to raise prices, she said, they'll need to cut costs elsewhere, automating where they can or planting less labor-intensive crops.

In general carbs and protein have much lower labor costs than fruits and vegetables. The states that are doubling the federal minimum wage and awarding overtime and family leave to seasonal workers will inevitably hurt those the wage floor is intended to help. U.S. growers of melons, rutabagas, asparagus, onion, garlic, cut flowers, peppers, oranges, cherries, broccoli, Brussels sprouts, spinach and strawberries are already forced to compete globally against countries in which workers are paid in a week what they're paid in a day in the United States. The two crushing forces – globalization and the regulatory state – all but ensure future gluts in grain, corn, beef, pork and plant-based "milks," as they ensure future scarcities of domestic fruits and vegetables.

As key farm states like Washington, New York, California and Oregon experiment with wages by *diktat*, expect the production of more mechanically harvested crops over hand-harvested ones, more grains than veggies, more nuts than fruits, more starches than fiber.

We've taken food abundance for granted for too long. The generation old enough to remember the Great Depression is dying off; soon there will no living connection to a time when hunger and widespread farm failures gripped America.

While we were living the good life, terrific monocrops formed at the cost of our food security. Government is shirking one of its most basic functions in a free society – keeping markets on a level playing field and free from stultifying, initiative-killing concentration of ownership. What's happening is not in line with our ideals as Americans. Still other corners of government are enforcing New Deal policies – a testament to how hard it is to extinguish bureaucracies after the problems they were set up to address have long been solved. Amid these many failures, politicians have not failed to find new ways to tax, regulate and demonize ag at the state and local levels. Bullying state governments are a big threat and are inadvertently resulting in a poorer diet for all Americans with more starches, more corn sugars, more cheap protein and fewer fruits and vegetables as farmers re-crop to survive. Those who can't re-crop, disappear. Soon there will be fewer than two million farms in America. America cannot allow more of its farmers to be plowed under.

But even as the noose has slowly tightened, there have been success stories. That's encouraging. We can only hope audacity, imagination and determination remain alive in the farmyard. We cannot forget who we are.

Index

Abboud, Fadi, 229, 230
ABCDs, 274
Abernathy, Kevin, Milk
   Producers Council, 202
Adam Johnston, 217
ADM, 274
Aduba, Uzo, 135
African runner, Carolina
   peanut, 245, 246, 247
Agricola La Campana, 219
Agricultural & Applied
   Economics Association,
   147
Ahmed, Nesar, 267, 268
Alacqua, Bob, 184
All The King's Men, 55
Allayaud, Bill, 86
allergies, 248
   lactose, 97, 205
Almond Board of California,
   96, 101
almond orchard
   life cycle, 96
Amen, Todd, 127
Andean Trade Preference Act,
   24
Anheuser-Busch InBev, 176,
   177, 180
Ansolabehere, David, 85
apple, 27, 78, 94, 95, 100, 237,
   280
Arax, Mark, 107, 108, 109
Armengolli, Jaime, 219
Arvin-Edison Water Storage
   District, 109

Ascochyta blight, 229
Athenos, 227
Australia, 111, 112, 157, 159,
   160, 219, 281
average age, American farmer,
   22, 281
Avery, Jill, 153
Avi Crane, 126
baba ganoush, 227
baijiu, 161
Bailey Lauerman, 68, 92, 93
Baker, Geoff, 177
Barkley, Noelle, 252
Barr, Roseanne, 134
BASF, 27
Bayer Crop Science, 24, 25,
   26, 30, 35, 38
Bearss, John, 232
Bee++, 33
Belk, Adolphus, 131
Benson, Ezra Taft, 143
Betti, Matt, 33
biennial crop, 27
Bierlink, Henry, 16
Blaser, Martin, 260
boll weevils, 169, 245, 246
Boone, Pat, 145
boysenberries, 27
Bradford, Nat, 247
Brandi, Gene, 78, 79
Brazil, 237, 269
Brenneis, Lisa, 65, 67
Briggeman, Brian, 23
British Commonwealth, 225

Brown, Jerry, California Governor, 51, 97, 202
Brown, Jim, 134
Brown, Karlanea, 270
Brown, Louie A., Jr., 81
Bryan, William Jennings, 2
Bud Light, 176, 177, 178, 185
Buffalo Wild Wings, 132, 136
Buffett, Jimmy, 243
bumble bee, 31
Bunge, 274
Burford, Tom, 94
Butz, Earl, i, 142, 143, 144, 145
Cal Poly San Luis Obispo, 81, 194, 282
Calder, Vanessa Brown, 48, 179
California Asparagus Commission, 24
California Citrus Mutual, 79, 81
California Coastal Commission, 86
California Council on Science and Technology, 86
California Garlic and Onion Research Committee, 29
California Water Project, 106
canola, 38, 79, 229
Cargill, 274
Carleton, Mark A., 252
Carolina Gold Rice Foundation, 247
Carson, Rachel, 143
Cartel Land, documentary, 125, 235

Cawelo Water District, 85, 86, 87, 88, 89, 90
Cena, John, 104
Center for Biological Diversity, 213
Centers for Disease Control and Prevention, 4, 207, 248
Central America, 28
Central Coast, California, 18, 65
Changyu, 161
ChemChina, 27, 274
Cheng, Tso-Hsin, 15
Chicken Wing Dilemma, 132, 136
chickpea, 227
chickpeas, 228, 229, 230
Chile, 118, 153, 160, 219, 263
China, 161, 188, 193, 203, 261, 263, 265, 266, 268, 269
Christopher Ranch, 46, 52, 54
Christopher, Ken, 46, 57
Churchill, Jim, 65, 66, 67, 68
Cisneros, Mario, 234, 236
citric acid, 149
citrus canker, 239, 240, 241
clothianidin, 38
Cockrell, Mike, 135
Colangelo, Michael, 155
Connor, Hannah, 213
Copeland, Ray, citrus consultant, 80
Corden, James, 59
Cork Quality Council, 155, 158
Corticeira Amorim, 158

cotton, 11, 29, 38, 95, 99, 114, 255
Cregan, Melissa, 63, 64, 65
Critser, Greg, 144
Cromwell, James, 136
crop insurance, 19
Cuervo, Jose, 170
Cuomo, Mario, 151
daisy (cocktail), 171, 172
Davies, R.W., 13
Dean, John, 145
Deen, Joey, 237
DeGeneres, Ellen, 135, 153
Denimpex, 237
Dhaliwal, Rob, 6
Di Justo, Patrick, 141
DiCaprio, Leonardo, 228
Diddy (rapper), 134
Dilly Dilly, 176, 177, 178
Dorito dust, 150
Doritos, 139, 140, 141, 149, 150, 151, 152, 153, 154
Dow Chemical, 274
DowDuPont, 27
Draper, Don, "Madmen", 139
Dresler, Jenny, 290
Dreyfus, 274
DuPont, 274
Duvick, Don, 146
Dylan, Bob, 2
Eastern Filbert Blight, 219, 220
EB-5 Visa Program, 187, 188, 189
Ecuador, 266
Edward Jones Dome, 181
Ehn, Robert, 29, 102
Ellis, Curt, 144

Elmhurst Milked, LLC, 205, 206
E-logs, 236
EPA, 32, 38, 79, 83, 84
Ernst, Falko, 125
espadín, 172, 173, 174
Farm Aid, 2
Farris, Kendrick, 192
Fat Land: How Americans Became the Fattest People in the World, 144
Federal Marketing Order No. 955, 29
Federal Milk Marketing Order System, 200
Feinstein, Dianne, 189
Ferrero, 215, 216, 217, 218
Fiscalini, Brian, 194, 195, 196, 283
Flanagan, Graham, 177
Food & Water Watch, 213
food-pleasure equation, 149
Four Pests Health Campaign, 14
Fournier, Valérie, 34
Franz, Hilary, 263
Freeworld Trading, 217
Fresh Alliance, 243
Friedman, Matt, CEO, Wing Zone, 132
FrieslandCampina, 193
Frito-Lay, 139, 150, 151, 152
Fundación Agaves Silvestres, 174
Fusarium (wilt), 166
Gale, Jason, 261
Game Changers, The, 192
garbanzo beans, 225

Gastelum, Rick, 8
Genasci, Laura, 194
Goeler, Andy, 177
Gomez-Pinilla, Fernando, 148
Graham, James, 171
grapefruit, 27, 72, 239
Grassley, Charles "Chuck", 2,
    189, 276
Great Britain, 224
Great Depression, 142
Great Leap Forward, 13
Greenspan, Alan, 144
Grey's Anatomy, 135
Guatemala, 232, 237
Guenther, Robert, 21
Hacker, Jana, 139
Haley, Nikki, 245
Halperin, Marc, 231
Hamburg Consumer
    Protection Center, 216
Harkinson, Josh, 72, 106
Harpur, Brock, 33
Harris, Glen, UGA, 255
Harvey, Paul, 1
Heather Davis, Nuveen, 112
H-E-B, 41
Heineman, Matthew, 125
Heinzen, Tarah, 213
Henry, Lois, 13, 106, 107, 114
Heritage Foundation, 179,
    276
Hill, Craig, Iowa Farm Bureau
    president, 147
Hippeas, 228
HLB, 63, 64
honeybees, 31
Howard, Phil, 274
Huanglongbing, 63, 241

imidacloprid, 31, 38
isoamyl acetate, 167
Jacobsen, Randy, 74
jimador, 162
John Birch Society, 143
Johnson, Lyndon, 26, 28
Judkis, Maura, 26, 152
Kaepernick, Colin, 135
Kahn, Carrie, 124
Karlin, Joel, 203
Karp, David, 62, 241
Kasich, John, Ohio governor,
    189
Keats, Adam, environmental
    lawyer, 106
Kemerait, Bob, 254
Kempner, Matt, reporter,
    Journal-Constitution, 132
key lime, 232
Khulna district, Bangladesh,
    267, 268
Kimball, Mary, 22
King Corn, 144
King County, 8
Kissinger, Henry, 144
Klein, Jeff, 98
Klemp, Gordon, 127
kohlrabi, 27
Kong, Lincoln, 161
Kowalski, Dan, 146
Kraft Foods, 227
Kroenke, Stan, 181
Kuper, Judah, 174
La Cucaracha Bar, 171
lactic acid, 149
Lactococcus lactis cremoris,
    141
Lamb, Marshall, 257

Land-Based Learning, Center for, 22
Landrieu, Mitch, New Orleans mayor, 190
Lange, Chris, 80
Lange, Lisa, Senior Vice President, PETA, 137
Le Cour Grandmaison, Romain, 124, 125
Ledford, Alex, 177
Levenstein, J.J., M.D., 249
Lewis and Clark, 208
long hang-time flavors, 149
Lost Valley Farm, 208, 209, 211, 213
Love, David, Ph.D., 270
Lower Umatilla Basin Groundwater Management Area, 211
Lummi, 262
Lupita, 171
Macklin, Ken, H.R. Macklin and Sons, 103
Madden, Henry, 171
Magdaleno, Marco Polo, 163
Mao Zedong, 14
Marderosian, Jim, 70
Margaritaville (brand), 243, 244
Mariano Gonzalez, 194
Marks and Spencer, 225
Marquis of Altamira, 170
Marshall, Jason, 83
Matt Joyce, 231
Mayahuel, Aztec fertility goddess, 168, 170
McCandless, James, UBS AgriVest, 95

Mehlenbacher, Shawn, 220
Mellencamp, John, 2
Mena, Ana Maria Romero, 164
Metropolitan Water District of Southern California, 109, 110
Mexican Firing Squad, 171
Meyer lemons, 27
Michailides, Themis, UC Davis plant pathologist, 100
milk cows
  Holstein, 197, 198
  Jersey, 197, 222
Millerton Lake, 109
Mills, Anson, 247
minimum wage, 51, 99, 101, 227, 285, 286, 287, 288, 289, 290
Mireles, Dr. Jose Manuel, 125
Molnar, Tom, 222
monarch butterfly, 115
monoculture, 17, 167, 172
Monsanto, 26, 27, 30, 274
Moo, academic farce, 145
Mr. Peanut, 245
MRSA (Methicillin-resistant Staphylococcus aureus, 264
Mulvany, Lydia, 261
Nahuatl, 121, 162
Naranjo, Hugo, 124
National Center for Germplasm Preservation, 252
National Clonal Germplasm Repository, 250, 251

National Germplasm System, 252

National Marine Fisheries Service, 260

National Onion Association, 26, 28, 29

National Peanut Board, 247

National Plant Germplasm System, 251

National Tequila Industry Chamber, 163

nematodes, 38, 104, 167, 254

neonicotinoids, 30, 34, 38

Nestle, Marion, 217, 279

New Jersey, 219, 222

Nickelsburg, Jerry, 47

Nieves, Cinthia Garcia, 126

Ningxia, autonomous region of, 160

Nitty Gritty Dirt Band, 2

Nooyi, Indra, 151

North American Free Trade Agreement, 24, 233

Nutella, 215, 216, 217

oats, 38, 205

Obama administration, 21, 98

Oceana, 261

Odometer.com, 44

Ojai, California, 65, 66, 67

Oktay, Sarah, water-testing expert, 90

Olmecs, 169

onion, iv, 9, 10, 18, 25, 26, 28, 29, 30, 38, 39, 40, 41, 56, 150, 224

Owen, Polly, 220

Owens Valley, 110

Pacific flatheaded borer, 221

Palermo, Mike, Roswell, Georgia, councilman, 191

Paltrow, Gwyneth, 120

Panama disease, 166, 167

Papa John's, 135

Parker, Forrest, 245, 248

Patecatl, 170

Patricio, Miguel, 177

Paz, Ramon, 117

Pearl River, 261

Penaeus stylirostris densovirus (aka IHHNV), 260

People for the Ethical Treatment of Animals, 136

PepsiCo, 150, 151, 153, 227, 228

Percival, Albert, 169

Perry, Mark J., 288

Persian lime, 232, 243

Peru, 56, 120, 236

PETA. See People for the Ethical Treatment of Animals

Phillips, Harley, 81, 103

Pierce County, 8

Pierson, David, 187

Placentra, N.J., 177

Porter, Sarah, 151

Post, Emily, 151

propionibacterium, 141

Psihoyos, Louie, 192, 193

pulque, 168, 169, 170

Pyeongchang Winter Olympics, 192

pythium, 38

Rabe, Etienne, 81

Rabinowitz, Adam, 248

Rabobank, 200, 212, 265

Rangan, Urvashi, Ph.D., 259, 264
Raw Milk Institute, 206
RDM Aquaculture, 269, 270
Reaser, Lynn, Ph.D., 287
Red Delicious, 94, 95
Reel, Monte, 261
Renton, Washington, 7
Resnicks, Stewart and Lynda, 72, 104, 105, 106, 107, 110, 111, 244
rhizoctonia, 38
Rhoten, Brandon, 135
Richards, Ann, 151
Riggs, Bonnie, 136
Ringling Bros. and Barnum & Bailey Circus, 246
Ritchie, Bryce (golf editor), 178
Roark Capital Group, private equity firm, 132
Robert Penn Warren, 55
Roberts, Glenn, 247
Rockwell, Norman, 2
Rodakowski, Garry, 220, 221, 223
Rodgers, Clay, 88
Roethlisberger, Ben, 177
Rolling Stone, 145
Rossow, Seth, 281, 282
Ruffalo, Mark, actor, 89
Rusty Wagon, 15
Rutgers, 222
rye, 38
Sabra, 227, 228, 229, 231
Sabra Dipping Company, 227
Sainsbury's, 225
Saldaña, Rebecca, 7

Samish, 262
San Benito County, 48, 49, 50
San Jose, 44, 47, 54, 60
San Miguel Neighborhood, 45
Sanderson, Joe, Jr., 134
Sanschagrin, Grover, 163, 164, 168
Santa Clara County, 42
Sauza, Don Cenobio, 170
Scheper, Richard, 199
Schwartz, Henry, 206
Schwartz, Max and Arthur, 205
Seacrest, Ryan, 59
Senapathy, Kavin, 249, 250
sensory-specific satiety, 149
Serbia, 219
Serpico, Frank, 135
SGMA (Sustainable Groundwater Management Act), 101, 102
Shaanxi, Chinese province, 160
Shandong, 160
Sheeran, Ed, 58, 59, 60
Shepherd, David, 175
Sherman, Richard, 105
Shields, David, 247
Shirk, David, 235
Silbernagel, Terry, 212
Silent Spring, 143
Silicon Valley, 11, 44, 46, 47, 49
Simon, Bill, former Secretary of the Treasury, 144
Smiley, Jane, 145
Smith, Scott, chief scientist, Water Defense, 89

SNAP (Supplemental Nutrition Assistance Program), 277
Snohomish County, 8
South Africa, 219, 255
South Carolina Peanut Board, 247
South Korea, 52, 203
Southern root-knot nematode, 255
Southern Shrimp Alliance, 260, 265, 268, 269
soybean, 38, 141
sparrow, campaign against, 14, 15
Spink, John, 57
Stark, Willie (literary character), 55
Steinmetz, Katy, 238, 241, 242
Stevenson, Mark, 115
stink bug, brown marmorated, 222
Stoner, Allan K., 284
Strunk, Delaney, writer, BuzzFeed, 131, 132
suicide, 4, 170
Sumbal Matah, 225
Sun Pacific, 59, 60, 61, 71, 72, 81
sunflower, 38, 141
Sunion, 24, 25, 26, 27, 30, 38, 40, 41
Sunrise Cocktail, 171
Super Bowl, i, 1, 2, 122, 124, 129, 136, 137, 151, 225
Super Bowl XLVII, 1
Suro, David, 168
Surrey, 224

Swedish Society for Nature Conservation, 268
Swift, Taylor, 58, 68
Swinomish, 262
Syngenta, 27, 274
Tahiti lime. *See* Persian lime
Take a Knee (movement), 130, 131, 132, 134
Take Me Out to the Ball Game, 246
Tancítaro, 122, 123, 124, 125
TCA (Trichloroanisole), 159
Tequila Interchange Project, 168
Tequila Regulatory Council, 163, 164
Tequila Sauza, 170
Teresa's, Mexican restaurant, 77, 78
Tesco, 225
Texas A&M AgriLife Extension, 31
Thacher Ayala, Emily, 67
thiamethoxam, 31
Threemile Canyon Farms, 209
Tillamook County Creamery Association, 208, 210, 211
Tillamook Creamery, 207
Toom, 231
toum, 231
Travis Love, 211
Traynor, Joe, 80
Traynor, Joe, bee broker, 80
Triple Site, 45
Triple V Dairy, 200
Troell, Max, 267, 268
Trump administration, 21, 98, 213

Tubbs, Scott, UGA agronomist, 255
Turkey, 28, 217, 218, 219
U.S. Federal Motor Carrier Safety Administration, 235
U.S. Food and Drug Administration, 263
United Nations Department of Economic and Social Affairs, 275
Urner Barry, 134
USA Dry Pea & Lentil Council, 228
Valadao, David, Congressman, 200, 202
Valderrama, Sergio del Castillo, 237
Valentine, Howard, 250
vanishing caloric density, 150
vibrio, 264
Vidalia Onion Committee, 29
Villa, Joy, 134
Vinolok, 158
Vogel, Jerry, 151
Ward, Brian, 247
Washington Farm Bureau, 8
Washington Post, 2, 21, 26, 35, 279
Washington Red Raspberry Commission, 16
Watson, Bart, 185
Waycott, Richard, 101
Wenger, Paul, 51
West, Archibald Clark "Arch", 139

Whatcom County, 16, 78
wheat, 4, 8, 38, 119, 145, 172, 256
Wheatcroft, S.G., 13
Wheeling, Craig, 238, 240
Wilks, James, 192, 193
Williams, Ken, owner Willitts Pump Co., 102
Wiman, Nik, 221, 222
Wine Intelligence, 158
Wing Zone, 132, 136
Witherly, Steven A., Ph.D., 149
Wonder, Stevie, 134
Wonderful (Company), 61, 69, 72, 73, 104, 107, 108, 242, 243
Woods, James, 134
Woolf, Aaron, 144
World Ag Expo, Tulare County, 203
Xanthomonas axonopodis, 239
Xerces Society, 32
Xinjiang, Uyghur autonomous region, China, 160
Xufa, Liao, 161
Yakima Valley, Washington, 18
Zayed, Amro, 32
Zenovich, Marina, 106, 107, 108, 109
Zolezzi, Stephen, 287
Zork, 158